# ZBIG

# ZBIG

## THE STRATEGY AND STATECRAFT OF ZBIGNIEW BRZEZINSKI

*Edited by*

**Charles Gati**

*With a Foreword by*

**President Jimmy Carter**

The Johns Hopkins University Press

*Baltimore*

The Johns Hopkins University Press
2715 North Charles Street
Baltimore, Maryland 21218-4363
www.press.jhu.edu

Library of Congress Cataloging-in-Publication Data

Zbig : the strategy and statecraft of Zbigniew Brzezinski / edited by
Charles Gati ; with a foreword by President Jimmy Carter.
pages     cm
Includes bibliographical references and index.
ISBN-13: 978-1-4214-0976-4 (hardcover : acid-free paper)
ISBN-10: 1-4214-0976-3 (hardcover : acid-free paper)
ISBN-13: 978-1-4214-0977-1 (electronic)
ISBN-10: 1-4214-0977-1 (electronic)
1. Brzezinski, Zbigniew, 1928– 2. Brzezinski, Zbigniew, 1928– —Political
and social views. 3. United States—Foreign relations—1977–1981. 4. United
States—Strategic aspects. 5. Statesmen—United States—Biography.
6. National Security Council (U.S.)—History—20th century.
7. International relations—History—20th century. 8. Intellectuals—
United States—Biography. 9. College teachers—United States—
Biography. I. Gati, Charles.
E840.8.B79Z24 2013
327.730092—dc23
[B]      2012041893

A catalog record for this book is available from the British Library.

*Special discounts are available for bulk purchases of this book.
For more information, please contact Special Sales at 410-516-6936 or
specialsales@press.jhu.edu.*

The Johns Hopkins University Press uses environmentally friendly
book materials, including recycled text paper that is composed of
at least 30 percent post-consumer waste, whenever possible.

# CONTENTS

# PART III    The Policy Advocate

# PART IV    Portraits

Illustrations follow page 111

## FOREWORD by Jimmy Carter

In *Keeping Faith: Memoirs of a President*, I described Zbigniew Brzezinski as my favorite seatmate (with the exception of certain members of my family) on long-distance trips, because "we might argue, but I would never be bored." I trust that the contributors to this book convey a sense of why I wrote this: Zbig's first-rate intellect, his incisive analysis, and his provocative style of presentation. As my national security advisor, he provided me a wide range of options and ideas that were frequently incisive and innovative, sometimes too much so. That was what I wanted, because I had plenty of humdrum and conventional advice from the Department of State.

I knew what to expect from Zbig. I had first met him in 1973 when I joined the Trilateral Commission, of which he was the executive director. This group had fifty members from North America, Western Europe, and Japan. I was invited as a governor who had indicated that a priority was increasing trade. I also was interested in increasing my knowledge of international affairs, and I paid very close attention in the meetings I attended. The next year, after I announced my candidacy for president, Zbig wrote to me offering help. He may not have expected much to come of this, because I was definitely considered a long shot by the national media, but I took full advantage of his offer. During 1975, he became my chief foreign policy advisor. After winning the 1976 election, I asked him for advice on my future national security advisor. He gave me alternatives, but I knew that I wanted him for this job.

He put together an excellent staff to support him and me. Zbig, of course, was the direct source of most information and advice. My first scheduled meeting each morning was with him as he brought me the Presidential Daily Briefing. He usually would be part of other meetings during the day. When special knowledge was needed on a particular topic, he would bring in the appropriate members of his staff and other members of the administration. He was an effective manager and highly efficient.

Zbig did what I asked him to do, and at times I asked him to go beyond the role of an advisor. I expected Cyrus Vance, my secretary of state, to be the public voice of the administration on issues of foreign policy. However, this turned out not to be a role he always enjoyed playing. Zbig proved more willing and able to explain our policy, and sometimes I encouraged him to do so. On one very sensitive political issue, normalization of relations with China, I decided to manage the effort from the White House. After a State Department mission failed, I sent Zbig as an envoy to meet with Deng Xiaoping to explain exactly how I wished to move ahead. His mission was successful.

He also served as a key member of the American negotiating team for the Israeli-Egyptian summit meeting at Camp David. This was an extraordinary event of diplomatic history. I personally took the lead and worked directly with President Anwar Sadat and Prime Minister Menachem Begin, but members of the teams for all three of us also played vital roles in the negotiations over the thirteen days that resulted in the Camp David Accords.

At the beginning of the administration, Zbig led in drafting a memo setting forth our agenda in foreign affairs. It was highly ambitious, which was what I wanted. Working toward a comprehensive peace in the Middle East and establishing diplomatic relations with the People's Republic of China were only two of ten broad goals we pursued. Enhancing human rights throughout the world was a goal to which we gave special attention, along with a nuclear arms agreement with the Soviet Union. I am proud of what we achieved, although I recognize as legitimate criticism that we took on too many controversial issues and that they hurt me in domestic politics. The Panama Canal Treaties proved especially damaging politically, but we were absolutely right to pursue them, and their achievement has been to the benefit of the United States and of Latin America.

Whatever agenda a president pursues, he always has to face the unexpected in foreign affairs. One of the duties of the national security advisor is to be prepared for the unexpected. Zbig always gave me strong support in times of crisis. We managed to survive the two major challenges, the Soviet invasion of Afghanistan and the Iranian Revolution, without being drawn into war, and in neither case did the Soviet Union benefit. Some critics at the time and afterward have blamed Zbig for a revival of the cold war during this period. While it is true that he was the most skeptical among my advisors regarding the conduct of the Soviet Union, I reject the idea that he somehow convinced me to retreat from détente. The actions of the Soviet Union clearly had to be addressed. Nevertheless, we continued to honor the SALT Treaty, despite the political impossibility of achieving ratification. Even my successor in office continued to observe the agreement until the end of its scheduled term, despite having criticized it. The Soviet leadership at this time made truly disastrous decisions that required us to take a more confrontational position.

In the years after my presidency, Zbig has continued to be a valuable advisor. In 1982 when I decided to create the Carter Center, he attended a meeting at Sapelo Island, Georgia, to contribute his good advice. He has participated in several of our projects, and he just joined me in California the week before I wrote this foreword to recount to our financial supporters some unpublished details of the negotiations at Camp David. I am grateful to him for his service.

This book about him is long overdue. In the late twentieth and early twenty-first centuries, he has been one of the most significant thinkers and actors in the field of international affairs.

# PREFACE by Charles Gati

Zbigniew Brzezinski has become a celebrity. He's stopped at street corners and at airports. People want to know how he and his daughter, TV news anchor Mika, are doing. When he speaks about the state of the world and the state of America, an old television advertisement comes to mind. *When E. F. Hutton speaks, people listen.* E. F. Hutton, a stock brokerage firm, is long gone, but Brzezinski—looking rested, quick-witted, and vigorous in his eighties—holds forth on television, writes a bestseller every three or four years, and still travels around the world to lecture and meet the high and mighty. More than ever, *when Brzezinski speaks, people listen.*

He remains a significant voice in foreign affairs. When a head of state visits Washington, Brzezinski is frequently invited for lunch or dinner. After such events, illustrious participants often testify that the visitor was particularly curious to find out what Brzezinski thought about some event or trend. Decades ago he was still confused with Henry Kissinger; I witnessed an amusing encounter then in New York, near Columbia University, where a taxi driver addressed him as "Dr. Kissinger." This is unlikely to happen today. On a recent occasion, in fact, the manager of a Washington restaurant approached him with a proposition: bring Mika to the restaurant some day, and lunch would be on the house. Brzezinski seemed very proud of his daughter.

His celebrity status is due, in part, to lucid observations during frequent television appearances. More importantly, however, his early opposition to the Iraq War—when most Democrats hesitated to take on the Bush administration's foreign policy—was widely perceived as candid and even bold. Offended by lies that were put forth to explain the rationale for the war, and without any personal ambition to play a role again in the U.S. government, he's been more willing than in the past to show his blunt and often feisty personality. How many Washington insiders would call Joe Scarborough—better known as "Morning Joe," the prominent TV anchor and Mika Brzezinski's cohost on the show—"stunningly superficial," to his face? How many Democrats would claim that President Obama had "caved" to political pressure on the Arab-Israeli conflict?

Dismayed by America's excessive concern about domestic security after 9/11, Brzezinski also enjoys poking fun at unnecessary security measures by relating how he once signed in as "Osama bin Laden" in a Washington office building, where no one stopped him. The story, which is obviously meant to shock, represents a metaphor for an America that's flustered, unable to decide what really matters. This is why the "new" Brzezinski, worried about the future, calls a spade a spade, in contrast to the "old" Brzezinski of the past century, who was also outspoken but who nonetheless carefully positioned himself to remain more or less within the mainstream of Washington's foreign policy elite. Brzezinski of the twenty-first century cares far less about the mainstream, or the received wisdom of the moment. He seeks to cut through diplomatic double-talk to tell it like it is (or at least the way he sees it). What he's eager to tell nowadays is as simple as its solution is difficult: *America is experiencing a systemic crisis.* Once an unreserved optimist about the United States overcoming domestic deadlock and prevailing over adversaries abroad, he has come to appreciate much more than in the past the very real limits on what today's America can hope to achieve. Brzezinski has become neither a pessimist nor a "declinist," but it's clear that since the end of the cold war he's been less willing to support the use of American military power, particularly in the Middle East. His message resonates well with his audiences.

⁘ After a successful teaching career at Harvard, Columbia, and Johns Hopkins's School of Advanced International Studies (SAIS), Brzezinski now works at the Center for Strategic and International Studies (CSIS), a prominent Washington think tank. He earns a living as a writer and lecturer. Whether he speaks to a group of foreign policy specialists or an audience of business people or university students, in the United States or abroad, he relates to them by weaving a few reasonably well known details into his presentations—but the context is fresh, the analysis logical, the formulations insightful, and the delivery invariably disciplined. His forty- to forty-five-minute lectures are crisp, the words carefully chosen; he speaks in perfect paragraphs. He usually begins with a story that serves to illustrate his main message. At the time of the Cuban Missile Crisis in 1962, according to one such introductory story, President John F. Kennedy asked Dean Acheson, President Harry S Truman's secretary of state, to brief Charles de Gaulle on the evidence that would justify U.S. military action. But the French president didn't look at the pictures that Kennedy's distinguished emissary had come to present. Although he detested Kennedy, de Gaulle pushed aside the pictures with the comment that an American president's word was good enough for him to appreciate the situation. And he assured Kennedy of France's support. Brzezinski relates the story to make the point that the United States has lost much of its credibility in the world, and he adds, somewhat wistfully, that it should be recovered.

Focusing far more often than in the past on America's domestic circumstances in the twenty-first century, Brzezinski's lectures, essays, books, and television and newspaper commentaries all expose his concern about partisanship, polarization, and the resulting political paralysis. He's troubled by the divisive gap between the rich and the poor, about how greed has come to rule the American way of life. More than anything else, perhaps, he's distressed by the prospects for peace and stability in an increasingly unguided and unguarded world. At times, he isn't even happy with his audiences. So many of you, he notes in a professorial sort of way, haven't learned elementary geography because it's not part of the curriculum in most schools. And yet the audiences treat him well. The applause he gets isn't just polite; it's enthusiastic. Back in 2008, when he spoke to a large political gathering in Washington, Senator Joe Biden, the future vice president, followed him on the podium. Seldom lost for words, Biden paused uncomfortably for a few seconds and then turned to the organizers with a complaint: "You didn't tell me I'd have to speak right after Zbig, did you?" The audience broke into laughter and applause.

Still, Brzezinski remains a controversial figure. Many Republicans distrust him for being a Democrat and for becoming such an influential early opponent of the foreign policy of President George W. Bush and the war in Iraq. There are Democrats who can't forgive him for his past as a cold warrior, a Russophobe, and a supporter of the war in Vietnam, and some even recall that he publicly favored the Republican candidate for president in 1988. Among Washington insiders with a long memory, there is some residual hostility toward Brzezinski for being a combative (though effective) bureaucratic infighter as President Jimmy Carter's national security advisor, winning the battle for control of the foreign policy agenda against the less contentious secretary of state, Cyrus Vance. Neoconservatives and many others portray his proposal for a solution of the Arab-Israeli conflict as lacking in consideration of Israeli vulnerabilities and empathy for Israeli sensitivities, wondering why he doesn't lean on the Palestinians to at least recognize the right of Israel to exist. Supporters of a U.S. foreign policy based on human rights find his wholehearted espousal of U.S.-China rapprochement, and the corresponding de facto endorsement of China's Communist government in particular, perplexing if not hypocritical for a professed advocate for universal human rights.

Such mixture of admiration and controversy notwithstanding, this is still the first book about Brzezinski. Dozens of studies have been published about Henry Kissinger; many about Dean Acheson and John Foster Dulles; at least as many about George F. Kennan (whose prominence in the academic literature exceeds his actual influence that ended around 1950); and a few about Madeleine Albright, J. William Fulbright, Henry "Scoop" Jackson, Walter Lippmann, and Condoleezza Rice—but not one about Brzezinski. The brief bibliography at the end of this book could list only a couple of studies in Polish, which stress his roots and focus on his activities related to Poland during the cold war. Of the unpublished academic studies and dissertations written about him, Justin Vaïsse's (in French) and Patrick Vaughan's (in Polish) stand out; they're scheduled to be published in English as well. (Happily, each has also contributed a chapter to this volume. Chapter 1 by Vaïsse offers a comparative study of Kissinger and Brzezinski, two naturalized U.S. citizens who rose to top foreign policy positions once reserved for financial and legal luminaries with prominent WASP backgrounds and connections. Chapter 10 by Vaughan presents detailed evidence about the curious collaboration of the Polish-born national security advisor and the Polish-born Pope John Paul II to undermine Poland's Communist regime.) This book, then, intends to fill the proverbial gap in the all-but-nonexistent literature on Brzezinski by covering his academic and policy-related contributions from the time he was a Sovietologist at Harvard and Columbia, to the White House years when he joined the Carter administration, to his writings in the 1980s and 1990s as communism collapsed in the Soviet sphere and a transition to something different began, to his outspoken criticism of the war in Iraq early in this century, to his latest books and articles that have further enhanced his reputation as a prominent foreign policy strategist.

❖ The idea for this book originated with Dean Jessica Einhorn and her colleagues at SAIS. After Brzezinski stopped teaching regular classes there, Einhorn asked me if I'd put together a volume of original essays dealing with his career. I agreed, and we also agreed that the book should not be a *Festschrift*. While Brzezinski deserves a book that consists only of tributes and celebratory essays, I wasn't interested in editing one. I didn't think too many people would read it; for that matter, I didn't think even Brzezinski would read all of it. With the dean's support, then, I ended up with full editorial control over the selection of authors. I also edited each chapter, primarily with a view toward eliminating duplications.

I requested that all contributors prepare "respectful but not uncritical" studies or essays. In two or three cases I did feel the need to ask authors to temper ill-mannered criticism or excessive praise, but I didn't discourage four of his former colleagues at the National Security Council (NSC; chapters 6–9) and one in academia (chapter 16) from submitting brief portraits and stories that put Brzezinski in a favorable light. As a whole, I think the book—written by leading scholars and experts, some who knew him and some who never met him—consists of serious, well-documented assessments. My purpose was to prepare the first wide-ranging and balanced study of Brzezinski's career as a scholar, policy maker, policy advocate, and commentator, as well as a colleague.

As for my own relationship with Brzezinski, I didn't consult with him about who should be asked to address various aspects of his activities, scholarly and political. When the table of contents was ready, I showed it to him, but he didn't read any of the chapters in advance of publication. The only obvious exception was chapter 17, a condensed version of two conversations the two of us had about himself; he reviewed and edited his responses to my questions.

⁘ From the time he arrived at Harvard in the early 1950s, Brzezinski was seen as a gifted and an ambitious scholar. As chapter 1 amplifies the similarities and differences between them, Henry Kissinger was the *other* gifted and ambitious scholar there. Contrary to conventional wisdom then and later on too, the evidence suggests that the two men were and remained rivals but not adversaries. Chapter 2 deals with Brzezinski as the Sovietologist he was, the author, most prominently, of comparative studies exploring the totalitarian qualities of the fascist, Nazi, and especially Communist dictatorships of the twentieth century. In contrast to old-fashioned authoritarian regimes that used to issue only *prohibitions*—instructing their citizens of what they must *not* do—Brzezinski stressed that the new totalitarians of the twentieth century issued both *prohibitions* and *imperatives* on what their citizens *must not* as well as what they *must* do. In other words, the totalitarians didn't simply repress and control their subjects; they also sought to mobilize them toward promoting both internal and international objectives. In lengthy treatises full of fine distinctions and academic jargon, Brzezinski argued that the very essence of these regimes had to do with capturing political power and then consolidating it at home and exporting it elsewhere. This is why, after the demise of the fascists and the Nazis, the Communist totalitarians of the Soviet Union and China represented such a serious threat to American interests and values.

In response to this threat, as chapter 3 shows in considerable detail, Brzezinski sought to blend scholarship on the Soviet Union and Eastern Europe with policy advice, infusing the intellectualism of the Ivy League with the influence of New York's financial and legal elites in order to advance his ambitious policy and career goals. He was gradually becoming a "public intellectual." *The Soviet Bloc*, published in 1960, was his last major study of Communist political systems without explicit policy advocacy. Other books and articles he published in the 1960s and 1970s were also informed by scholarly research, but they clearly aimed at influencing U.S. foreign policy. Moreover, after he moved from Harvard to Columbia in 1960, Brzezinski could and did use the New York–based Council on Foreign Relations and the newly established Trilateral Commission as platforms for the promotion of a more dynamic—but not necessarily more militant—foreign policy to weaken the Soviet imperial domain by driving a wedge between Moscow and the Eastern Europeans.

Thus, as Muska and Zbigniew Brzezinski were raising their three children—Ian, Mark, and Mika—in New Jersey, he was working in New York while eyeing Washington. Mastering the art of preparing crisp talking points, he reached out to almost all Democratic presidential hopefuls with advice and help. Of the then-current crop of candidates and presidents, he was in touch with John F. Kennedy, Hubert H. Humphrey, Lyndon B. Johnson, Henry "Scoop" Jackson, and Edmund Muskie, but he was probably closest to Humphrey, the winner of the 1968 primaries. Aside from their ideological proximity—in the idiom of the era, both Humphrey and Brzezinski were liberal on domestic issues and strong anti-Communist internationalists—they shared an almost fatalistic belief in America's duty to shape a better world. To both of them, such a better world entailed the transformation and eventual demise of communism—what Brzezinski would later call proof of its "grand failure." Importantly, for neither Humphrey nor Brzezinski did the notion of an anti-Communist foreign policy signify any concern, as it did for Richard Nixon and of course Senator Joseph McCarthy, about domestic Communist activity, real or illusory.

When President Jimmy Carter appointed him as his national security advisor, Brzezinski moved to Washington. Chapter 4 is a comprehensive and at the same time critical overview of what was and what was not accomplished during his four years at the White House. The coauthors of chapter 5 deal with the normalization of U.S. relations with China. They approve and praise the *results* of Brzezinski's dealings with China, but they're critical of his willingness to overlook China's human rights stance and to trade Taiwan's full sovereignty for a quasi-alliance with China against the Soviet Union, as well as his treatment of Secretary of State Vance and his colleagues at the Department of State. Chapters 6–9, written by Brzezinski's colleagues on the NSC staff, offer an altogether different perspective. Unwittingly (as the authors didn't preview chapter 5), these four essays amount to a vigorous if indirect defense of the boss they respected and the policies he pursued. Let the reader decide!

With respect to the Carter administration's China policy, the controversy about Brzezinski centered around two major questions.

First, was he correct to support a delay in arms control negotiations with Moscow until after the normalization of U.S.-China relations? The Department of State's view that midlevel officials there leaked to the elite press in Western capitals was that something was better than nothing: a minor deal with Moscow was within reach, and that's what should be sought and achieved as soon as possible. President Carter, who had campaigned against the step-by-step approach pursued by Nixon and Kissinger, wanted a breakthrough and therefore instructed Vance to press the Soviet leaders for an agreement that would include major cuts in the two countries' arsenal of nuclear weapons. For his part, Brzezinski initially tended to agree with Vance, but he soon modified his position, believing that Moscow would consent to substantial reductions only after the U.S. and China had come to terms about establishing normal relations. The upshot of these differences was that Vance's 1977 mission to Moscow failed, in part because the Soviet leaders were surprised by the change from one U.S. administration to another, and they questioned the motivation of the unfamiliar new team in Washington. Vance's subsequent mission to Beijing also failed to produce results, in part because the profoundly anti-Soviet Chinese preferred to deal with the similarly anti-Soviet Brzezinski rather than the presumably more pro-détente Vance.

Second, did Brzezinski fight for principle or for turf? In his memoir and in his foreword to this book, President Carter sides with Brzezinski. In a letter published in *Foreign Affairs* in 1999, he said he had instructed Brzezinski to approach the China negotiations without full advance consultation with officials at the Department of State. In an unusually blunt rebuttal of Brzezinski's critics, some of whom are cited in chapter 5, Carter wrote,

> I was leery of channeling my proposals through the State Department, because I did not feel that I had full support there and it was and is an enormous bureaucracy that is unable and sometimes unwilling to keep a secret. It seemed obvious to me that premature public disclosure of our intensifying diplomatic effort could arouse a firestorm of opposition from those who thought that Taiwan should always be "one China." I decided that no negotiating instructions to Ambassador Leonard

Woodcock [in Beijing] would ever be channeled through the State Department; they would be sent directly from the White House.

Like most if not all of his predecessors, Carter was also dissatisfied with the quality of the State Department's policy recommendations and with its slow procedures. By contrast, Brzezinski's NSC prepared recommendations to the president on time and accommodated the president's preferred style of administrative modus operandi. Moreover, Carter, mindful of Republican criticism of Democrats as weak on national security issues, seems to have favored Brzezinski's confrontational style over Vance's conciliatory approach in order to quiet the Republicans. Put another way, there *was* a bureaucratic tussle between the street fighter, as Leslie Gelb called Brzezinski, and the soft-spoken Vance, who was more at home as a mediator than as an advocate, but there were also differences about policy priorities. To Vance, an arms control agreement with the Soviet Union—a country with sufficient nuclear muscle to destroy the world—mattered more than anything else, with the possible exception of strengthening transatlantic relations. For his part, Brzezinski was neither opposed to nor enthusiastic about early negotiations with Moscow. His concern was that the United States was too weak in the aftermath of Vietnam (and Watergate), while the Soviet leadership seemed too confident to be willing to make concessions. For these reasons, he was willing to wait in the hope that a U.S. accord with China would make Moscow more acquiescent. To the extent that a friendly U.S.-China relationship could put additional pressure on the Soviet Union, Brzezinski believed that his principal objective would be met.

After the White House years, Brzezinski remained an influential advocate of the type of policies he favored at the NSC. In the 1980s, as chapter 10 shows, he was deeply involved with Poland. He worked closely with Pope John Paul II, U.S. labor unions, and Radio Free Europe to destabilize Poland under martial law. In a sense, the Soviet leadership's claim about a "plot" to liberate Poland from Communist rule was true, for coordination among a variety of groups and individuals did take place behind closed doors. Out of office, Brzezinski remained very active indeed. Chapter 11 offers an eyewitness account of his 1989 visit to Moscow on the eve of the collapse of communism in the Soviet Bloc. He was in Moscow to participate in an unofficial, off-the-record dialogue between American and Soviet experts about the future of Eastern Europe. His hosts sensed the imminent breakup of the bloc, and they gave him—the notorious, anti-Soviet Dr. Brzezinski—an opportunity to speak to hundreds of officials there about how to navigate peacefully toward an uncertain but non-Communist future. This

American strategist with a Polish heart refrained from "lecturing" his audience, but privately he could congratulate himself for contributing to what he was witnessing, which was the grand failure of the Soviet experience and the impending independence of Poland.

In the 1990s, the main issue that occupied Brzezinski was the enlargement of NATO to include new members from Central and Eastern Europe, but the Middle East remained on his agenda. Chapter 12 presents a detailed description and analysis of his unambiguous critique of U.S. policies toward Iraq in the new century. Did he turn into a dove, as the chapter's subtitle suggests? In point of fact, Brzezinski disclaims both the designation of dove after the end of the cold war and the designation of hawk during the cold war. "I was always for a policy that allowed us to prevail in the cold war, and to do it by a strategy of what I called peaceful engagement," he explains in our conversation as recorded in chapter 17. Yet as he considers America's relative standing in the twenty-first century, it is clear that he has reduced expectations, particularly as far as *military* interventions are concerned. Chapter 13 shows that he has consistently pressed for a more activist U.S. *diplomatic* involvement in the Arab-Israeli conflict; his support for a two-state solution there goes back to the mid-1970s. He put forth a four-part plan as the basis for a comprehensive agreement between the Israelis and the Palestinians. In recent statements on the subject, Brzezinski still regards Washington—and the president, in particular—as the key to bringing the two sides together in order to avert a larger Middle East conflagration, but he appears to have shied away from the idea of the United States trying to impose a settlement.

Brzezinski's criticism of President Obama in this respect (see chap. 17) makes him one of the few bipartisan voices in the midst of the kind of partisan and disruptive debates that have come to dominate America's political landscape. Bipartisanship aside, Brzezinski is also guided by a desire to take a longer-term view as a strategist focusing on the *consequences* of doing too much or too little. Chapter 14 identifies him as a strategic thinker, and his most recent book is titled *Strategic Vision*. He's always been preoccupied with the future, trying to understand and anticipate what matters and what doesn't. In one book, he once dealt with what was then the impending "technetronic" era and its implications for foreign policy. In another, he analyzed the "grand failure" of communism and its implications for foreign policy. In *Strategic Vision*, the main subject is America's domestic condition, including political deadlock and its implications for foreign policy. For Brzezinski, it seems, the future is history that needs to be written by sane and wise people who listen to educated advice and who are not easily swayed by angst about the next election. The otherwise liberal Brzezinski has probably moved closer to the conservative Edmund Burke's theory of representation—that politicians should be elected in order to do what *they* consider best for their country and their constituents. This, of course, is different from what most Americans, conservative or liberal, embrace, which is the mirror theory of representation—that politicians should mirror the views of their constituents as closely as possible.

In part four, the shortest part of this book, chapter 15 presents a portrait of Brzezinski as a professor for more than half a century. Although some of his students wished for more personal attention from him, those receiving an "A" were thrilled to have received a handwritten note of congratulations from the demanding and seemingly standoffish professor. In chapter 16, Francis Fukuyama, a widely respected colleague, describes Brzezinski's luncheon seminars with a few carefully chosen specialists from think tanks and SAIS faculty. The sessions always featured a guest speaker who would talk about a current event and its ramifications, followed by discussion moderated by Brzezinski. Finally, chapter 17 offers an abridged and edited version of two conversations I had with him in the spring of 2012. In this self-assessment, Brzezinski speaks candidly about people who made a difference in his life—among them his father, Pope John Paul II, and President Carter. In greater detail than ever before, he also reacts to the charge that his disapproval of certain Israeli policies stems from his "Polish-Catholic," and presumably anti-Semitic, heritage. Of all foreign countries he visits, Brzezinski says, after Poland he feels most at home in Israel. He also relates the reasons why he didn't Anglicize his name when he had an opportunity to do so. It's an unusual discussion for a very private man who much prefers to discuss policy alternatives to reflections about himself.

❖ In the pantheon of major American foreign policy thinkers and practitioners, where is Zbigniew Brzezinski's place? It is only a slight overstatement that, since at least the end of World War II, the practice of self-interest and the rhetoric of idealism have guided U.S. foreign policy. Such influential thinkers as Walter Lippmann, Hans Morgenthau, George Kennan, J. William Fulbright, Henry Kissinger, and Zbigniew Brzezinski have all stressed the national interest as the guidepost to be followed, and at one time or another they all warned against the overextension of American power. As early as 1943, Lippmann summed it up in one memorable sentence: "The nation must maintain its objectives and its power in equilibrium," he wrote, "its purposes within its means and its means equal to its purposes, its commitments related to its resources and its resources adequate to its commitments." In 1951, writing along the same lines, Morgenthau appealed to the American people to forget "the crusading notion that any nation, however virtuous and powerful, can have the mission to make the world over in its own image," and to remember "that no nation's power is without limits, and hence that its policies must respect the power and interests of others." It's more difficult to characterize George Kennan's positions. His famous "X" article in 1947 was a clarion call for the use of military force whenever and wherever needed to counter Soviet expansion, and in 1948 he pressed for an aggressive program of covert warfare against the Soviet Union. However, after Lippmann criticized him in a series of articles, Kennan claimed he was misunderstood, namely, that his notion of containment in the "X" article didn't amount to the application of military force against communism. He subsequently embraced Lippmann's limitationist perspective.

For Brzezinski, it seems that the gap between the practice of mostly carefully limited goals and rhetoric informed by political opportunism and wishful thinking became evident in the mid-1950s. It was the time when the Eisenhower administration, and particularly Secretary of State John Foster Dulles, delivered one speech after another proclaiming the goal of the "liberation" of Eastern Europe from Communist domination. In election years, in particular, both Republicans and Democrats talked about the "rollback" of Soviet power. Yet, behind the scenes, Vice President Nixon in mid-1956 considered a Soviet military intervention in Eastern Europe, as happened in Hungary later that year, "not an unmixed evil"—because it would be good propaganda for the West. This is when Brzezinski, more interested in actual gains than in propaganda victories, began to devise his notion of *peaceful engagement*. It was containment plus. It was the rejection of what was jokingly identified in the West as the Soviet concept of peaceful coexistence: "what's mine is mine, what's yours is negotiable." If Moscow was competing with the West outside the Soviet Bloc, Brzezinski seemed to be saying, the West should compete inside the Soviet Bloc.

Except for a few articles during the Vietnam War when he backed the Johnson administration's "globalist" outlook, Brzezinski consistently held up the competitive "containment plus" paradigm. While he accepted the commonly held version of containment that stressed the goal of maintaining a military balance that would nonetheless tilt toward the United States, Brzezinski understood Soviet vulnerabilities. He believed that while the Soviet Union was a military giant, it was an economic and political dwarf. Neither the nations of the Soviet Union, such as the Baltic countries or Georgia, nor the nations of Eastern Europe, such as Poland and Hungary, joined the Soviet Union or the Soviet Bloc voluntarily.

Their integration was incomplete if not altogether unsuccessful. Their common institutions were ineffective. Permanent shortages of elementary necessities proved the failure of their centrally planned economies.

To exploit these weaknesses, Brzezinski's proposed "peaceful engagement," also called "differentiation," was adopted by the Johnson and Kennedy administrations. In Eastern Europe, Moscow's backyard, the policy signified a strong opposition to Communist rule, combined with economic enticements and educational exchanges, activities aimed at cultivating intellectuals eager for renewing contact with the West, and even favors extended to Communist regimes that showed signs of either domestic liberalization or a modicum of foreign policy detachment from Moscow. The goal was thus limited in scope: liberalization rather than liberty, diversity rather than democracy, partial detachment from the Soviet Union rather than complete separation, and support wherever possible for nationalist aspirations. Brzezinski offered a realistic, evolutionary alternative to empty political rhetoric.

The opportunity to apply this alternative to China was the ultimate test of Brzezinski's *realpolitik*. Once in the White House, Brzezinski's approach—rooted in the maxim "the enemy of my enemy is my friend"—was as self-evident as it was simple. After all, China had left the Soviet orbit since the early 1960s—some 15 long years earlier—and it was now ready to cooperate with the United States against the "hegemonists" in Moscow. Brzezinski's anti-Sovietism, learned at home and nourished by studies of totalitarianism and the Soviet system in particular, made the choice of reconciliation with China relatively easy. It was a choice made by a strategist who approached each issue, then and since, with America's long-term interests in mind.

## PART I

# From the Ivy League

# Zbig, Henry, and the New U.S. Foreign Policy Elite

## JUSTIN VAÏSSE

Cambridge, January 23, 1964

Dear Zbig: I just read in the latest issue of LOOK Magazine that you were elected as one of the Ten Outstanding [Young] Men of the Year. I knew you were outstanding but I had never thought of you as that young. No wonder Muska prefers you to me.

Let me take this opportunity to congratulate you and Muska on the new baby.

Warm regards.
Sincerely, Henry Kissinger
PS—I thought your article in *The New Leader* was splendid. I have only one comment: do you think the Germans are clever enough for the policy you suggest? It may be too subtle. Let's discuss this sometime.

New York, January 30, 1964

Dear Outstanding '58: Muska prefers me because I am vintage '63. I am told that this year was a particularly good breeding year.

I looked you up in Cambridge yesterday, but you were not there. Too bad because I would have liked to talk to you about the state of the world—otherwise known as the accelerating process of disintegration of American foreign policy.

Warm regards,
Sincerely, Zbigniew Brzezinski[1]

This is not the correspondence between two enemies. It is, by all standards, a cordial exchange where mutual respect, intellectual appreciation, and personal proximity are evident. Observers have it wrong when they write about the "long-standing mutual coolness" between Zbigniew Brzezinski and Henry Kissinger. They are even more mistaken when they depict the pair as lifelong foes harboring "smoldering resentment" toward one another, sworn enemies locked in an epic battle for fame and power in America's postwar decades. Typical of this misrepresentation is Walter Isaacson's portrayal of Zbigniew Brzezinski as "Kissinger's old nemesis at Harvard" in his landmark biography of Henry Kissinger.[2]

There may have been a dose of friction alongside camaraderie at Harvard, where the German-born Kissinger arrived in 1947 and the Polish-born Brzezinski in 1950. Both students were ambitious and competitive. Even though they didn't move in the exact same circles (Kissinger was in international studies, Brzezinski a Sovietologist at the Russian Center), they both strained toward the same goal—rise fast in the Harvard hierarchy, make their mark, and have a political impact beyond academia. In the 1950s, Kissinger was described by his peers as brilliant but also clumsy and sometimes arrogant. One day, in the mid-1950s, Brzezinski was waiting to see his thesis director, Carl Friedrich, sitting in the lobby along with Stanley Hoffmann (another brilliant Central European immigrant, born in Vienna). Kissinger arrives, sails through the lobby, knocks on the door, and, without waiting for an answer, proceeds into Friedrich's office. Before he enters, however, he catches Brzezinski's furious stare at him and needles him: "Zbig," he asserts with his strong German accent, "that's how junior faculty should be treated."[3]

But such frictions don't create durable enmity, and there are also traces of friendly cooperation between them. In 1956 and 1957, Brzezinski writes to "Henry" to recommend Polish candidates for the Harvard International Seminar, a cold war summer program for Europeans and Asians created by Kissinger and his mentor Professor William Yandell Elliott (whose rivalry with Carl Friedrich in the Department of Government was well known), and receives a kind acknowledgment.[4] Both men deny they saw each other as rivals during their Harvard years, and if there ever existed some competition on Brzezinski's side, Kissinger insists, it's because it was "built into the system, in the sense that I was two or three years ahead of him as a graduate student and in every job I got.[4] I got the jobs that he wanted and deserved—I didn't get them at his expense, but that sort of put him in an inherently competitive position with me and imposed the need to come up with some differences."[5]

With this remark, Kissinger introduces the second reason behind the widely shared cliché of their supposed "intense rivalry": the striking similarity of their life stories. Kissinger, born in Fürth in 1923, is five years older than Brzezinski, born in Warsaw in 1928. Both sailed from Europe to New York in the fall of 1938—Kissinger a Jewish refugee fleeing persecution from the Third Reich, Brzezinski the son of a Polish diplomat to be posted in Montreal as consul general. Both went to Harvard and soon made a name for themselves by their intellectual and political acumen. In spite of their accents, both would ascend to the top of American society, lifted by the enormous needs of strategic expertise that came with America's rise to globalism.

Both men got prominent academic positions early on: Kissinger as a tenured professor at Harvard in 1959, Brzezinski at Columbia in 1960 because the Department of Government at Harvard was clogged with talented young men and couldn't offer him tenure early enough. At that time, he was identified solely as a brilliant Ivy League Sovietologist, "a Harvard Professor with the unbelievable name of Zbigniev [*sic*] Brzezinski, who reads Pravda with his morning coffee and delights in following the intricacies of Kremlin politics," in the words of a *Wall Street Journal* article of 1960.[6] Both men were co-opted early on into the Council on Foreign Relations, widely known as "the Council." Kissinger published his first article in *Foreign Affairs*, the journal of the Council, at age 32, Brzezinski at age 33, and both became regular contributors, among the most prolific of all times.[7] As demonstrated by the correspondence cited at the beginning of this chapter, the U.S. Junior Chamber of Commerce didn't miss the early signs of their promising careers. It selected Kissinger as one of the "Ten Outstanding Young Men" of 1958, at age 35, and Brzezinski in 1963, at age 35 as well. After a first experience as a consultant to the National Security Council under Kennedy, around age 38, Kissinger was named national security advisor by Richard Nixon in 1968. Brzezinski, after having worked at the State Department's Policy Planning Staff under Lyndon Johnson (around age 38 as well), was named national security advisor by Jimmy Carter in 1976. Both men have regularly published widely read and widely debated books and have retained considerable intellectual and political influence until their retirement, which both have so far refused to take. How could these twin titans of American foreign policy not be rivals?

But perhaps the question of their relationship is not the one we ought to ask first. And perhaps their parallel biographies tell us something more important than the captivating success story of two immigrants. For Kissinger and Brzezinski did not simply conform to a familiar pattern of upward social mobility. They were trailblazers in a profoundly transformed landscape of international policy making, the pioneers of a new model of American foreign policy elite. And if Kissinger came first, because, as he pointed out himself, he was older, it took Brzezinski to validate this now-familiar pattern of the academic intellectual turned Washington strategist and diplomat.

To understand this transformation, it is useful to take a point of reference in the world that preceded them. On a snowy day of December 1960, president-elect John F. Kennedy received banker Robert Lovett for lunch at his Georgetown house. Lovett, born in 1895, was the son of the chairman of the Union Pacific Railroad. He had followed the perfect *cursus honorum* of the WASP elite—the Hill School, Yale University, the Skull and Bones society, and Harvard—and married well. A partner in the powerful New York investment bank Brown Bros., Harriman & Co., Robert Lovett was the embodiment of the foreign policy Establishment and its values: moderation, aversion to publicity and self-promotion, devotion to public service. He knew international affairs because of his business activities, and because he had served the United States as a commander of the first naval air squadron during World War I, a special assistant to Secretary of War Henry Stimson during World War II, an under secretary of state under George C. Marshall, and finally as the fourth secretary of defense. Although he was a Republican, Kennedy offered him not one but three secretary jobs in his administration: defense, state, or treasury—his pick. But Lovett declined, citing poor health, and recommended in his stead Robert McNamara for the Pentagon, Dean Rusk for Foggy Bottom, and Douglas Dillon for the Treasury. All three were hired.[8]

Such was the power and prestige of the Establishment, of the "wise men" who created the American world in the mid-twentieth century—including Henry Stimson, Dean Acheson, Averell Harriman, John McCloy, and Chip Bohlen.[9] But by the end of the turbulent 1960s, the world of foreign policy making had dramatically changed, and that sociological transformation was embodied by the nomination of immigrant PhD-holding Henry Kissinger as national security advisor, eight years before immigrant PhD-holding Zbigniew Brzezinski got the same job at the White House. Interestingly, both men competed for influence with secretaries of state who personified the old Establishment (and whom they tellingly dominated): William Rogers in the case of Kissinger, Cyrus Vance in the case of Brzezinski, two WASP New York City lawyers who played by the old rules.

The old elite was naturally called to power through their connections and social hegemony; Kissinger and Brzezinski had to conquer their own positions—and they played by the new rules. They were ambitious, hardworking, and brazenly self-promoting, and they relied on three key developments of the postwar decades: the Cold War University; the rise of a gray zone between academia and policy making where media, policy organizations, and think tanks played key roles; and the increasing politicization in the selection of foreign affairs officials. They didn't create these developments, but they were the first to take full advantage of them—and by doing so, they helped bring about the Washington we know today.

The Harvard Kissinger and Brzezinski entered, respectively, in 1947 and 1950 was no longer a sleepy elite Ivy League institution. It was the bustling epitome of the Cold War University.[10] With an existential battle to fight in two parts of the world after 1941 and then global responsibilities in the cold war, the United States suddenly found itself in urgent need of knowledge on a range of issues, from nuclear physics to economics and foreign languages—to develop an atomic bomb, promote economic development in Third World countries, and administer faraway lands. To do this, it turned to universities, pouring huge amounts of federal money into the likes of Harvard, Columbia, and Stanford. This money had the effect of turning top universities into powerful research institutions (sometimes to the detriment of teaching students), granting a formidable international advance to the United States in many sciences. It also transformed the nature of academic work itself: "The free university, historically the fountainhead of free ideas and scientific discovery, has experienced a revolution," warned President Eisenhower in his famous 1961 farewell address in which he also blasted the military-industrial complex. "The prospect of domination of the nation's scholars by Federal employment, project allocations, and the power of money is ever present—and is gravely to be regarded."[11]

It is precisely these "compromised campuses" with their inflow of federal money and their blurry borders with the government that the student revolt would denounce in the 1960s.[12] But to Kissinger and Brzezinski, the Cold War University, with its direct channels to Washington and policy-oriented scholarship, was the blessed milieu that allowed them to flourish. The field of area studies, for example, was born of the necessities of waging war and guarding peace in faraway and unknown countries, by combining language skills with the multidisciplinary knowledge of one region. In 1946, the Russian Institute was created at Columbia with money from the Rockefeller Foundation and former OSS (Office of Strategic Services) official Geroid Robinson as its director, and in 1948, the Russian Research Center at Harvard, financed by the Carnegie Corporation and the federal government (including the Air Force, the State Department, and the Central Intelligence Agency), was inaugurated.[13] In the summer of 1950, when McGill graduate student Zbigniew Brzezinski didn't have enough money to go to Harvard, Merle Fainsod gave him a research assistant job with Alex Inkeles, noted sociologist at the Russian Research Center, which made it possible for him to go to Cambridge.[14] Brzezinski would spend the entire decade there, becoming a "graduate student fellow" before his 1953 PhD, then a "research fellow," and lastly a "research associate" of the center, and fully participating in its collective research projects.[15] That is where he wrote not only his dissertation, published in 1956 (*The Permanent Purge*), but also the book on totalitarianism co-authored with Carl Friedrich (1956), which first made him visible in the field of Sovietology, as well as the first edition of his most important book, *The Soviet Bloc: Unity and Conflict* (1960).[16]

Kissinger, for his part, benefitted from the rise of international relations as a discipline in its own right, with realism as its dominant tendency, and of the particular attention given to America's image abroad. The International Seminar, mentioned above, was created by Elliott and Kissinger in 1950–51. It was aimed at countering Communist influence by having forty young students and leaders from Europe and Asia attend seminars at Harvard and visit the region and Washington over the summer.[17] Both the seminar, which provided Kissinger with a vast rolodex of alumni he would later put to good use, and its attending magazine *Confluence*, which put him in touch with the prestigious intellectuals he published (Reinhold Niebuhr, Raymond Aron, James Burnham, Hannah Arendt, etc.),[18] were financed by private foundations and by the CIA—a fact that became public only in the 1960s—in the cold war context of winning hearts and minds.

The Cold War University was also the incubator of many research centers on international affairs, combining scholarship with a policy-oriented approach. Both Kissinger and Brzezinski were involved in the creation of Harvard's Center for International Affairs (CFIA, later the WCFIA) in 1958.[19] McGeorge Bundy, the dean of the Faculty of Arts and Sciences, oversaw the birth of the center, made possible by the Ford Foundation. He asked Robert Bowie, director of policy planning at the Department of State from 1953 to 1957, to become its first director and Kissinger, then a rising star, to be his deputy. The two men didn't get along, and the tension between them became legendary.[20] Bowie, however, really liked the younger Brzezinski, who divided his time between the Russian Research Center and the CFIA in 1958–60, writing his book *The Soviet Bloc* under the auspices of both centers, and mingling with the foreign visiting fellows Bowie and Kissinger gathered each academic year. The CFIA was quite an impressive place: in the late 1950s and early 1960s, one could run into people like Thomas Schelling, Samuel Huntington, Stanley Hoffmann, Joseph Nye, Morton Halperin, Walt Rostow, and Kenneth Waltz in its meetings. In spite of the best efforts of Robert Bowie and Merle Fainsod to retain Brzezinski at Harvard, Dean Bundy was not able to create a new chair for Brzezinski in 1959, and he left for Columbia in 1960, following in the footsteps of his friend Samuel Huntington (who returned to Harvard a few years later, while Brzezinski declined two offers to get back—as did Kissinger in 1977).[21]

The Cold War University thus produced, starting in the 1950s, a generation of young men who were professionals, true experts of international affairs—rather than enlightened amateurs like the Old Establishment types—and who were policy oriented. But for the most ambitious ones, like Kissinger and Brzezinski, academia was not fully satisfying, and they aspired to get closer to power, to share a piece of the action. For Brzezinski, the turning point came in 1960, when he decided to go to Columbia. "Had I been given tenure at Harvard," he later explained, "I would have been delighted and I would have stayed. But then I was forced to think, what do I really want to be? I said to myself I don't want to be crossing the Harvard yard year after year carrying a folder, lecture number 7, 'joke used last year,' 'class reaction,' with a tweed jacket. I want to influence the world, shape American policy. And New York was better for that."[22] This is what Kissinger had concluded four years earlier: "The rarefied world of academe was not as enticing as the power-charged precincts of Manhattan. The realization that life as a professor would not sate his ambitions represented a major turning point in Kissinger's career," writes Walter Isaacson.[23] Thanks to a recommendation by Arthur Schlesinger Jr., Kissinger had become the director of a study group on nuclear strategy at the New York–based Council on Foreign Relations in 1955. Two years later, he published *Nuclear Weapons and Foreign Policy*, based on the discussions of the group. The book became a surprise best seller and started to put Kissinger's name on the map, facilitating his selection as deputy director of the CFIA in 1958.[24]

This is where the second important development of the postwar decades comes in: the creation of a vast gray zone between academia and foreign policy making, an in-between world of think tanks, journals, mass media, and policy organizations that Kissinger and Brzezinski were among the first to navigate and use to their advantage.

A step closer to actual policy making than university research centers like the CFIA, think tanks started to make their presence felt in the 1960s and 1970s: old ones like Brookings reinforced their work on international affairs, younger ones like RAND grew more influential, and new ones appeared, such as the Center for Strategic and International Studies (CSIS). But in the 1950s and early 1960s, the New York–based Council on Foreign Relations ("the Council") was still reigning supreme. Created in the wake of the rejection of the Treaty of Versailles, it embodied the foreign policy Establishment—its preferences (internationalism, Atlanticism, and a prudent but determined American leadership), its social values (consensus, discretion, responsibility), and its connections with the outward-oriented New York business community of the biggest investment banks and law firms. The Council was a membership organization, but, when enough recommendations were provided, it was open to new talents, as we just saw with Kissinger, who benefitted tremendously from his association with the Council. Brzezinski, for his part, was made a member in 1961. Hamilton Fish Armstrong, the legendary editor of *Foreign Affairs*, took him under his wing when he arrived in New York City and had him write several articles that bolstored his nascent reputation as a specialist on Eastern Europe and the Soviet Bloc.[25]

In 1964, the Council asked both Brzezinski and Kissinger to give a series of seminars on transatlantic relations and to publish their thoughts. A year later, two influential books resulted from this initiative.[26] In *The Troubled Partnership*, which focused on political-strategic issues inside NATO, Kissinger made the case for a better American understanding of European, especially French and German, diplomatic positions, warning against American tendencies to simplify or ignore them, and he crushed the idea of a nuclear Multilateral Force pushed forward by his enemy Robert Bowie. In *Alternative to Partition*, Brzezinski elaborated on the idea of peaceful engagement with Eastern Europe he had laid out in *Foreign Affairs* four years earlier.[27] Since "rollback" and "liberation" were chimera and resignation over the division of Europe was not an acceptable option, he argued, the United States should take the lead in hugging Eastern European countries closer, encouraging cultural and economic exchanges, so as to decrease cold war tensions—and increase the inner contradictions and centrifugal tendencies of the Soviet Bloc (the latter objective, although not explicit, is easy to discern between the lines).

The formidable platform for visibility, quality information, and useful contacts offered by the Council was complemented by the association of both Kissinger and Brzezinski with other think tanks. Kissinger worked with RAND, for which Brzezinski consulted in the mid-1960s. Brzezinski took part in several initiatives of the Brookings Institution's foreign policy program under Henry Owen, most notably a 1974–75 study group on the Israeli-Palestinian conflict that recommended Palestinian self-determination (subject to Palestinian acceptance of the sovereignty and integrity of Israel), resulting in either an independent Palestinian state or autonomous Palestinian self-government in Jordan.[28] On top of think tanks, foundations played an important role in creating this in-between world in expansion. Not only did the Ford Foundation help build the Cold War University, including Kissinger's International Seminar and Brzezinski's Research Institute on Communist Affairs at Columbia, but it also financed important foreign policy seminars in its center in Bellagio, Italy, which both men attended, and it provided a grant for the year Brzezinski spent in Japan in 1971—which led to the creation of the Trilateral Commission.

The evocation of the Trilateral Commission invites an exploration of another aspect of the nascent in-between world of foreign policy which Kissinger and Brzezinski navigated, that of policy groups and networks in the United States and beyond. Kissinger, as we saw, acquired an extensive network of contacts abroad with the Harvard International Seminar, which he directed from 1951 to 1965 (and again in 1967). He also got a powerful political boost from his work for the Rockefeller Brothers Fund as director of its Special Studies Project and from his association with the governor of New York and presidential hopeful Nelson Rockefeller. Brzezinski benefited from his association with another Rockefeller, Nelson's brother David, chairman of the Chase Manhattan Bank and of the Council on Foreign Relations (starting in 1970). In 1972, David Rockefeller and Brzezinski, along with Robert Bowie, Henry Owen, McGeorge Bundy, and others, cooperated to create the Trilateral Commission, a private group of elites from Europe, North America, and Japan which had the objective of weighing in collectively, through their public reports and networks, on the global challenges brought about by increasing interdependence. Interestingly, this creation is partly due to the refusal of another organization created at the height of the cold war, the Bilderberg Group, to add the Japanese to their transatlantic conversation.[29] Both Kissinger and Brzezinski, of course, attended several Bilderberg meetings among the European and American wealthy and powerful members and were part of this transatlantic network created in the postwar decades which included the Atlantic Council, the Aspen Institute, the Salzburg seminars, and the Munich Wehrkunde Conference.

If in these leadership circles the Old Establishment values of discretion and effacement were still valid, the situation was rapidly changing. In the course of the 1960s and 1970s, another key development contributed to shaping the in-between world of foreign affairs in which Kissinger and Brzezinski thrived: the rise of the media. While there had always been high-level journalism and commentary on foreign affairs by the likes of Walter Lippmann or Joseph Alsop, radio and television expanded tremendously, and the press became more active and assertive (the Vietnam War and Watergate were key moments) and also more open to outside perspectives—that is, for example, the period when op-ed pages first appeared. Kissinger and Brzezinski both became active and sought-after commentators on international issues well beyond *Foreign Affairs*, by writing for journals like the *New Republic, Newsweek*, and of course the *Washington Post* and the *New York Times*. They knew how to write the trenchant op-ed, the pithy and timely analysis of international events, and offer the catchy quote—and they enjoyed the publicity that furthered their fame.

Both became early commentators on television. In June 1965, for example, Brzezinski was live on CBS, alongside a RAND researcher, to help his former Harvard dean McGeorge Bundy, then national security advisor for Lyndon Johnson, make the case in favor of the Vietnam War. The three men were countered by Hans Morgenthau, a famous professor at the University of Chicago and father of the realist school of international relations, flanked by two other antiwar experts.[30] Two years earlier, a humorous exchange had taken place between Kissinger and Brzezinski: "I understand from the New York educational station," Kissinger complained, "that you recommended me to be on a program with you as a proponent of the "hard" line [on U.S.-Soviet relations]. I am flattered, of course, that you should think of me. But I loathe labels, and I was not aware of the fact that you were notoriously more moderate than I am. Moreover, how can I get a reputation for being wize if you will not let me pretend to be of the middle road?" A few days later, Brzezinski shot back with a tongue-in-cheek reply: "Since some Eric [Erich] Fromm type was to be the 'soft,' you were only natural as the exponent of the 'hard-headed,' statesmanlike, realist approach. I was only to make a middle of the way opening statement to set up the 'softie' for decapitation. So your reputation for being 'wize' (at Columbia we spell it with an 's,' like in 'Soviet' and 'Stalin') would not have been impaired."[31]

Robert Lovett or John McCloy would never have been caught dead in a TV studio, but the new elite were competing for exposure in a changed environment where the media was becoming increasingly important in the discussion of foreign affairs. In that new social system, social networks and visibility reinforced each other. After a scholarly book, publishing a more policy-oriented piece in *Foreign Affairs* made you an interesting potential contributor to the *New York Times*. An op-ed in the *Times* or a piece in *Newsweek* (where Brzezinski was a columnist in 1970) would then catch the eye of the administration, which would consult you. That would lead a think tank to invite you into its task force and the Bilderberg to admit you as a member, offering in turn new social connections, increasing your value as a prominent university professor, and ultimately making you an influential public expert. Thanks to his work at the Council on Foreign Relations and his books and articles, Kissinger was selected by McGeorge Bundy as deputy director of the CFIA in 1958, as we saw, and then offered to be a part-time consultant for the National Security Council (that 1961 experience, however, did not go well, as Kissinger was sidelined by Bundy). Similar assets led Henry Owen, then director of the Policy Planning Staff, and Walt Rostow, who had replaced Bundy as national security advisor, to offer Brzezinski a position at the Policy Planning Staff in 1966–68.

But in order to get to the top positions of America's foreign policy decision making, rather than being relegated to serving the Establishment in secondary jobs, success in another field was required—that of electoral campaigns. In 1960, Kennedy was still offering cabinet-level positions to Robert Lovett and the old elite, by virtue of their prestige and connections, and regardless of partisan affiliation. But that time was coming to a close, and Kennedy himself started hiring new professional elites, such as Walt Rostow—academics and experts who had been advising him on foreign affairs during his campaign.

Kissinger and Brzezinski played the foreign policy adviser game early on, and with so much talent they became advisers to multiple candidates. The former, as we saw, worked for Nelson Rockefeller, who unsuccessfully tried to get the Republican nomination in 1960, 1964, and 1968. Once he lost the 1968 campaign, the campaign staff of the vice president and Democratic candidate Hubert Humphrey, through its foreign policy chief adviser Brzezinski, asked Kissinger if he would be willing to share the "Nixon files"—the negative research on its main opponent that the Rockefeller operation accumulated over the years. Kissinger said he would, thereby showing its good will to the Humphrey camp and potentially positioning himself in case of a Democratic victory. But when Brzezinski made arrangements to go pick up the files at the Rockefeller Center, the operation got cancelled. Kissinger had just officially become a Nixon foreign policy advisor.[32] Nine years later, at a ceremony in honor of Hubert Humphrey at the U.S. Senate, Brzezinski would make a cryptic and ironic reference to this episode. "The greatest opportunity in my life was to serve in your 1968 campaign," he said to Humphrey. Then, pointing to Kissinger in the audience, he added: "And I want to publicly thank Dr. Kissinger for the assistance he offered during that campaign."[33] But that was not all: before he became an official advisor to Nixon, Kissinger, who had been a consultant and even an emissary for the Johnson administration on Vietnam and had good contacts in the U.S. delegation in Paris led by Averell Harriman, offered inside information on the ongoing negotiation with the North Vietnamese to the Nixon campaign.[34]

He had, in other words, managed to position himself in three campaigns, across party lines. This paid off when Nixon offered him the job of national security advisor a few weeks later. This crucial decision of late 1968 marked the true changing of the guard between the Establishment and the new foreign policy elite. Many were not quite expecting it, and even Brzezinski was caught by surprise.

> In 68, I worked for Hubert Humphrey, I was his principal foreign policy advisor.... To give you a sense of how...modest my expectations were, I thought maybe I might become an Assistant Secretary of State for Europe. Well, it may be strange, but I wasn't ready, and what suddenly boosted my expectations was Henry. Nixon won, he made Henry. It never occurred to me he would get that. It never occurred to me when I was Humphrey's principal advisor that I could be National Security Advisor. It was not in my sense of what was feasible in America at that time.[35]

Zbigniew Brzezinski had come to know the vice president during his stint at the Policy Planning Staff, and he had accepted the invitation to lead his foreign policy campaign team. After Humphrey's defeat, Brzezinski kept advising him on international issues during the following years, and when Humphrey ran for the Democratic nomination again in 1972, Brzezinski sent him analyses, talking points, and suggestions through David Fromkin and Max Kampelman, who were managing foreign affairs in his campaign.[36] If he was not as close to Humphrey as in 1968, this was compensated by the fact that he also positioned himself in other campaigns for 1972. Some of the memos and talking points he sent to Humphrey were the exact same ones he sent to Edmund Muskie and Ted Kennedy, in an older version of cut and paste, and he also sent material to Scoop Jackson.[37] Like Kissinger four years earlier, Brzezinski was hedging his bets (although within the same party), but the truth is that none of the candidates, apart from Humphrey, were really to his liking. And he was extremely critical of the one candidate who won the nomination, George McGovern, whom he saw as way too far to the left on foreign policy. Some of the senator's advisers nonetheless tried to get his endorsement in August 1972, but he remained cautious and even had to make public in a letter to the editor of the *Washington Post* that he was not a McGovern supporter as had been alleged.[38] A few weeks later, McGovern suffered the crushing defeat Brzezinski had predicted long ago against Nixon, thereby prolonging Kissinger's position of power (Kissinger would soon be named secretary of state on top of national security advisor).

Brzezinski thus returned to his life as a Columbia professor, an influential writer on foreign affairs, and the director of the nascent Trilateral Commission —the embodiment of the new foreign policy elite. In the 1970s, however, Brzezinski considerably expanded his horizons: from his specialization on the Soviet

Bloc and Europe to an opening to Asia (through his year in Japan in 1971 and his book *The Fragile Blossom*),[39] from his emphasis on politics and diplomacy to a broader sociological perspective on international relations, including the impact of technology on both advanced societies and the Third World (through his 1970 book *The Technetronic Era*),[40] and from academia to the in-between world of foreign affairs elite, with the creation of the Trilateral Commission.

And it is precisely through the Trilateral Commission that he met Governor Jimmy Carter of Georgia. In 1973, while composing the American membership, he and his colleagues needed a Democratic governor from the rapidly industrializing South, and they picked Carter, who proved an eager student at the Commission meetings, since he was lacking international experience. Brzezinski started offering his services, as he was doing for other politicians, and during 1975, he educated the fast-learning governor with his articles and memos, before becoming himself convinced by Carter's acumen and strength and pledging his support.[41] This time, however, he would be a monogamous adviser. In early 1976, Brzezinski had imposed himself as Carter's chief foreign policy advisor, with the help of Richard Gardner, a fellow Trilateralist and Columbia professor, and ran a solid campaign in foreign policy which contributed to Carter's victory against Gerald Ford in November, paving his own way to the White House.

Thus groomed by the Cold War University in the 1950s, charting new waters in the nascent in-between world of foreign affairs in the 1960s and 1970s, and skillfully positioning themselves in electoral campaigns, Kissinger and Brzezinski, by reaching the White House, helped usher in a new age of the American foreign policy elite, relegating the Old Establishment—already discredited by the Vietnam War—to history. In the second chapter of their 1984 book *Our Own Worst Enemy*, I. M. Destler, Leslie Gelb, and Anthony Lake offer a description of this changing of the guard and the advent of what they aptly call the "Professional Elite."[42] Their account is the best so far and is also, on this precise point, partly autobiographical: Gelb and Lake were themselves part of the new professional elite. But on closer examination, Kissinger and Brzezinski were not quite the typical representatives of this new class. Rather, they were early pioneers, hard-to-emulate role models setting higher standards for future generations, especially in terms of intellectual production. By at least one crucial biographical feature, Kissinger and Brzezinski are closer to one another than to anyone in the "professional elite": their relationship to politics.

Both men, as we saw, got to prominent positions thanks to their participation in electoral campaigns. But neither was very partisan. Kissinger certainly has conservative leanings, but he was comfortable working for the Kennedy and

Johnson administrations (even if at the margins), and he was close to Nelson Rockefeller, who gave his very name to a moderate or even liberal strand of the GOP ("Rockefeller Republicans"). Although he rejected the neoconservative worldview and was seen as a villain by the New Right, he was flexible enough to send friendly signals to the Reagan right and even make a tough anti-Soviet speech at the Heritage Foundation. While this wasn't really enough to get re-hired by the Reagan administration, and although he was kept at bay by George H. W. Bush, who didn't like him personally, this allowed him to keep some access to all Republican administrations, especially the George W. Bush one. Brzezinski, for his part, is a lifelong Democrat and a traditional liberal as far as his views on domestic politics are concerned. But his foreign policy opinions are what really matters. As we saw, he refused to endorse McGovern in 1972. He maintained friendly relations with the hawkish Reagan and publicly endorsed George H. W. Bush in the 1988 campaign because he saw Michael Dukakis as too much to the left (much to the dismay of his former Columbia student and National Security Council staffer Madeleine Albright, who acted as Dukakis's foreign policy adviser) and a reincarnation of McGovern. All in all, he was involved in one way or the other with all U.S. presidents between Kennedy and Obama except for George W. Bush, whom he strongly opposed.

These attitudes do not quite coincide with one feature of the "professional elite": heavy politicization. This is largely a question of generation. While Kissinger and Brzezinski were born in the 1920s, the bulk of the "professional elite" were born in the 1940s and after. World War II was the formative experience for Kissinger, as a young soldier, and for Brzezinski, as a teenager anxiously following every development of the war on the family radio and keeping a daily diary. But the formative experience of the new professional elite was the Vietnam War and the divisive 1960s, ushering in an age of ideology. Was the United States an inherently imperialist country too quick to emphasize military force? Or was it a righteous nation betrayed by its liberal elite? Political divisions about the very meaning of the American experience in the light of Vietnam became paramount, dividing new professionals of foreign affairs on the left (such as Tony Lake, Leslie Gelb, Richard Holbrooke, or Morton Halperin) from their counterparts on the right, often originally coming from Democratic ranks (such as Jeane Kirkpatrick, Richard Perle, Paul Wolfowitz, or Elliott Abrams). The in-between world of foreign affairs quickly became polarized, with powerful think tanks and magazines on the right (Heritage Foundation, American Enterprise Institute, *Commentary*, etc.) battling those on the left (Carnegie; Brookings to some extent; *Foreign Policy*, which represented, however, a variety of viewpoints; *World Policy*

*Journal*; etc.), while the Council on Foreign Relations, which chose to straddle the ideological divide and open its ranks more widely in the 1970s, saw its influence wane with the disappearance of the Old Establishment.

Kissinger and Brzezinski inaugurated the historical breakup with the traditional Establishment, but they never became an integral part of the heavily politicized landscape of the new professional elite, never quite fitting in. A good case can be made that they constitute, in effect, a sociological category by themselves, a crucial transition group. And perhaps this explains the enduring quality of their personal relationship over the decades: they inhabited the same world. After all, in spite of all the good reasons they had to be antagonists over the decades, one finds very little animosity, personal attacks, or name-calling among the two men.

Moreover, their outsider status could occasionally get them closer together. "For all his fame and power, Kissinger remained an outsider to American society," writes Jeremy Suri. "His German Jewish background was essential for his rise to power, but it detracted from his public legitimacy."[43] Brzezinski suffered from the constant suspicion that his views on U.S.-Soviet relations were entirely determined by his Polish-Catholic origin. The attacks from the Old Establishment could be incredibly harsh. "We shouldn't have a National Security Adviser like that who's not really an American," sneered Robert Lovett once Brzezinski was at the White House. "I can't imagine anyone negotiating with the Russians with his loathing and suspicion."[44] A few years earlier, as was his usual strategy in such circumstances, Brzezinski had written a blistering letter to another figure of the aging Establishment, Averell Harriman (a close friend of Lovett's):[45]

> June 21, 1974
>
> Dear Mr. Harriman:
>
> I have been told by some friends that you expressed the view that my Polish background somehow disqualifies me from dealing objectively with the US-Soviet relationship. . . . Since you are a blunt man, let me also say quite bluntly that I do not feel that Henry Kissinger's background disqualified him from dealing effectively with the Middle Eastern problem, nor do I think that your background as a millionaire capitalist prevents you from dealing intelligently with the Soviet communists.
>
> Yours sincerely,
>
> Zbigniew Brzezinski

Brzezinski and Harriman later reconciled, to the point that the newly appointed national security advisor, in 1977, was invited to stay at Harriman's apartment in Washington for a few months while he was relocating his family, along with Marshall Shulman, Richard Holbrooke, and other Carter officials. But the suspicion about his origins remained, and it remains to this day. On December 6, 1973, Secretary of State Kissinger hosted nine academics at Foggy Bottom for a discussion, including Marshall Shulman, Stanley Hoffmann, and Brzezinski. Having painted a very dark prospective picture of an isolated America in a hostile world for the years 1976–80, he joked that in any case this would only happen after Brzezinski had inherited his job, thanks to the precedent he himself established of having a foreign-born official holding this prestigious function. Brzezinski simply added, "I hope this has become a firm tradition!"[46]

The fact of the matter is that Kissinger and Brzezinski remained on good terms, despite their increasingly diverging views and their inherent situation of competition that produced occasional tension in the years 1969–80. To an outside observer, these two could only be archrivals and sworn enemies. But to the historian who gets access to their correspondence and pays attention to the larger sociological forces that drove them closer together, the picture is different.

Kissinger received Brzezinski regularly at the White House and the Department of State, often for face-to-face meetings. When they had dinner in July 1969, for example, they talked about all the burning issues of the day—the planned reengagement with China, relations with Moscow, and what to do with Vietnam, of course. The next day, at Kissinger's request, Brzezinski sent ideas for a speech on "the meaning of peace" for Nixon to use in a toast in New Delhi later that month.[47] In May 1970, the two men had a long discussion about the domestic repercussions of the invasion of Cambodia. Kissinger stated his fears of domestic divisions—less the agitation from the left than the possibility of a reactionary swing to the right by Nixon—and confided that he was envisaging leaving his job before the end of Nixon's term, but not to get back to Harvard. He was very bitter vis-à-vis his former colleagues, whom he saw as endorsing student unrest. They also talked about the Middle East, Germany (neither saw much of a chance for *Ostpolitik* to be successful), and the situation of Radio Free Europe / Radio Liberty (RFE/RL), whose activities the West German government in Bonn wanted to curb to please Moscow.[48]

Such meetings kept happening in spite of Brzezinski's public criticism of the administration's performance. For example, the day after the two men spoke about the Cambodian crisis, and while he was sending him a confidential memorandum of advice on how to handle the fallout from the crisis, Brzezinski published an op-ed in the *Washington Post* entitled "Cambodia has undermined our vital credibility," in which he criticized the intellectual world but more pointedly Nixon's decision, as well as "some of Mr. Nixon's assistants." "Today," he lectured, "the situation is infinitely more complex and calls for a much more subtle appreciation of international realities."[49] But Kissinger thanked him for the confidential memo and promised in a handwritten postscript that he would "keep a sharp eye on the RFE matter."[50]

Of course, there also might have been a dose of calculation in their relationship. By receiving Brzezinski regularly, Kissinger ensured that his comrade would remain moderate in his public criticism, so as not to jeopardize his access to the administration, and that he would keep him informed of relevant developments and ideas. Brzezinski, by feeding memos, ideas, and advice to the administration, could get access to firsthand information and also have his specific issues of concern taken care of, such as the fate and budget of the RFE/RL radio, which was one of the causes he defended throughout the cold war.[51] Still, their correspondence betrays more than just a mutually convenient arrangement.

These regular meetings continued until the electoral year 1976, in Washington or abroad. In April 1973, for example, they lunched together at Sans-Souci, near Berlin: Kissinger was anxious to know more about the nascent Trilateral Commission. Occasionally, however, tensions flared up. In his famous scorecard of the administration's international performance for *Foreign Policy* magazine, Brzezinski had given Nixon and Kissinger an overall B in the summer of 1971.[52] But in March 1974, he got markedly more critical. The overall grade, a C+, did not bother Kissinger as much as the pointed attack on détente and his own personal style of diplomacy. In the sharply penned article, Brzezinski stigmatized the triple predilection shown by the administration (read: Kissinger) for "the personal over the political," "the covert over the conceptual," and "acrobatics over architecture." He charged that the administration's diplomacy was unresponsive to the new global, rather than just international, challenges, especially North-South relations, and that the détente policy was a one-way street. It relegated the democratic allies and unduly elevated the USSR (Brzezinski detected in Kissinger "fascination with enemies and ennui with friends"), while the United States was not getting much in return on Strategic Arms Limitation Talks (SALT) negotiations, the Middle East, or trade.[53]

This time, Kissinger shot back with an irritated three-page letter marked *"Personal"* and *"Not for Publication,"*[54] which began this way: "Since I will be leaving for Moscow this evening to continue the pursuit of a detente which you either support or decry (depending on which Brzezinski you read), my thoughts will necessarily be both hasty and brief. I find it difficult to accept that the author of *Peaceful Engagement in Europe's Future*[55] can now claim that we were too soft in the Strategic Arms Limitation Agreements we have thus far reached." Kissinger was particularly baffled by what he saw as Brzezinski's criticism of Brzezinski's own strategy of hugging Communist countries closer, recommended by him in the early 1960s, and mirrored by Kissinger's détente policy. The letter continued with a specific rebuttal of each attack and expressed dismay at the idea that Brzezinski's article seemed to adopt "the same line of attack on detente that used to be the privileged property of the extreme right." In closing the letter, however, he ended on a conciliatory note. "Perhaps when I have returned from Moscow and we both have more time for reflection, we could sit down and go over in more detail some of our apparent areas of disagreement. With warm regards, Henry Kissinger."[56]

The similarities between "peaceful engagement" and détente were only superficial, as the first policy was aimed at subverting Moscow's hold on Eastern Europe while the latter was largely aimed at stabilizing the overall U.S.-Soviet relationship. And Brzezinski had a point about the lack of reciprocity and growing Soviet confidence: this would become a constant theme of criticism until 1977 (even if the case could be made that it was also about "the need to come up with some differences," as Kissinger later put it).[57] There is no recorded meeting or letter between the two men in the following seven months, an unusually long time. But a delegation of Europeans, Americans, and Japanese from the Trilateral Commission, led by Brzezinski, visited Kissinger at the State Department in December, and the regular exchanges resumed. Brzezinski, in his warm thank-you letter, even asked a favor from Kissinger in a postscript: "You may be amused that the following request comes from me, but two of my boys very much want to have your autograph.... Their names are Ian and Mark. I never thought at Harvard that someday I would be asking you this!"[58]

If the exchanges between the two men were particularly dense in 1975 ("Even for those of us who live in Newcastle, coals are important.... Your observations are always welcome," encouraged Kissinger[59]), they sharply slowed down in the fall and completely stopped in 1976. The reason is easy enough to guess: the electoral campaign had begun, and Kissinger was a key asset in Gerald Ford's campaign. "At some point it will be necessary to take the Kissinger foreign policy head-on," Brzezinski advised Jimmy Carter in a confidential strategy memo of late October 1975. "Blaming its shortcomings on Nixon or on Ford will not do, while Kissinger is likely to become one of the major pillars of the Republican pitch for re-election. Accordingly, Kissinger's foreign policy ought to be attacked directly, and his personal role in shaping it and giving it its somewhat dubious moral-political outlook ought to be the major focus of such a speech."[60] No wonder, in these conditions, that Kissinger grew increasingly irritated during the

course of 1976, to the point of making—in private—the only derogatory comment about Brzezinski that has come to our attention. While discussing campaign politics during a meeting with National Security Advisor Brent Scowcroft
and two others, he exclaimed, "Brzezinski is a total whore. He's been on every
side of every argument. He wrote a book on *Peaceful Engagement* and now that we
are doing most of what he said in the book, he charges us with weakness."[61] But
the pressure on Ford and Kissinger kept coming. In the course of 1976, Carter
delivered two main speeches on foreign affairs. The first one, given at the Chicago Council on Foreign Relations in March, was indeed critical of Kissinger's
secretive diplomacy. James Reston, the legendary columnist for the *New York
Times* and a Kissinger confidante, defended the secretary of state and wrote that
"Carter was the speaker, but Zbigniew Brzezinski was the principal writer"[62]—
a line that may well have been inspired by Kissinger himself, according to an
editor of the *Times* (or so Brzezinski reported to Jimmy Carter).[63] However, the
most robust attack came in the main speech given in June in New York. "Under the Nixon-Ford administration, there has evolved a kind of secretive single
'Lone Ranger' foreign policy—a one-man policy of international adventure."
That "Lone Ranger" line, which apparently came not from Brzezinski but from
George Ball, was the one that stuck and made the headlines, even though Brzezinski had argued against it.[64] Ironically, when Carter was elected in November,
the anti-Kissinger mood played against the selection of Brzezinski as national
security advisor: it was feared that he would replicate Kissinger's bureaucratic
omnipotence over foreign policy. And while there was good internal balance and
teamwork in the first year of the Carter administration, this is more or less what
happened subsequently. During the Carter years, contacts between Brzezinski
and Kissinger continued on the same pace. After all, Brzezinski and the Carter
administration efficiently sealed the deal on unsuccessful diplomatic attempts
dating back to the Kissinger years—the Panama Canal treaties, the normalization of diplomatic relations with China, the Camp David Accords, and even the
SALT II Treaty. There were also, of course, occasional tensions. In 1979, David
Rockefeller, John McCloy, and Kissinger lobbied for the shah of Iran to be admitted for treatment in the United States after his ouster by the Iranian Revolution—a very sensitive point, as the new regime in Tehran was considering it a
grave provocation. But it was one on which Brzezinski largely agreed with Kissinger. Relations with NATO and the SALT II Treaty were other points of contention.

But by and large, the pattern observed in the previous eight years continued:
the two men, with the table turned, continued their exchange. Occasionally,

Kissinger was even able to provide advice to Brzezinski, as when Cyrus Vance resigned in April 1980. "You are now in the same position that I was when Jim Schlesinger was forced out as Secretary of Defense," he warned him. "The press and everyone else saw me as completely in charge and turned against me in full fury. You, Zbig, never had the press behind you the way I had, and thus you are even more vulnerable to the attacks that now will concentrate on you." "How right he was," Brzezinski noted in his memoirs.[65]

It is then no wonder that in the next three decades, the two men continued to maintain good relations, sparring on television sets while attending each other's important birthdays. Because they were so similar, perhaps they could not become more intimate friends. But perhaps they secretly knew that beyond their motives of disagreement, they shared essential features and a common achievement. Together, these two immigrants invented a new model that many would later emulate, and they made a profound mark on American foreign policy, one that resonates to this day.

Both continue to be very sought-after commentators of U.S. foreign policy—on the airwaves, in op-eds, or in the corridors of power. Yet Brzezinski also remains a regular reader of Russian websites and publications and an insightful analyst of Russian politics and society, true to his beginnings as an academic Sovietologist in two Ivy League universities, the milieu that propelled him to the commanding heights of American foreign policy.

NOTES

1 Henry Kissinger to Zbigniew Brzezinski, January 23, 1964; Zbigniew Brzezinski to Henry Kissinger, January 30, 1964, folder "Kissinger, Henry 1956–1969," box I.16, Zbigniew Brzezinski Papers, Manuscript Division, Library of Congress, Washington, D.C. (hereafter Brzezinski Papers). The article mentioned by Kissinger is "The Danger of a German Veto," *New Leader,* January 20, 1964, 13–15.

2 Walter Isaacson, *Kissinger: A Biography* (New York: Simon and Schuster, 1992), 715 ("mutual coolness"), 699 ("nemesis"), 80 ("among the most intense rivalries"), 706 ("smoldering resentment").

3 Stanley Hoffmann, interview with author, December 4, 2009.

4 Brzezinski to Kissinger, February 28, 1956, and February 16, 1957; Kissinger to Brzezinski, March 15, 1957, folder "Kissinger, Henry 1956–1969," box I.16, Brzezinski Papers.

5 Zbigniew Brzezinski, interview with author, June 22, 2010; Henry Kissinger, interview with author, January 27, 2012.

6 Robert Novak, "Kennedy's Braintrust: More Professors Enlist but They Play Limited Policy-Making Role," *Wall Street Journal,* August 4, 1960, 1.

7 Henry Kissinger, "Military Policy and Defense of the 'Grey Areas,'" *Foreign Affairs,*

April 1955; Zbigniew Brzezinski, "The Challenge of Change in the Soviet Bloc," *Foreign Affairs*, April 1961.

8  See the account in David Halberstam, *The Best and the Brightest* (New York: Random House, 1974), 3–10; Walter Isaacson and Evan Thomas, *The Wise Men: Six Friends and the World They Made* (New York: Simon and Schuster, 1986), 594; and I. M. Destler, Leslie Gelb, and Anthony Lake, *Our Own Worst Enemy: The Unmaking of American Foreign Policy* (New York: Simon and Schuster, 1984), 92.

9  The best description of the foreign policy Establishment remains Isaacson and Thomas, *Wise Men*.

10  Jeremy Suri was first to make the point about Kissinger and the Cold War University in *Henry Kissinger and the American Century* (Cambridge, MA: Harvard University Press, 2007), 102. On the Cold War University, in addition to Suri, see the books mentioned in David Engerman, "Rethinking Cold War Universities, Some Recent Histories," *Journal of Cold War Studies* 5, no. 3 (Summer 2003): 80–95.

11  Dwight D. Eisenhower, Farewell Address, January 17, 1961, http://nas.ucdavis.edu/Forbes/Efarewell.html.

12  See Sigmund Diamond, *Compromised Campus: The Collaboration of Universities with the Intelligence Community, 1945–1955* (New York: Oxford University Press, 1992).

13  See David Engerman, *Know Your Enemy: The Rise and Fall of America's Soviet Experts* (New York: Oxford University Press, 2009).

14  Reginald Phelps to Brzezinski, August 17, 1950, folder "Harvard University 1950–1953, 1959–60," box I.12, Brzezinski Papers.

15  Brzezinski to Prof. William Langer, February 25, 1958 (actually 1959), folder "Harvard University 1950–1953, 1959–60," box I.12, Brzezinski Papers.

16  Zbigniew Brzezinski, *The Permanent Purge: Politics in Soviet Totalitarianism* (Cambridge, MA: Harvard University Press, Russian Research Center Studies 20, 1956); Zbigniew Brzezinski and Carl Friedrich, *Totalitarian Dictatorship and Autocracy* (Cambridge, MA: Harvard University Press, 1956); Zbigniew Brzezinski, *The Soviet Bloc: Unity and Conflict* (Cambridge, MA: Harvard University Press, 1960).

17  On the International Seminar, see Isaacson, *Kissinger*, 70; and Suri, *Kissinger and the American Century*, 117.

18  On *Confluence*, see "Confluence Magazine: General Records, 1951–1969 (inclusive)," boxes 1–8, UAV 813.141.75, Harvard University Archives.

19  On the CFIA, see David Atkinson, *In Theory and in Practice: Harvard's Center for International Affairs, 1958–1983* (Cambridge, MA: Harvard University Press, 2007).

20  As late as 2009, Robert Bowie asked me to discontinue recording our interview when he turned to a discussion of his relationship with Kissinger; R. Bowie, interview with author, July 7, 2009.

21  See Brzezinski to Albert Mavrinac, February 28, 1959, folder "Mavrinac, Albert A., 1959–1965," box I.20, Brzezinski Papers.

22  Zbigniew Brzezinski, interview with author, June 2, 2011.

23  Isaacson, *Kissinger*, 83.

24  Henry Kissinger, *Nuclear Weapons and Foreign Policy* (New York: Harper, for the Council on Foreign Relations, 1957).

25  Nabil Mikhail, "Zbigniew Brzezinski: The Scholar and the Statesman. A Study of the Thoughts and Policies of the National Security Adviser and His Staff in the Carter Administration" (PhD diss., University of Virginia, 1996), 92–93.

26  Henry Kissinger, *The Troubled Partnership: A Re-appraisal of the Atlantic Alliance* (New York: McGraw-Hill, for the Council on Foreign Relations, Atlantic Policy Studies Series, 1965); Zbigniew Brzezinski, *Alternative to Partition: For a Broader Conception of America's Role in Europe* (New York: McGraw-Hill, for the Council on Foreign Relations, Atlantic Policy Studies Series, 1965).

27  Zbigniew Brzezinski and William Griffith, "Peaceful Engagement in Eastern Europe," *Foreign Affairs*, July 1961.

28  "Toward Peace in the Middle East—Report of a Study Group" (Brookings, 1975). The conclusions of that report are reproduced in Zbigniew Brzezinski, *Power and Principle: Memoirs of the National Security Adviser 1977–1981* (New York: Farrar, Straus, Giroux, 1983), 85–86.

29  Zbigniew Brzezinski, interview with author, June 2, 2011; also "Minutes of the May 9th meeting on the proposed Commission for Peace and Prosperity," in George Franklin to Brzezinski et al., May 11, 1972, folder "Correspondence File: 5/11/72–2/28/73," box 33.1, Donated Historical Material, Zbigniew Brzezinski Collection (33), Trilateral Commission File, Jimmy Carter Library, Atlanta, GA. Also see David Rockefeller, *Memoirs* (New York: Random House, 2002), 416.

30  "The Debate," *Time*, unsigned editorial, July 2, 1965.

31  Kissinger to Brzezinski, October 24, 1963; Brzezinski to Kissinger, October 30, 1963, folder "Kissinger, Henry 1956–1969," box I.16, Brzezinski Papers.

32  Ted Van Dyk, *Heroes, Hacks and Fools: Memoirs from the Political Inside* (Seattle: University of Washington Press, 2007), 101. In his biography of Kissinger (p. 133), Walter Isaacson mentions that Samuel Huntington, another expert working for the Humphrey campaign, also got the offer to share the Nixon files from Kissinger at Martha's Vineyard during the summer.

33  Isaacson, *Kissinger*, 133.

34  David Halberstam, "The New Establishment: The Decline and Fall of the Eastern Empire," *Vanity Fair*, October 1994. The Kissinger source is confirmed by Richard Nixon, *RN: The Memoirs of Richard Nixon* (New York: Grosset and Dunlap, 1978), 323. Henry Kissinger is known to disagree with this interpretation of his role in the 1968 campaign.

35  Zbigniew Brzezinski, interview with author, February 15, 2011.

36  See, for example, Brzezinski to Max Kampelman, March 6, 1972, and May 6, 1972, including draft of speech entitled "Community of Industrial Nations," folder "Presidential Election Campaigns 1972, Humphrey, Hubert H. 1971–72, n.d.," box I.94, Brzezinski Papers.

37  See, for example, Brzezinski to Humphrey, May 25, 1970, folder "Humphrey, Hubert H. 1970–1977," box I.13; Brzezinski to Muskie, May 26, 1970, folder "Muskie, Edmund S., 1969–1975," box I.21; Brzezinski to Edward Kennedy, June 3, 1970, folder "Kennedy, Edward Moore, 1964–1976," box I.16, Brzezinski Papers. In the course of 1972, the use of the same material for multiple candidates is restricted to Muskie and Humphrey: see Brzezinski to Max Kampelman, March 6, 1972, folder "Presidential Election Campaigns 1972, Humphrey, Hubert H. 1971–72, n.d.," box I.94; and Brzezinski to Tony Lake, March 6, 1972, folder "Presidential Election Campaigns 1972, Muskie, Edmund M. 1972, nd," box I.94, Brzezinski Papers.

38  Rowland Evans and Robert Novak, "McGovern's Odd Braintrust," *Washington Post*, September 3, 1972, C7; and Zbigniew Brzezinski, "Not In Agreement" (Letter to the Editor), ibid.

39  Zbigniew Brzezinski, *The Fragile Blossom: Crisis and Change in Japan* (New York: Harper and Row, 1972).

40  Zbigniew Brzezinski, *Between Two Ages: America's Role in the Technetronic Era* (New York: Viking Press, 1970), 334.

41  See, for example, Brzezinski to Carter, December 17, 1974, folder "Zbigniew Brzezinski Correspondence: 12/1/74–12/31/74," box 33.7; Brzezinski to Carter, June 17, 1975, folder "Zbigniew Brzezinski chronological file: 6/1/75–6/30/75," box 33.6, Donated Historical Material, Zbigniew Brzezinski Collection (33), Trilateral Commission File, Jimmy Carter Library, Atlanta, GA.

42  Destler, Gelb, and Lake, *Our Own Worst Enemy*, chap. 2.

43  Suri, *Kissinger and the American Century*, 11.

44  Isaacson and Thomas, *Wise Men*, 736.

45  Brzezinski to Averell Harriman, June 21, 1974, folder "Harriman, W. Averell 1964, 1974–1976," box I.12, Brzezinski Papers.

46  The nine academics were Stanley Hoffmann, Marshall Shulman, David Landes, Nick Wahl, Richard Ullmann, Stephen Graubard, Robert Pfaltzgraff, Walter Laqueur, and Brzezinski. Memo of conversation, "Meeting with Secretary of State, luncheon given by Henry Kissinger, Dec. 6 1973, 1pm–3:15pm," folder "Kissinger, Henry 1970–1973," box I.16, Brzezinski Papers.

47  "Talk + dinner with Henry Kissinger," July 14, 1969; Brzezinski to Kissinger, July 15, 1969; Kissinger to Brzezinski, July 22, 1969, folder "Kissinger, Henry 1956–1969," box I.16, Brzezinski Papers.

48  Memo of conversation with Henry Kissinger, May 23, 1970, folder "Kissinger, Henry 1970–1973," box I.16, Brzezinski Papers.

49  Memorandum "The Cambodian Crisis," May 25, 1970, folder "Kissinger, Henry 1970–1973," box I.16, Brzezinski Papers; Zbigniew Brzezinski, "Cambodia Has Undermined Our Vital Credibility," *Washington Post*, May 24, 1970, 35.

50  Kissinger to Brzezinski, June 22, 1970, folder "Kissinger, Henry 1970–1973," box I.16, Brzezinski Papers.

51  See, for example, Kissinger to Brzezinski, November 14, 1970, folder "Kissinger, Henry 1970–1973," box I.16, Brzezinski Papers.

52  Zbigniew Brzezinski, "Half Past Nixon," *Foreign Policy*, no. 3 (Summer 1971): 3–21. Also see "The Balance of Power Delusion," *Foreign Policy*, no. 7 (Summer 1972): 54–59.

53  Zbigniew Brzezinski, "The Deceptive Structure of Peace," *Foreign Policy*, no. 14 (Spring 1974): 35–55.

54  Emphasis in the original.

55  Emphasis in the original. The correct title of Brzezinski's 1961 *Foreign Affairs* article, coauthored with William Griffith, is "Peaceful Engagement in Eastern Europe."

56  Kissinger to Brzezinski, March 23, 1974, folder "Kissinger, Henry 1974–1975, n.d.," box I.16, Brzezinski Papers.

57  Brzezinski to Kissinger, April 16, 1974, folder "Kissinger, Henry 1974–1975, n.d.," box I.16, Brzezinski Papers.

58  Brzezinski to Kissinger, December 12, 1974, folder "Zbigniew Brzezinski Correspondence: 12/1/74–12/31/74," box 33.7, Donated Historical Material, Zbigniew Brzezinski Collection (33), Trilateral Commission File, Jimmy Carter Library, Atlanta, GA.

59  Kissinger to Brzezinski, April 21, 1975, folder "Kissinger, Henry 1974–1975, n.d.," box I.16, Brzezinski Papers.

60  Brzezinski to Carter, October 28, 1975, folder "Internal memoranda 1975," box I.38, Brzezinski Papers.

61  "Memorandum of Conversation, Washington, March 13, 1976, 10 a.m.," Office of the Historian, Department of State, *Foreign Relations of the United States, 1969–1976*, vol. 37, *Energy Crisis, 1974–1980* (2012), 336. Available at http://static.history.state.gov/frus/frus1969–76v37/pdf/frus1969–76v37.pdf.

62  James Reston, "When Jimmy Pretends," *New York Times*, March 19, 1976, 32.

63  Brzezinski to Carter, March 23, 1976, folder "Zbigniew Brzezinski chronological file: 1/1/76–4/30/76," box 33.6, Donated Historical Material, Zbigniew Brzezinski Collection (33), Trilateral Commission File, Jimmy Carter Library, Atlanta, GA.

64  Brzezinski, *Power and Principle*, 8. This is confirmed by Richard Gardner, *Mission Italy: On the Front Lines of the Cold War* (Lanham, MD: Rowman and Littlefield, 2005), 19.

65  Quoted by Brzezinski, ibid., 502.

# CHAPTER 2

# The Fall of Totalitarianism and the Rise of Zbigniew Brzezinski

DAVID C. ENGERMAN

Few scholars are important enough to account for either the spread of academic terminology or its demise. Zbigniew Brzezinski has the unusual distinction of contributing to a concept's rise as well as its fall. The term in question is, of course, *totalitarianism*, a term that dominated American (and to a lesser degree Western European) studies of the Soviet Union in the early decades of the cold war. This chapter tracks Brzezinski's role in Sovietological debates over *totalitarianism* from the early 1950s through the late 1960s—from the term's absorption in the scholarly literature to its controversial expulsion almost two decades later. It will show how Brzezinski's views attempted to account for changing conditions in the USSR, as well as the impact of Weberian notions of "industrial society" on American studies of the cold war enemy. In the process, the chapter will demonstrate Brzezinski's unusual ability to assimilate new academic perspectives without abandoning his core beliefs about the Soviet Union and its development.

Sovietology in 1950, when Brzezinski entered the scene, was still a field in formation. The leading centers at Columbia and Harvard were still in their infancy, while the major projects that would define the field's early years had yet to appear in print. Columbia's Russian Institute established its distinctive MA in Russian Studies, which attracted a wide group of future scholars and government experts. The institute also housed collective efforts such as the Joint Committee on Slavic Studies and published the *Current Digest of the Soviet Press*—but struggled to build a strong research program. Harvard's Russian Research Center was off to a slow start in its economic and political studies, but the hallmark of its early years, the sociologically oriented Refugee Interview Project, was in full data-collection mode. There were a handful of other American universities with respectable Russian/Soviet Studies programs—at least partly because the Rockefeller Foundation, for instance, had included the USSR in its "Far West Looks to the Far East" grant initiative. However, none of the other programs had the size, resources, or impact of these two Ivy League programs.

Meanwhile, just north of the border, at Montreal's McGill University, Brzezinski was completing his MA thesis on Russian nationalism within the USSR. It was a perspicacious work, addressing themes that would receive fuller scholarly attention only decades later. Studies of nationalism in the USSR in the early cold war years amounted to a search for ethnic nationalisms that might weaken Soviet rule over a multiethnic citizenry—not for nationalism in Russia itself. In his thesis, Brzezinski sought to move beyond what he derided as the "paint job" approach to studying the Soviet Union, in which everything ended up "either highly red or snow-white"—either highly sympathetic or unremittingly harsh toward the USSR. At the same time, Brzezinski conceded, "It is not easy, in the present times, to write in an impartial manner on any topic involving the Soviet Union. One is quite liable to fall victim to his prejudiced, preconceived opinions." Brzezinski's way of avoiding such traps was to focus on the political functions of Soviet nationalism, noting in particular the integrative functions that Soviet patriotism served in the USSR. True to psychological approaches to mass society that were gaining popularity in American social science, Brzezinski also elaborated on the ways in which Soviet patriotism offered psychological benefits to the population while concurrently incorporating or channeling Russian nationalism in nonparty institutions like the Orthodox Church. The thesis concluded with the sorts of gestures toward Western policy that were ubiquitous in early cold war studies of the USSR, suggesting that the rise of Russo-Soviet nationalism, by alienating non-Russians, might provide a basis for a "multi-national anti-Soviet version of the Comintern [Communist International]" and thus may ultimately "help a great deal the cause of freedom."[1]

The thesis introduced two patterns that would remain important in Brzezinski's later work: first, an effort to use reigning social-scientific concepts while at the same time remaining focused on broader political visions of the USSR during the cold war; and second, a focus on the complex relationship between ideologies and institutions. He carried both of these tendencies into a brief introduction to émigré analyses of party activity within the Red Army. Like many scholars of his day—and particularly those under the sway of the sociological vision of Harvard's Talcott Parsons—Brzezinski emphasized that tendencies toward professionalism could ultimately challenge Soviet authority. Thus, officers' esprit de corps was a threat to the Soviet system—an argument that would soon appear in the analysis of the Refugee Interview Project data.[2]

The year 1956 would mark a big change for the Soviet Union, as well as for Soviet experts like Brzezinski. In early February, Nikita Khrushchev consolidated his rise to power with his withering "Secret Speech"—soon available around the world—on "The Crimes of the Stalin Era." That year, encouraged by winds of change in Moscow, efforts to loosen the party's tight grip over Polish society— the original Polish Spring—and Hungarian society, too, soon followed. While events in Poland soon petered out, a newly empowered party leadership during Hungary's anti-Soviet revolt demanded the departure of Soviet troops, resulting in Soviet invasion in early November. The events of February 1956 and November 1956 established the new parameters of Soviet politics, including the primacy of the Communist Party of the Soviet Union (CPSU) within and beyond Soviet borders. (Beyond these headlines, 1956 also marked the founding of the first organization promoting scholarly travel to the USSR: the Inter-University Committee on Travel Grants—the predecessor to IREX [International Research and Exchanges Board]—came into being only two days before Khrushchev's speech.)[3]

Brzezinski's place in the Sovietological profession changed dramatically in 1956—when Brzezinski was only 28 years old—with the appearance of two books. One was Brzezinski's first solo-authored monograph, *The Permanent Purge*. The other volume, which Brzezinski coauthored with his advisor and early mentor, the Harvard political scientist Carl Friedrich—*Totalitarian Dictatorship and Autocracy*—built on Friedrich's work on totalitarianism over the previous few years.

The term *totalitarian* dated back to the 1920s, when Benito Mussolini used it to describe his aspirations of Fascist Party rule in Italy. In the 1930s, it appeared occasionally in scholarly and non-scholarly comparisons of Stalin's Soviet Union, Mussolini's Italy, and Hitler's Germany. But the use of the term exploded in the early 1950s, prompted in part by a heightened sense of the Soviet threat— in the aftermath of the Soviet atomic tests, the creation of the People's Republic of China (both in the fall of 1949), and North Korea's invasion of its southern neighbor in the summer of 1950. These events set the tone for the enthusiastic reception in 1951 of Hannah Arendt's pathbreaking work, *The Origins of Totalitarianism*. Arendt's book brought the Frankfurt School's critique of totalitarianism—as an aspect of modern society—into American political usage, focusing on the USSR. She attributed totalitarianism's rise to the dissolution of the integuments of nineteenth-century society, nation-states, political parties, and hereditary classes. The result was a modern mass society ill equipped to govern itself but equipped with new technologies of power. Under totalitarianism, individuals were completely atomized, bereft of affective ties to each other; the state was not just the dominant but the sole force shaping society. The fact that her historical account fit the Soviet case poorly did not reduce the book's resonance or reach.[4]

Carl Friedrich, the German-born political theorist teaching at Harvard and a friend of Arendt's, offered his own definition of totalitarianism, reformulating some of her ideas so they might better account for the USSR. Friedrich had sketched out a project along these lines in the 1930s—a comparative analysis of Nazi and Communist political systems—but World War II had interfered.[5] He returned to the topic in 1953 by bringing together an impressive group of scholars and public intellectuals—which convened, ironically, on the very day that American newspapers announced Stalin's death.[6] The essay Friedrich prepared for the conference, a touchstone for future scholarship, enumerated five distinctive features of totalitarian societies: an official ideology, a "single mass party of true believers," monopolies of both the means of violence and mass communication, and a "system of terroristic police control." Like Arendt and the Frankfurt School, Friedrich identified totalitarianism as a syndrome of modernity. Yet in many other ways, his definition marked a departure from Arendt's: Friedrich focused on systems of control and left aside, at least in this essay, the question of atomization, and he admitted the possibility (albeit unlikely) of "evolution," while Arendt saw few ways for a totalitarian society to change.[7]

Three years later, in 1956, the volume Friedrich coauthored with Brzezinski held fast to his notion of totalitarianism after Stalin's death and Khrushchev's rise; it did not seem to take into account the critical reception his article had received at the 1953 conference he hosted. *Totalitarian Dictatorship and Autocracy* deviated little from his original article: totalitarianism was a distinctly modern phenomenon that took fundamentally similar forms in interwar Germany, Italy, and USSR; the five features of totalitarianism remained intact, joined now to a sixth: total control over the economy. In the process, Friedrich and Brzezinski dismissed the central concerns of other political scientists stressing the role of ideologies, governance structures, and links between politics and society. They placed little importance on totalitarian ideologies, calling them nothing but "trite restatements of certain traditional ideas, arranged in an incoherent way that makes them highly exciting to weak minds." Constitutions and government structures—the focus of Friedrich's aborted prewar project—were "of very little importance." There was no society to speak of; the family constituted the only "oasis in the sea of totalitarian atomization."[8] To the extent that *Totalitarianism Dictatorship and Autocracy* reflected Friedrich's ideas, it suggested a convergence with Arendt on the issue of atomization while keeping the old formulations despite changes evident in Soviet politics after Stalin's death.

One of the book's innovations—absent from Friedrich's original article— might reasonably be attributed to Brzezinski. The book offered a schema for the evolution of totalitarianism over time. Diverging from Friedrich's article, the book incorporated the evolutionary sensibility that Friedrich's colleague, Merle Fainsod—Brzezinski's other key mentor—had suggested in his landmark study *How Russia Is Ruled* (1953). According to Fainsod, the Bolshevik revolution did not immediately establish totalitarianism, even if it set Russia on a path in that direction: "out of the totalitarian embryo," Fainsod famously wrote, "would come totalitarianism full-blown." The totalitarian future was thus foreordained because it was "implicit in the doctrinal, organizational, and tactical premises" of bolshevism.[9] Very much in the spirit of Fainsod's analysis, *Totalitarian Dictatorship and Autocracy* argued that while totalitarianism was inevitable after 1917, the "totalitarian breakthrough" did not occur until the late 1920s. Once in place, though, totalitarian states could evolve only in the direction of "becom[ing] more total."[10]

Brzezinski's first solo book, *The Permanent Purge*, shared much with *Totalitarian Dictatorship and Autocracy*, not least a 1956 publication date. Brzezinski completed the dissertation on which *The Permanent Purge* was based in April 1953, one month after Stalin's death and Friedrich's totalitarianism conference. In spite of the tumult of the intervening three years—including the succession struggle and the execution of Stalin's henchman Lavrenti Beria—the published version varied little from the dissertation. The book added an additional chapter on post-1953 events but made few significant alterations to the argument or even the language of the dissertation. Both versions—like his coauthored work, *Totalitarian Dictatorship and Autocracy*—defined totalitarianism in terms of the Soviet Union. *The Permanent Purge*, as the title suggests, took the purge as the essence of Soviet totalitarianism. While some observers considered the purges paroxysms of chaos and irrationality, Brzezinski saw them as a "technique" used "for the achievement of specific political and socio-economic objectives." Denunciations, similarly, were not the result of "the perversity of human nature" but a "calculated effort to realize ambitions of upward mobility." Because purges were functional—serving political and economic needs, facilitating the rotation of elites, and providing individual opportunities for advancement—they would not disappear.

While the show trials of the late 1930s had come to symbolize Soviet tyranny in widely read accounts (most notably Arthur Koestler's *Darkness at Noon,* first published in 1940), Brzezinski dismissed those trials as "the frosting on the cake" because the real work of the 1930s purges was already completed by the time of the famous show trials of the Old Bolsheviks. Furthermore, Brzezinski credited the purges with facilitating the transformation of the economy (and the demise of any serious opposition to Stalinist economic policy) as well as the transformation of the party into a "Stalinist mode."[11] As he had done in his MA thesis, Brzezinski was interested in exploring the functions served by even such extreme events as the purges. He used the purge as a metaphor for Soviet society, then, not to prove its irrationality but to measure its utility.

Acknowledging the decline of such widespread purges and public spectacles since the 1930s, Brzezinski argued that the show trials had been replaced by what he called the "quiet purge." But he warned against confusing volume with essence. Just because the purges had quieted, "to expect . . . a fundamental mellowing in the political system of the USSR [was] to show a great misunderstanding of totalitarianism and to engage in a dangerous underestimation of the compelling logic of totalitarian rule."[12]

As with the volume Brzezinski coauthored with Friedrich, *The Permanent Purge* received strong criticism from academic reviewers. One noted that the empirical—though not the theorizing—material in the book offered "further refutation" of the notion that totalitarian states were static in form and function. Another questioned Brzezinski's insistence that the system—rather than its individual leader, Stalin—was the appropriate unit of analysis.[13] It was clear, nonetheless, that by 1956, despite important similarities, Brzezinski's approach to totalitarianism differed from that of his mentor and coauthor. Brzezinski was interested in the implications of totalitarian rule and the structures and functions of paradigmatic institutions such as the purge. And the course of events in the USSR and Eastern Europe, together with his continued study of the Sovietological scholarship, led Brzezinski and Friedrich in different directions.

Perhaps inevitably for a scholar ensconced in Harvard's Russian Research Center in the 1950s, Brzezinski had to come to terms with the sociological or Weberian strand of Sovietology then dominating the center. The Refugee Interview Project took this sociological strand as its core. As Raymond Bauer—the project's field research director—later observed, "The Soviet Union is a modern

industrial society (or at least in the last stages of becoming one), and all industrial societies have many features in common." Social structure, in this vision,
trumped political differences.[14] The project's emphasis on Soviet society worked
against the reigning notions of totalitarianism, especially as expressed by Arendt;
indeed, Arendt's version would not even allow for the existence of "society" in a
totalitarian polity. But Bauer and the other leaders of the interview project, such
as anthropologist Clyde Kluckhohn and the sociologist Alex Inkeles, insisted in
*How the Soviet System Works* that the Soviet Union, in terms of social organization, "resemble[d] . . . the large-scale industrial society in the West." While their
book acknowledged "a great deal of dissatisfaction," it noted that there was
"very little disaffection and even less active opposition." The lack of opposition
was not just the result of the effectiveness of the secret police. *How the Soviet
System Works* insisted on the centrality of the Soviet citizens' "techniques of accommodation." To the extent that there were cleavages in the USSR, Kluckhohn,
Inkeles, and Bauer argued, they were the same ones that divided Americans from
each other—social class and economic status.[15] Indeed, when Bauer and Inkeles
eventually published their final accounting of the interview project data, they
framed the book as fundamentally a contribution to "general social-psychology
of industrial society"; the fact that they were focusing on a nondemocratic state
and America's cold war antagonist was secondary.[16]

Although the interview project's leaders did not make predictions about the
Soviet future, beyond insisting that the USSR was not on the verge of collapse,
others in the early 1950s argued that the need for "technical rationality" in an
industrial society—even the USSR—could threaten Communist Party rule. The
British writer Isaac Deutscher expected that the repressive aspects of the system
would have to ease as the Soviet Union reached higher levels of industry and education.[17] More important were the contributions of Barrington Moore Jr., a Harvard sociologist and an erstwhile (and halfhearted) participant in the interview
project who nevertheless sought to use its data to contemplate possible Soviet
futures. In his 1954 book *Terror and Progress*, Moore claimed that Soviet leaders had to reckon with the challenges of maintaining their power while building a modern industrial system. He enumerated three trends that would shape
the Soviet future: the pursuit of power, the imperatives of technical rationality,
and what Moore called "traditionalism." Like other Russia experts of the time,
Moore saw Soviet terror as a crucial barometer for the future. The post-Stalin regime "still requires terror as an essential aspect of its power," yet terror created
such uncertainty that it led to inefficiency. A more rational system, according to
Moore, would maintain power not through terror but through "conformity to a

code of law." While Moore outlined three possibilities for the Soviet future—i.e., those based on power, technical rationality, or traditionalism—he devoted most of his attention to the second possibility: that the Soviet system would "adapt to the technical requirements" of modern industrial society "even at some sacrifice in political control."

Moore wondered, what would a Soviet society that is more receptive to the demands of industrialism look like? It would replace political aims with "technical and rational criteria," allowing rapid economic growth to continue without maintaining the economy as a "servant" of the political system. It would still be a centralized society, but one that no longer relied on organized terror. It could even evolve into "technocracy—the rule of the technically competent," including an ascendant "technocratic aristocracy" within the political elites. The rise of "technical and rational criteria of behavior and organization," he argued, would "by definition . . . imply a heavy reduction of emphasis on the power of the dictator." Rationality could, Moore concluded, "do [the] work of erosion upon the Soviet totalitarian edifice."[18] In a later article, Moore dropped the uncertainty of *Terror and Progress*, arguing unequivocally that the USSR was moving toward technical rationality.[19]

Given the eventual importance of this work to political scientists, it is worth noting that Moore's vision of technical rationality happened *within* rather than *in opposition to* continued rule by the Communist Party. The nature of the party elite might change, but the party would not relinquish the reins of power. Moore suggested that the imperatives of a modern industrial society existing in a complex international environment would not just encourage but even require such changes. These industrial imperatives would yield the demise of "totalitarianism" by rendering it into a less ambitious despotism—or perhaps into a more stable and rational form of single-party rule. Moore would continue to contemplate the relationship between totalitarianism and industrialization in his later work, including his celebrated *Social Origins of Dictatorship and Democracy* (1966)—a study that he originally called an exploration of "how . . . industrialism affects the structure of authority and the possibilities of freedom in modern society."[20] Following Moore's book, American scholars often returned to these questions, specifically about the USSR. Thus, the talk of American-Soviet convergence—a popular theme in the 1960s—developed from Moore's and others' claims that in the long run totalitarianism would be incompatible with industrial society.

Brzezinski began to reckon with the implications of Weberian Sovietology soon after Moore's book appeared. Indeed, in late 1956—even before *Totalitarian*

*Dictatorship and Autocracy* appeared—Brzezinski published an extended rumination on "Totalitarianism and Rationality." While singling out Deutscher's arguments for special criticism and praising Moore in a footnote, Brzezinski challenged the notion (which appeared in both Deutscher and Moore) that technical rationality would erode totalitarianism. Such a prediction, Brzezinski insisted, failed to address the "problem of power": after all, "the rationalist tomorrow, if it ever comes, will therefore not be an introduction to a democratic form of government, but rather a stage in further totalitarian evolution."[21] Industrial organization might bring about changes in Soviet society, Brzezinski insisted, but it would not reshape Soviet politics.

In the early 1960s, Brzezinski expanded on these insights in two very important works. The first appeared in 1961 in the first issue of *Slavic Review*, the flagship journal of the American Association for the Advancement of Slavic Studies. *Slavic Review* editors created a "Discussion" section featuring a broad scholarly article along with responses. Brzezinski's article, "The Nature of the Soviet System," inaugurated this section. His essay was in many ways an expansion of "Totalitarianism and Rationality," and some paragraphs appeared in nearly identical form in both articles. But "The Nature of the Soviet System" also revealed Brzezinski's continuing effort to assimilate social-scientific notions of the Soviet system into his own understanding. He described four phases of Soviet rule, building on the evolutionary framework he had introduced in 1956. The first phase, Leninism, set the stage for the second—Stalin's "totalitarian break-through," which Brzezinski termed "the all-out effort to destroy the basic institutions of the old order and to construct at least the framework for the new." Late Stalinism, from the end of World War II until the dictator's death, was a "repetition . . . and extension" of the prewar years: the reconstruction of Soviet society made visible by the demise of the party and the rise of secret police. The fourth—post-Stalin—stage, Brzezinski argued, included the "maturation" of totalitarian rule as the liquidation of alternative loci of power under the preceding stages "paved the way for the relative leniency" that marked the USSR after 1953.[22]

Acknowledging the relaxation of Stalinist methods in the 1950s, Brzezinski had no illusions that the Soviet leadership was relinquishing its power. As he had claimed in *The Permanent Purge*, the threat of future purges would be sufficient to keep social actors in line. Indeed, reduced reliance on ideological mobilization meant that the firebrands and intellectuals who battled with Stalin before World War II gave way to bland technocrats: while Stalin had battled with the "brilliant and articulate [Nikolai] Bukharin" in the prewar decades, his postwar counterpart was "the hulking, sullen, and anything but effervescent [Lazar] Kaganovich." For Brzezinski, the decline of the quality of the leaders suggested the decline of the system.[23]

In examining the uneven "thaw" after Stalin's death, Brzezinski identified significant advantages for the effectiveness of the Soviet system; once again, he was interested in the social and political functions of various forms of rule. Noting the demise of terror as a "dominant feature of the system," Brzezinski observed that the emerging "voluntarist totalitarianism can be more effective than [the preceding] terrorist one." Yet the transition from "terrorist" to "voluntarist" rule was merely a change *within*, not a departure from, totalitarianism. He criticized scholars who analyzed the thaw in terms of "liberalization" or "democratization"—categories, Brzezinski added, that described the transformation of "Western societies under entirely different conditions." In his view, the party still remained at the helm of the Soviet Union, and whatever socioeconomic changes took place did so in a system in which "politics are still supreme." To the extent that socioeconomic changes brought about competing worldviews within the Soviet system, the result would be "erosion" and not transformation. (Brzezinski, who published this article just after completing his remarkable book *The Soviet Bloc*—discussed in chapter 3 in this book—made a similar claim about increasing ideological diversity within Eastern Europe.) The "relativization of ideology" under way at home and abroad, Brzezinski predicted, carried "dangerous implications" for Soviet rule.[24]

Two leading scholars of Soviet politics, Alfred Meyer and Robert C. Tucker, responded to Brzezinski's essay by calling for deeper immersion in comparisons and theorization. Meyer's essay, "USSR, Incorporated," amounted to a catalogue of possible analogies between the Soviet Union and American institutions. Over eight pages, Meyer compared Soviet leadership to C. Wright Mills's "power elite," to a Western corporation's board of directors, and—in a very different vein—to European absolutist rulers; he also drew analogies between Soviet society and a "company town" or an "industrial bureaucracy." This wealth of comparisons suggested, to Meyer at least, that Brzezinski had overemphasized the role of politics in the Soviet future and had "paid insufficient attention to the importance of . . . industrialization as the driving force of the Soviet system." Meyer, in short, put forth the precise argument that Brzezinski was challenging in his essay.[25] Tucker, meanwhile, offered a broadside against totalitarianism as it was used in contemporary social science—and in Brzezinski's essay in particular.[26] Here, too, Brzezinski held firm, insisting on the relevance of totalitarianism as a category of political analysis.

Within a few years, however, Brzezinski reconsidered Tucker's criticism if not Meyer's. In *Political Power, USA/USSR*, jointly authored with his erstwhile colleague Samuel Huntington, Brzezinski completely dispensed with the terms *totalitarianism* and *totalitarian*. The authors' comparison of the two cold war antagonists addressed the notion of Soviet-American convergence, an argument implicit in the notion of "technical rationality." If the logic of modern industrial societies promoted certain social structures (bureaucratic organization), priorities (economic efficiency), and mentalities (productivity oriented), then the future would bring the convergence of all modern industrial societies. Huntington and Brzezinski set out to write *Political Power* in this vein, but the book eventually made the opposite argument: that convergence could result only from a "drastic alteration of course." Indeed, the authors concluded that the "undramatic pattern for the future" would be "the evolution of the two systems"—but not their convergence. Perhaps more striking was that the book never used the word *totalitarian* to describe the USSR.[27] It was not that Brzezinski suddenly doubted the ability or desire of Soviet leaders to stay in power, only that he had come to find the term *totalitarian* distracting for the analysis of the Soviet system.

Brzezinski's wariness about the term *totalitarian* was evident elsewhere as well. In the early 1960s, after Brzezinski—significantly—declined Carl Friedrich's invitation to work on a new edition of *Totalitarian Dictatorship and Autocracy*, Friedrich had to plunge ahead on his own. Despite headline-making changes in the Soviet Union under Khrushchev, Friedrich saw little reason to modify his theory. Khrushchev's efforts at de-Stalinization, Friedrich argued, "tended to confirm" the totalitarian argument because it was but part of an effort to maintain or augment power. In short, Friedrich made few fundamental amendments to totalitarianism as an analytic category.[28] Publicly, he described Brzezinski's decision to stay away from the revision of their joint effort as the result of other "pressing commitments," though Friedrich hinted that their intellectual trajectories had increased the distance between their views.[29] Brzezinski recalled much later that it "would be a stretch" to maintain the book's basic position given the evolution of the Soviet system in the decades since the publication of its first edition.[30]

Having abandoned the concept of totalitarianism, Brzezinski continued to emphasize the "question of power" while taking into account the growing scholarly literature describing changes in Soviet socioeconomic structures. His efforts culminated in an essay that served as the fulcrum of extended academic debate on Soviet politics in the late 1960s, after Khrushchev was deposed and Leonid Brezhnev consolidated his rule. Brzezinski's essay, "The Soviet Political

System: Transformation or Degeneration?," appeared in *Problems of Communism* in early 1966. The journal, sponsored by the State Department, brought together scholarly essays and policy-related commentary. Brzezinski's essay prompted almost two dozen responses, appearing intermittently in *Problems of Communism* from 1966 through late 1968.

Brzezinski's article sought to account for Brezhnev's rise on the one hand and the increasing scholarly attention to industrial societies on the other. The Soviet Union, Brzezinski conceded to the sociologically inclined, was "an increasingly modern and industrial society." Yet industrialization, he argued (echoing his 1961 essay), would not produce liberalization, democratization, or any other kind of political transformation; it would produce instead degeneration. Maintaining a "doctrinaire dictatorship" in an industrial society, Brzezinski claimed, "has already contributed to a reopening of the gap that existed in pre-revolutionary Russia between the political system and the society." (Here Brzezinski was invoking the work of his Columbia colleague Leopold Haimson, whose *Slavic Review* articles on "The Problem of Political and Social Stability in Urban Russia on the Eve of War and Revolution" had recently appeared.) In Brzezinski's view, the most important way for Soviet leaders to reduce that gap was to change the nature of senior leadership, giving it "broader representation of social talent"— i.e., scientists, economists, and managers—at the top. But, far from predicting such a radical redistribution of power and privilege, Brzezinski foresaw the "beginning of a sterile bureaucratic phase"—stagnation. As he had done in his earlier writings, Brzezinski compared the declining quality of Soviet leadership to the declining prospects for the nation they led. In one memorable footnote, Brzezinski contrasted Leon Trotsky to Georgii Malenkov. He wondered what three-volume trilogy could track Malenkov's career much as Isaac Deutscher had done for Trotsky in his trilogy, *The Prophet Armed*, *The Prophet Unarmed*, and *The Prophet Outcast*. A prospective Malenkov trilogy would lack elegance and drama: *The Apparatchik Promoted*, *The Apparatchik Triumphant*, and *The Apparatchik Pensioned*.[31]

Brzezinski, in sum, had abandoned the totalitarian model without losing the notion of party control. He had solved the "problem of power" analytically, but he doubted that the Soviet leadership could solve it practically. Brzezinski thus responded to a growing number of scholars' sociological challenge to totalitarianism by returning to the principal topic for political scientists: power.

⁙ The variety of responses to Brzezinski's article on "transformation or degeneration" gave a clear sense of how American experts understood Soviet politics in the late 1960s. The respondents included some of the leading academic and governmental specialists on Soviet politics, including Frederick Barghoorn, Robert Conquest, Fainsod, and Friedrich. Brzezinski, in his reply, conveniently mapped out these responses graphically, on a continuum divided into those expecting evolutionary and revolutionary change. Two-thirds of the respondents were on the "evolutionary" end of the scale. Four of the respondents even saw "renovative transformation" as the most likely outcome, with another four seeing that as possible. In other words, a good number of Soviet experts saw the possibility, even the likelihood, that the Soviet regime would lose power without having it "wrenched from their hands," in Merle Fainsod's memorable phrase.[32]

Brzezinski diverged from this emerging scholarly consensus in the late 1960s, insisting instead that any socioeconomic changes would contribute to the degeneration, not the transformation, of the Soviet political system. Looking back, his ultimate conclusion in the *Problems of Communism* essay suggested a future that serves as an apt description of Putin's Russia. The disintegration of Soviet power, Brzezinski predicted, could easily lead to an "assertive ideological-nationalist reaction, resting on a coalition of secret police, the military and the heavy industrial-ideological complex."[33]

### NOTES

1 Zbigniew K. Brzezinski, "Russo-Soviet Nationalism" (MA thesis, McGill University, 1950), 2, 1, 145–46.

2 Zbigniew Brzezinski, introduction to *Political Controls in the Soviet Army* (New York: Research Program on the Soviet Union, 1954); Clyde Kluckhohn, Raymond A. Bauer, and Alex Inkeles, "Strategic Psychological and Sociological Strengths and Vulnerabilities of the Soviet Social System," Final Report to the Air Force (October 1954) in Refugee Interview Project Reports (Harvard University Archives), Series UAV759.175.75, box 5.

3 William Marvel, memorandum of conversation with Schuyler Wallace, February 20, 1956, Carnegie Corporation of New York Records (Columbia University Library), Series III.A, box 514, folder 6.

4 Hannah Arendt, *The Origins of Totalitarianism* (New York: Harcourt, Brace, 1951); Abbott Gleason, *Totalitarianism: The Inner History of the Cold War* (Oxford: Oxford University Press, 1997), chaps. 2–3; Margaret Canovan, *Hannah Arendt: A Reinterpretation of Her Political Thought* (Cambridge: Cambridge University Press, 1992), chap. 2.

5 Carl Friedrich and Zbigniew Brzezinski, *Totalitarian Dictatorship and Autocracy* (Cambridge, MA: Harvard University Press, 1956), vii; grant application, "Russian Constitutional and Administrative History in Modern Times and Its Relation to the Constitutional Development of the Rest of Europe" (1937–38), in Carl Joachim Friedrich Papers (Harvard University Archives), Series HUG (FP) 17.10.

6 Invitees in Friedrich Papers, Series HUG(FP) 17.12, box 33.

7 Carl Friedrich, "The Unique Character of Totalitarian Society," in *Totalitarianism: Proceedings of a Conference Held at the American Academy of Arts and Sciences, March 1953*, ed. Friedrich (Cambridge, MA: Harvard University Press, 1954), 52–53, 55–57.

8 Friedrich and Brzezinski, *Totalitarian Dictatorship and Autocracy*, 3, 7, 9–10, 81, 18, 246–47.

9 Merle Fainsod, *How Russia Is Ruled* (Cambridge, MA: Harvard University Press, 1953), 12, 47, 489, 31, 59.

10 Friedrich and Brzezinski, *Totalitarian Dictatorship and Autocracy*, 295–300.

11 Zbigniew Brzezinski, *The Permanent Purge: Politics in Soviet Totalitarianism* (Cambridge, MA: Harvard University Press, 1956), 8, 37, 89, 145, 62, 72; Brzezinski, "The Permanent Purge and Soviet Totalitarianism" (PhD diss., Harvard University, 1953).

12 Brzezinski, *Permanent Purge*, 8, 37, 89, 145, 165, 173.

13 John Stearns Gillespie, review of *The Permanent Purge*, by Zbigniew Brzezinski, *Journal of Politics* 19, no. 2 (May 1957): 293–95; Robert M. Slusser, review of *The Permanent Purge*, by Zbigniew Brzezinski, *American Slavic and East European Review* 15, no. 4 (December 1956): 543–46.

14 Raymond A. Bauer, *Nine Soviet Portraits* (Cambridge, MA: MIT Press; New York: Wiley, 1955), xv, 173.

15 Raymond A. Bauer, Alex Inkeles, and Clyde Kluckhohn, *How the Soviet System Works: Cultural, Psychological and Social Themes* (Cambridge, MA: Harvard University Press, 1956), 230, 218, 27, chaps. 8, 12–13, 19.

16 Alex Inkeles and Raymond A. Bauer, *The Soviet Citizen: Daily Life in a Totalitarian Society* (Cambridge, MA: Harvard University Press, 1959), 3–4.

17 Isaac Deutscher, *Russia: What Next?* (Oxford: Oxford University Press, 1953).

18 Barrington Moore, *Terror and Progress—USSR: Some Sources of Stability and Change in the Soviet Dictatorship* (Cambridge, MA: Harvard University Press, 1954), 178, 224, 185, 224, 191, 189, 225–26, 231.

19 Ibid., 288; Barrington Moore, "The Outlook," *Annals of the American Academy of Political and Social Science* 303 (January 1956): 9–10.

20 Barrington Moore, "Dictatorship and Industrialism" (n.d.—1953? 1954?), RRC Research Papers (Harvard University Archives), Series UAV 759.275, box 8.

21 Zbigniew Brzezinski, "Totalitarianism and Rationality," *American Political Science Review* 50, no. 3 (September 1956): 762, 761.

22 Zbigniew Brzezinski, "The Nature of the Soviet System," *Slavic Review* 20, no. 3 (October 1961): 354–55, 357.

23 Ibid., 361, 365.

24 Ibid., 362, 367.

25 Alfred Meyer, "USSR, Incorporated," *Slavic Review* 20, no. 3 (October 1961): 369–76. Zbigniew Brzezinski, "Reply," *Slavic Review* 20, no. 3 (October 1961): 383–88.

26 Robert C. Tucker, "The Question of Totalitarianism," *Slavic Review* 20, no. 3 (October 1961): 377–82.

27 Zbigniew Brzezinski and Samuel Huntington, *Political Power: USA/USSR: Similarities and Contrasts, Convergence or Evolution* (New York: Viking, 1964), xi, 436; H. Gordon Skilling, "Interest Groups and Communist Policy," *World Politics* 18, no. 3 (April 1966): 441n31.

28  Robert Burrowes, "Totalitarianism: The Revised Standard Version," *World Politics* 21, no. 2 (January 1969): 281–94.

29  Carl Friedrich, "Foreword to the Revised Edition," Friedrich and Brzezinski, *Totalitarian Dictatorship and Autocracy*, 2nd ed., Revised by Friedrich (Cambridge, MA: Harvard University Press, 1965), vii–viii; Friedrich, "The Evolving Theory and Practice of Totalitarian Regimes," in Friedrich et al., *Totalitarianism in Perspective: Three Views* (New York: Praeger, 1969), 153.

30  Zbigniew Brzezinski, interview with author, February 19, 2004.

31  Zbigniew Brzezinski, "The Soviet Political System: Transformation or Degeneration?" (1966) and "Concluding Reflections" (1968), both in Brzezinski, ed., *Dilemmas of Change in Soviet Politics* (New York: Columbia University Press, 1969), 31–33, 162, 153–54, 15n10.

32  Chart by Edward McGowan in Brzezinski, "Concluding Reflections," 157.

33  Ibid., 153–54.

# CHAPTER 3

# Anticipating the Grand Failure

## MARK KRAMER

Soviet-style communism was a dominant motif in Zbigniew Brzezinski's publications from the mid-1960s through the end of the 1980s, a period punctuated by his four years as national security advisor to President Jimmy Carter (1977–81). In numerous books and essays during this period, Brzezinski moved away from the totalitarian model he had developed earlier in conjunction with Carl Friedrich and focused instead on empirical analyses of the systemic inadequacies of Communist rule in the USSR and Eastern Europe. Although some of Brzezinski's writings included predictions of specific events (events that were ultimately shaped in part by the conscious actions of individuals and groups and in part by accidental circumstances), the main focus here is on his assessment of the underlying processes and trends in Soviet-style systems that potentially could lead to momentous political change or, instead, to enervating decline.

⁖ Whatever utility the totalitarian ideal-type may have had in understanding Josef Stalin's dictatorship, the model proved inadequate when applied to the post-Stalin era. Although Brzezinski initially tried to salvage the basic conceptual structure with slight modifications, he shifted course in the 1960s and early 1970s and replaced much of the old paradigm with a more viable framework that captured essential features of the Soviet system as it had evolved throughout its history. Brzezinski's new conception preserved a few elements of the totalitarian model and used them to explain how the USSR had metamorphosed into a bureaucratized, ossified polity. Looking ahead, he argued that the key question

was whether the Soviet Union would undergo "transformation" and revitaliza-
tion or would instead gradually succumb to "degeneration" and decay.

Brzezinski first propounded the notion that the Soviet Union was faced with
two alternative paths in the future—"transformation or degeneration"—in a
landmark article he published in early 1966 in the journal *Problems of Communism*.[1] The article touched off a long series of articles in the same journal that
responded to his essay and assessed the prospects for far-reaching change in the
Soviet political system. Brzezinski took an active part in these exchanges and
gathered his original article (in slightly updated form), thirteen of the responses,
and his "concluding reflections" for a book, *Dilemmas of Change in Soviet Politics*.[2]

Comparing the political situation under Stalin with developments after Stalin's death, Brzezinski emphasized the stifling role of the Soviet bureaucracy.
The Bolsheviks had come to power with an ideology that envisaged the withering
away of the state, but in reality the Soviet regime from its earliest days had built
up an elaborate bureaucracy. After Stalin's death, the USSR no longer had an all-
powerful, charismatic figure who could impose his will on the country. Brzezinski argued that the "new generation of clerks" who displaced Nikita Khrushchev
in October 1964—nearly all of whom had risen in the hierarchy in the 1930s and
1940s as beneficiaries of Stalin's purges—regarded "bureaucratic stability" as
"the only solid foundation for effective government." According to Brzezinski,
the Soviet Union was "unique" in being "led by a bureaucratic leadership from
the very top to the bottom," resulting in an "extremely centralized and rigidly
hierarchical bureaucratic organization" that was "increasingly set in its ways,
politically corrupted by years of unchallenged power, and made even more confined in its outlook than is normally the case with a ruling body by its lingering
and increasingly ritualized doctrinaire tradition." This lack of flexibility, Brzezinski contended, would "pose a long-range danger to the vitality of any political system" because "decay is bound to set in, while the stability of the political
system may be endangered." In particular, "the effort to maintain a doctrinaire
dictatorship over an increasingly modern and industrial society" would lead to
the "degeneration" of the entire system—a fate that, in Brzezinski's view, could
be avoided only if "the bureaucratic Communist dictatorship [were gradually
transformed] into a more pluralistic and institutionalized political system" that
would "confront major domestic issues" and accommodate the demands of "key
groups" whose "growing assertiveness" would otherwise debilitate the regime.[3]

Five points are worth noting about Brzezinski's argument.

First, he depicted the "degeneration" of the Soviet system as an exclusively political phenomenon. The process of decay, he believed, would stem not from economic inefficiency or a projected slowdown in economic growth (which he did not even mention in his initial article), but from the smothering impact of an oppressive bureaucracy that wanted to keep ordinary citizens from having any meaningful say in the political arena. Brzezinski's view about the relative weight of political and economic factors in the decline of the USSR changed in later years, but when he first devised his notion of "transformation or degeneration" in the Soviet Union, he was focusing solely on the political dimension of the problem, especially the Soviet "system's growing incapacity" to deal with a multitude of pressing political and social issues, the dearth of top-notch individuals who wanted to ascend to leadership positions in the Communist Party of the Soviet Union (CPSU), and the increasing gap between the stagnant, inflexible Soviet political system and the ever more restless and dynamic Soviet society.

Second, among the "key groups" in the Soviet Union whose "growing assertiveness" Brzezinski believed would pose a long-term challenge to the regime were "the non-Russian nationalities." Few Western analysts at the time ascribed much political importance to Soviet nationalities and ethnic groups, but Brzezinski raised the issue (albeit briefly) in his initial article and then addressed it much more directly in his concluding essay, where he criticized "the inclination of many Western scholars of Soviet affairs to minimize what I fear may be potentially a very explosive issue in the Soviet polity." He elaborated:

We still live in the age of nationalism, and my own highly generalized feeling is that it is going to be exceedingly difficult for the Soviet Union to avoid having some of its many nationalities go through a phase of assertive nationalism.... [The nationalities] can claim such things as political autonomy, constitutional reform, a greater share of the national economic pie, [and] more investment, without it appearing that they wish to secede from the Soviet Union. History teaches us, be it in Algeria or in Indonesia or in Africa, that these demands will grow rather than decline. If they are not met or are suppressed, it is likely that the demands will become sharper and more self-assertive. If they are satisfied, they will grow with the eating. I frankly do not see how the central authorities in the Soviet Union will be able to avoid having a prolonged period of fairly difficult relations with the non-Russian nationalities.[4]

Although the problem did not become acute until twenty years later, when the political liberalization under Mikhail Gorbachev permitted nationalist discontent to come to the surface, Brzezinski was right to stress the potential volatility of the issue. He came back to the nationalities question numerous times in his later writings.

Third, Brzezinski went astray in his assessment of Soviet leadership dynamics in the wake of Khrushchev's ouster. Arguing that "Khrushchev's fall provides . . . an important precedent for the future," Brzezinski underestimated the extent to which the Soviet system still permitted the leader of the CPSU to consolidate individual power, achieving a status as something more than simply *primus inter pares*. Although a form of "collective leadership" did exist for the first several years after Khrushchev's ouster, Leonid Brezhnev as the CPSU general secretary was always the preeminent leader and gradually removed his chief rivals, establishing a dominant position and dying in office after eighteen years. As Myron Rush pointed out at the time and later, the highly centralized nature of the Soviet polity and the lack of institutionalized succession procedures gave Brezhnev and those who came after him the ability to take steps to forestall any repetition of the conspiracy that resulted in Khrushchev's downfall.[5] Because Brzezinski (in generalizing from Khrushchev's dismissal) mistakenly viewed the leadership contest in Moscow in the early post-Khrushchev era as nothing more than "a protracted bureaucratic struggle" and a "depersonalized political conflict," he neglected the aspects of the system that still allowed power to be concentrated in the hands of a single leader. Brzezinski argued that the emergence of "an increasingly secure 'counter-elite' is likely to make it more difficult for a leader to consolidate his power," but events during the Brezhnev years contravened this assertion. The "counter-elite" were not actually as "secure" as Brzezinski had claimed, and the consolidation of power by a single leader, far from being "more difficult" than for Khrushchev, was in many ways easier. After seeing what had happened to Khrushchev, Brezhnev and his successors knew they must be on their guard and must head off any similar challenges to their own power.

Fourth, Brzezinski's analysis reflected and built on an eclectic mix of academic currents. His emphasis on the emerging divide between Soviet society and the Soviet regime reflected the approach to political order devised in the mid-1960s by Samuel Huntington, who subsequently brought together many of his ideas in his 1968 book *Political Order in Changing Societies*. (Brzezinski and Huntington were close friends and had coauthored a book comparing the U.S. and Soviet political systems.) Huntington argued that modernizing societies, as measured by higher rates of literacy, education, urbanization, industrialization, economic growth, mass media coverage, and other indicators, were apt to be plagued by political instability and violence unless strong political institutions were in place to maintain order. Brzezinski's argument about the Soviet Union reflected precisely this dynamic—the emergence of what he saw as a dangerous gulf between the Soviet regime and Soviet society. Brzezinski's thesis was also consonant with the work being done by scholars who sought to elucidate the deradicalization of erstwhile revolutionary regimes. Because China at the time was immersed in its chaotically violent Cultural Revolution, the contrast between Mao Zedong's revolutionary upheavals and the relative conservatism of the Soviet regime was striking. Some scholars, such as Richard Löwenthal, argued that unless a Soviet-style regime was willing to impose repeated "revolutions from above" (as Mao was doing in China), new social stratifications resulting from economic development would induce key individuals and groups to try to solidify their advantages, causing a gradual move away from proclaimed utopian goals.[6] Brzezinski's analysis was compatible with Löwenthal's, although Brzezinski went further in pointing out that the entrenchment of these new centers of social power (especially within the CPSU's highest organs and central apparatus) was one of the greatest barriers to political modernization and economic flexibility in the USSR.

Fifth, much of what Brzezinski wrote about the Soviet Union in the late 1960s and afterward, including his emphasis on the political and ideological stagnation of the Soviet system, the elimination of mass terror, the growing inability of Soviet leaders to contend with Soviet society, and the changing nature of Soviet leadership dynamics, eliminated core elements of the totalitarian model, essentially marking the de facto abandonment of that model except as an ideal-type of the brutal dictatorship fashioned by Stalin. Robert Tucker in a 1965 article had argued that the changes in Soviet politics after Stalin's death meant that the system "should be pronounced, at least provisionally, post-totalitarian."[7] Brzezinski by that time clearly agreed with this sentiment. As he later explained, he had come to see totalitarianism as "a particular phase in the system-society relationship in which the society is in almost complete subordination to the state. That phase may or may not persist for too long, depending on circumstances."[8] In the case of the USSR, he specifically dated this totalitarian period from 1929 to 1953. After Stalin's death, the "limited retraction of political control over society and the surfacing of societal pressures from below" had, he argued, moved the Soviet Union into a post-totalitarian phase.[9] Thus, long before the so-called revisionist critiques of the totalitarian model appeared in the late 1970s and 1980s, the proponents of totalitarianism had acknowledged that the model, even as an ideal-type, was unsuitable for analyzing the post-Stalin Soviet Union.

❖ Brzezinski returned to many of these issues in a lengthy chapter in his 1970 book *Between Two Ages*. The book, building on an article he published in *Encounter* two years earlier, explored the nature of the "technetronic" age (an age in which society "is shaped culturally, psychologically, socially, and economically by the impact of technology and electronics, particularly in the area of computers and communications"), the role of the United States in the world, the changing nature of political beliefs and ideologies, and the major challenges facing the United States.[10] Foremost among these challenges overseas was the cold war competition with the Soviet Bloc, and Brzezinski therefore devoted seventy pages to an assessment of the USSR and other Communist countries in the aftermath of the August 1968 invasion of Czechoslovakia.

His diagnosis of the fundamental problems confronting the Soviet regime was largely along the lines of his earlier critique, but in addition to analyzing trends in Soviet power, he provided a comparison with Western countries (a comparison distinctly unfavorable for the USSR) and laid out several scenarios of where the Soviet Union might be heading.[11] Brzezinski credited the CPSU with the "unique achievement" of "transforming the most revolutionary doctrine of our age into dull social and political orthodoxy." He contended that the Soviet political system, being "highly centralized but arrested in its development," had come to be perceived within the USSR as "increasingly irrelevant to the needs of Soviet society [and] frozen in an ideological posture that was a response to an altogether different age." The polity, he argued, had "become the principal impediment to the country's further evolution," causing "the relationship between the political system and the society [to] become dysfunctional." He predicted that the Soviet regime would find it "ideologically more and more difficult to justify" the "continued subordination [of Soviet society] to a political system embodying increasingly sterile nineteenth-century doctrines."

Brzezinski stressed what he saw as the increasingly adverse position of the Soviet Union relative to the United States, especially in overall economic strength. The "absolute gap between the two countries," he argued, "will widen even further." Soviet economic advances, he believed, would be "insufficient to satisfy the ideological ambitions of the political elite" or "to satisfy rising social aspirations"—aspirations that were "certain to escalate as comparison with the West makes it more and more apparent that major sectors of Soviet society have remained extraordinarily antiquated." Brzezinski averred that "Soviet backwardness is particularly evident in agriculture" and other areas suitable for the technetronic age. The Soviet Union, he pointed out, "has not been able to produce technologically advanced products capable of penetrating economically rewarding world markets in the face of Western competition" or to sate "more than the rudimentary needs of domestic consumption." He emphasized the shortcomings of Soviet scientific research outside the military sphere: "The Soviet lag is unmistakable in computers, transistors, lasers, pulsars, and plastics, as well as in the equally important areas of management techniques, labor relations, psychology, sociology, economic theory, and systems analysis." Brzezinski concluded that the "ideological-political centralization" of the Soviet system, which stifled innovation and resulted in a high degree of intellectual conformity, had produced science policies that were at best "capricious" and at worst "catastrophic."

After highlighting the deep-rooted problems facing the Soviet Union, Brzezinski laid out five "alternative paths" or "developmental variants" of the USSR's future course:

1. Oligarchic petrification: The CPSU's highest organs would retain their dominant "political control over society without attempting to impose major innovations." This "conservative policy [would likely be] masked by revolutionary slogans," but essentially it would amount to a continuation of the status quo.

2. Pluralist evolution: The CPSU would become a "less monolithic body" and would be "willing to tolerate within its own ranks an open ideological dialogue, even ferment." The party "would cease to view its own ideological pronouncements as infallible" and would instead be a "source of innovation and change."

3. Technological adaptation: The CPSU would become "a party of technocrats," with a premium on "scientific expertise, efficiency, and discipline." The party would use "cybernetics and computers for social control" and rely on "scientific innovation for the preservation of Soviet security and industrial growth."

4. Militant fundamentalism: The CPSU would revert to Marxist-Leninist orthodoxy and embark on policies analogous to Mao's Cultural Revolution in China. Even though the Soviet Union might not fall back into Stalinist mass terror or be engulfed by chaotic violence as in China, the hard-line reorientation of the Soviet system "in all probability . . . would necessitate the application of force to overcome both actual resistance and sheer social inertia."

5. Political disintegration: The CPSU would increasingly lose its influence over society in the face of "internal paralysis in the ruling elite, the ris-

ing self-assertiveness of various key groups within it, splits in the armed forces, restiveness among the young people and the intellectuals, and open disaffection among the non-Russian nationalities." Having lost faith in the "petrified ideology" of Marxism-Leninism, Soviet leaders would be unable to devise "a coherent set of values for concerted action" to avert a systemic crisis.[12]

Brzezinski averred that "the Soviet leadership will seek to strike a balance between the first and the third variants"—that is, the CPSU Politburo would try to maintain the political status quo overall but would integrate larger numbers of technical experts into key positions in the party apparatus, creating "a novel kind of 'technetronic communism.'" Brzezinski did not venture to surmise the long-term future of the Soviet Union, focusing instead on "the near future," "the 1970s," and "approximately a decade ahead." He asserted that "in the short run, development toward a pluralist, ideologically more tolerant system [in the USSR] does not seem likely," in part because the Soviet "political system is not in the near future likely to elevate to leadership a man with the will and the power to democratize Soviet society," and in part because Soviet "society lacks the cohesion and the group pressures necessary to effect democratization from below." In Brzezinski's view, "the Soviet problem with non-Russian nationalities" was a further crucial impediment to democratization because "the Great Russian majority would inevitably fear that democratization might stimulate the desire of the non-Russian peoples first for more autonomy and then for independence."

In predicting that "the thrust of Soviet social development and the interests of the present ruling elite" made it "unlikely that an effective democratizing coalition could emerge," Brzezinski indicated that he was talking only about "the 1970s." He hinted that a modicum of liberalization might be feasible in the 1980s after the leaders of Brezhnev's generation passed from the scene. "It is quite possible," he wrote, "that the emerging political elite will be less committed to the notion that social development requires intense concentration of political power." However, he did not expect liberalization to proceed very far because "evolution into a pluralist system is likely to be resisted by the entrenched political oligarchy." He concluded that unless a Soviet leader came along who was truly committed to "a major transformation of the system as a whole"—something Brzezinski regarded as highly unlikely—"the more probable pattern for the 1980s is a marginal shift toward [a] combination of the second (pluralist evolution) and third (technological adaptation) variants: limited economic-political pluralism and intense emphasis on technological competence, within the context of a still authoritarian government." Whether this limited shift would be enough to keep the system from being permanently mired in "oligarchic petrification" was doubtful.

Brzezinski saw a reversion to "militant fundamentalism under a one-man dictatorship" as "somewhat more probable than a pluralist evolution," but he did not regard it as especially likely because a dictator attempting to consolidate a militantly ideological regime "would have to overcome enormous inertia and the collective stake of the party oligarchs in preventing the reappearance of one-man rule." Although Brzezinski believed that "the fundamentalist alternative should not be dismissed out of hand, especially if it becomes the only alternative to political disintegration resulting from the petrification of the system" or if a Sino-Soviet war erupted (a scenario adumbrated by the armed clashes along the Sino-Soviet border in 1969), he did not expect a militant fundamentalist regime to be able to gain ascendance in the absence of such extreme circumstances. His bottom line was that with "the conditions prevailing in the early 1970s," the most likely outcome was "oligarchic petrification" combined with some degree of a "'technologization' of the Soviet political system," which would not alter the basic political contours of the USSR.

The broad thrust of Brzezinski's analysis was borne out in the 1970s and early 1980s when the Soviet polity seemed stuck in an ossified, gerontocratic mold, particularly during the final years under Leonid Brezhnev and the brief period under Konstantin Chernenko. Brzezinski accurately highlighted the formidable obstacles to far-reaching change. He did not anticipate the eventual emergence of Gorbachev and the dramatic changes that resulted, but *Between Two Ages* did not wholly foreclose that outcome. Although Brzezinski believed that the advent of genuine democratization and of "a domestic phase of open intellectual creativity and experimentation" was unlikely at best, he never ruled out the possibility. Moreover, he correctly specified the consequences that would ensue from "a transformation of the [Soviet] system."

Brzezinski was less astute, however, in foreseeing the way meaningful political change in the USSR might come about. He argued that change would be spurred by social unrest, including student protests akin to those in many countries around the world in the late 1960s and early 1970s. Brzezinski claimed that "the 1970s will witness the spread to the Soviet Union of convulsions similar to those that Spain, Yugoslavia, Mexico, and Poland began to undergo in the late 1960s." He believed that "more visible social and political tensions," especially "student unrest," would be the only thing that could spur the country's leaders to embark on a truly different course. None of this actually happened, however. No significant student protests occurred in the Soviet Union prior to the Gorbachev era, and in general Soviet society remained surprisingly quiescent throughout the 1970s and early 1980s. Even during the heyday of Solidarity in Poland in 1980–81, spillover into the Soviet Union was very limited. Stephen Kotkin has aptly noted that when Gorbachev took office in March 1985, "the Soviet Union was not in turmoil. Nationalist separatism existed, but it did not remotely threaten the Soviet order. The KGB [had] crushed the small dissident movement. The enormous intelligentsia griped incessantly, but it enjoyed massive state subsidies manipulated to promote overall loyalty."[13] Brzezinski's contention that major change in the Soviet Union would come only in response to growing social pressure had the causal arrow pointing in the wrong direction. What actually happened is that far-reaching liberalization during the Gorbachev years paved the way for protests and mass unrest, not the other way around.

One final small point about the analysis in *Between Two Ages* is worth noting. Brzezinski's proposition that Russian concerns about maintaining control over the Soviet nationalities militated against democratization in the Soviet Union was a striking augury of the view expressed in the late 1970s and 1980s by Jerry Hough, who repeatedly argued that "the multinational character of the Soviet Union" would preclude "any evolution toward constitutional democracy" in the USSR. In a textbook published in 1979, Hough asserted that Soviet leaders necessarily feared that sweeping liberalization would stimulate the rise of separatist movements in the non-Russian republics and that this in turn would provoke a Russian nationalist backlash. The mere threat of such a development, Hough insisted, deterred Soviet officials from considering the option of genuine democratization. "Even if a Russian prefers democratization for himself, he must know—perhaps unconsciously—that such a development might well produce a major decline in the world position of Russia.... [One] can well imagine the normal Russian reaction to the thought of the loss of so much of the country."[14] This line of reasoning essentially reiterated what Brzezinski had argued nearly a decade earlier. The emergence of mass separatist movements in several Soviet republics in the late 1980s after Gorbachev introduced far-reaching political liberalization bore out much of Brzezinski's assessment, with the main exception that he had overestimated the potential for a "Great Russian majority" backlash.

The fact that mass separatist movements emerged in Lithuania, Latvia, Estonia, Moldova, and Georgia does not necessarily mean that the Soviet Union could not have survived genuine democratization. Timely concessions, deal cutting, and side payments by Gorbachev might have altered the dynamic in his favor. The Soviet state would have ended up slightly smaller with the loss of several small republics but would still have existed. Instead of responding in this way, however, Gorbachev declined to grant independence to any republic. His unwillingness to brook the loss of even the smallest Soviet republics constrained his leeway for action and was perhaps a reflection of the sentiment to which Brzezinski was alluding.

❖ In the latter half of the 1980s, after Brzezinski had served four years as national security advisor in the Carter administration and had written an illuminating memoir of that period, he returned to his long-standing interest in analyzing Soviet-style regimes. The tenor of his assessments of the Soviet political system in the 1980s reflected the important events that were under way but also hewed closely to the themes he had developed in the late 1960s and early 1970s. The advent of Gorbachev and the dramatic changes that followed gave Brzezinski an opportunity to reflect anew on the innate deficiencies of Leninist systems.

The publication of Brzezinski's *The Grand Failure* in 1989 brought him full circle to where he had begun in 1960 with his landmark book *The Soviet Bloc*.[15] In that earlier work, which remains a classic more than half a century after its appearance, Brzezinski traced the shift away from a relatively monolithic Soviet Bloc toward a diverse and increasingly fractious Communist world.[16] Not only did he explore the Soviet rift with Yugoslavia during the Stalin era and (in the revised 1967 edition) the bitter splits between the USSR and China and Albania under Khrushchev, but he also traced the process of "de-satellitization" whereby the East European countries moved from a position of near-total subordination to Soviet power during the Stalin era to a less subservient and at times refractory posture vis-à-vis the USSR after Stalin's death.

By the time Brzezinski was working on *The Grand Failure*, the whole setting for the Soviet Union and the rest of the Soviet Bloc was undergoing momentous change. Events that had seemed inconceivable when he wrote *The Soviet Bloc* had suddenly become routine. The bounds of Soviet tolerance had not yet been fully tested, but the leeway for political liberalization and even democratization in Eastern Europe and the USSR had expanded so much that it gave Brzezinski freer rein to talk about the utter failure of Marxism-Leninism. The book, completed in August 1988, predicted that "by the next century communism's irreversible historical decline will have made its practice and its dogma largely irrelevant to the human condition" and "communism will be remembered largely as the twentieth century's most extraordinary political and intellectual aberration."[17] One of the major themes in the book, developed especially in the first several chapters and the final several chapters (sometimes with considerable repetition, which an editor should have weeded out), is that "the key to communism's historic tragedy is the political and socioeconomic failure of the Soviet system." Brzezinski's analysis of this issue echoed his earlier writings on the subject from the mid-1960s on, supplemented by some crisp judgments about events connected with Gorbachev's reforms and the changes that ensued. Brzezinski traced the origins of Soviet communism's decline back through Soviet history, showing how the extreme concentration of power under ruthless Bolshevik leaders, especially Stalin, had spawned a political system that long defied any attempts at genuine, lasting liberalization, much less wholesale transformation. "The terminal crisis of contemporary communism," he wrote, "is thus all the more historically dramatic for the very suddenness of its onset."

Brzezinski's assessment of Gorbachev's prospects touched on the economic and social dimensions of the crisis, but above all he stressed the multiethnic configuration of the Soviet Union, an issue he had been highlighting since the 1960s. Describing the "national problem" as the "Achilles' heel of [Gorbachev's] perestroika," Brzezinski argued that the long-standing dominance of the "Great Russian majority" in the USSR had created an intractable situation. "Genuine decentralization," he maintained, "would inevitably breed demands" in non-Russian republics for equitable treatment, but "central Russian control is so deeply embedded in existing arrangements that the needed corrective would require a massive upheaval." The result, in his view, was a "vicious circle," whereby the "lack of reforms breeds national resentments, but reforms would probably nourish an even greater appetite among the non-Russians for more power." In particular, he expected that "separatist attitudes" would surface promptly "among the Balts and the Soviet Moslems, the latter stimulated by the worldwide resurgence of Islam and the Soviet military failure in Afghanistan." Overtly separatist movements did indeed arise in the Baltic republics early on (in fact, they were already surfacing when Brzezinski was writing), but his prediction that Soviet Muslims would be at the forefront of the independence movements was unfounded. No separatist movements arose at any point in the USSR's Central Asian republics, all of which sought to remain part of the Soviet Union until the very end.

Brzezinski surmised that the intractability of the nationalities question would most likely doom the larger program undertaken by Gorbachev:

Great Russian fears of growing nationalist conflicts, by impeding the needed reforms, enhance the likelihood that the real prospect for Soviet communism is debilitating decay and not constructive evolution. A truly renovating success—one that results in a creative, innovative, and self-energizing Soviet society—could only happen through the dilution of doctrine, the dispersal of the party's power, and the gradual emancipation of the non-Russians from Moscow's centralized control. It is highly improbable that the party leadership and the ruling elite, no matter how eager for an economic revival, will be prepared to risk going politically that far.

Because public expectations in the Soviet Union had been steadily rising during the Gorbachev period, Brzezinski averred that a possible attempt to clamp down would create an "inherently explosive" and "potentially revolutionary situation." This in turn led him to expect "a progressive breakdown of order [that] could lead eventually to a coup at the center, undertaken by the military, with KGB backing"—a scenario that materialized largely along these lines with the abortive coup d'état in the USSR in August 1991.

Brzezinski also looked in some detail at the changing status of communism in Eastern Europe and China. Following up on the text of his Hugh Seton-Watson Memorial Lecture at the Centre for Policy Studies in January 1988,[18] he rightly characterized "Marxism-Leninism [as] an alien doctrine imposed on the region by an imperial power whose rule is culturally repugnant to the dominated peoples."[19] Brzezinski argued that changes under way in the Soviet Bloc amounted to "the organic rejection by the social system of an alien transplant. . . . The alien system, grafted on by force from outside, is being repudiated by the social organism." This process, Brzezinski argued, was potentially destabilizing because the region was undergoing "both political liberalization and economic retrogression, a classic formula . . . for revolution." In his memorial lecture, Brzezinski claimed that five of the six East European Warsaw Pact countries (East Germany was the exception) were "ripe for revolutionary explosion."[20] He expressed concern that Soviet troops would intervene if "a massive social explosion" occurred in one or more East European countries, and he therefore underscored the importance of seeking "gradual change" in Eastern Europe that would avert a violent upheaval:

> I do not believe for a minute that a massive revolutionary upheaval in the region is in our interest. Were that to occur in the foreseeable future, I still believe, despite what [Alexander] Dubček has said in his recent interview, that the Soviet Union would have no choice but to intervene. It is almost equally certain that the West would impotently stand by, and that reform in the region and perestroika in the Soviet Union would be the victims. Thus, I do not believe that an explosion is something which we should be fomenting, or simply waiting for, or welcoming. Gradual

change, I think, is desirable. It should be encouraged. It should be facilitated, and it is feasible.[21]

In the lecture (though not subsequently in *The Grand Failure*), Brzezinski urged a cautious Western strategy that would avoid the impression of trying to bring the East European countries into the Western camp. "Our strategic and histori-cal goal should not be the absorption of what was once called Eastern Europe into what is still called Western Europe." Instead, he called for "the progressive emergence of a truly independent, culturally authentic, perhaps *de facto* neutral Central Europe." He emphasized that he was not proposing the elimination of the Warsaw Pact or the removal of Soviet troops: "When I say *de facto* neutral, I mean mainly neutral in substance but not neutral in form. This would emerge in the context of the continued existence of the alliance systems that define the geo-political reality of contemporary Europe."[22]

Brzezinski's proposed course of action for U.S. policy toward the Soviet Bloc in his January 1988 lecture was similar to what some other observers were con-templating at the time. As late as January 1989, when Henry Kissinger met in an unofficial capacity with Soviet leaders in Moscow, he tactfully broached the possibility of a superpower accord regarding the neutralization of Eastern Eu-rope, implying that the incoming administration of George H. W. Bush might be interested.[23] (Gorbachev, however, declined to pursue the matter.) Nonethe-less, events in the region were moving so fast that Brzezinski did not include a similar strategy in *The Grand Failure*, a decision that proved wise. By refraining from offering policy recommendations, Brzezinski kept the book from being im-mediately overtaken by events. Even though he underestimated how rapidly and decisively communism would collapse in Eastern Europe, his diagnosis of the emerging crisis in the region and its connection with the fundamental crisis in the USSR held up well overall.

Similarly, Brzezinski was largely accurate in predicting that the economic reforms undertaken in China, unlike those in the Soviet Union, were "probably fated to be successful."[24] In four brief chapters, which are the most innovative part of the book, he gave a cogent assessment of the changes unfolding in China under Deng Xiaoping. Brzezinski claimed that Deng's willingness to dismantle China's collective farms and to allow peasants to grow their own products "car-ried profound ideological consequences" in a country like China, which was overwhelmingly agrarian when the reforms began. Brzezinski went so far as to claim that the agricultural reform was so important that it "meant that the over-whelming majority of the Chinese people [i.e., peasants] had ceased to live within a communist framework." This particular assertion may be problematic, but Brzezinski was on solid ground in pointing out that Deng's economic "reforms went further than those of the Soviet Union" not only in agriculture but also in "urban and rural industry, in foreign trade, in foreign investment, in consumer goods, and in private enterprise.... Last but not least, unlike the Soviet Union, China made significant cuts in the size of the army and in defense expenditures."

*The Grand Failure* appeared before mass protests began in China in the spring of 1989 and before the brutal crackdown in Beijing in early June 1989. The latter event belied Brzezinski's contention that "centralized political control" would steadily diminish "as China's overall economic power expanded." In fact, what has happened in China from 1980 to the present has defied all expectations, combining rapid economic growth sustained over three decades with a political system that remains tightly under the control of the Communist Party founded by Mao Zedong. Institutional modernization theory would indeed have led one to expect in the late 1980s that a burgeoning middle class in China would eventually push for democratization, but so far that has not happened in the wake of the Tiananmen Square massacre. Even though Brzezinski (like almost everyone else) underestimated the Communist regime's ability to preserve tight political control in China, other aspects of Brzezinski's assessment have been borne out remarkably well.

The chief prediction in *The Grand Failure*—that communism was in its "final agony" and would be gone by the end of the twentieth century—was largely, though not wholly, correct. The Soviet regime and all Communist regimes in Europe, including the Albanian and Yugoslavian, collapsed, as did the Mongolian regime. Elsewhere, however, Communist systems survived. North Korea, Cuba, China, Vietnam, and Laos remain Communist to this day. One can debate the extent to which China and Vietnam remain truly Communist in light of their adoption of important capitalist reforms and institutions (a few of which are now also being slowly adopted in Cuba), but there is no denying that they remain repressive, one-party dictatorships headed by Communist rulers. Hence, even though communism in most parts of the world, especially Europe, has been thoroughly discredited and will not be revived, the system does remain extant in five countries containing roughly one-quarter of the world's population, far more people than in the more numerous countries in which Communist regimes once held power but ceased to exist after 1989–91.

❖ When Zbigniew Brzezinski began studying the Soviet Union in the early 1950s, the Soviet regime seemed destined to stay in power indefinitely. The

USSR enjoyed wide prestige from its major role in the victory over Germany in World War II. Under Soviet auspices, Communist rule had spread into Eastern Europe and East Asia, bringing nearly one-third of the world's population under the sway of Soviet-style regimes loyal to Moscow. Many newly independent countries in the developing world looked to the Soviet Union as a natural ally against the West, and the leaders of those countries were often attracted by the Soviet state-led model of development. The USSR seemed to be increasingly on a par with the United States in overall power.

After Stalin's death, however, fissures began to emerge within the Communist Bloc, and by the end of the 1950s a bitter rift had opened between the Soviet Union and China. Internally as well, the challenges facing the Soviet regime multiplied. As Brzezinski observed these shifts in the 1960s, he focused on the stultifying impact of the Soviet bureaucracy, which seemed to be depriving Soviet Marxist-Leninist ideology of all its vitality. The theme Brzezinski developed in his 1966 *Problems of Communism* article and his companion book, *Dilemmas of Change in Soviet Politics*—that the Soviet Union would undergo either transformation or degeneration—remained at the heart of his inquiries over the next two and a half decades.

Brzezinski's publications analyzing the Soviet political system from the mid-1960s through the late 1980s, especially the work he produced before he served as national security advisor, were perspicacious and nuanced, reflecting an impressive grasp of Soviet and Russian history and culture and the nature of Communist regimes elsewhere in the world. Despite rarely making explicit use of political science techniques, he was able to shed valuable light on the Soviet system. Brzezinski's basic ideas and arguments remained consistent over time, though he suitably adapted them as conditions markedly changed. He pinpointed the systemic weaknesses of the Soviet Union and Soviet-style regimes early on, and this helped him in the late 1980s to understand the depth of the crisis facing Soviet-style communism. His books and essays after he had served as national security advisor were intended for popular audiences, but most of these writings, especially *The Grand Failure*, also contained insights useful for experts. Brzezinski's analyses over time cogently explained how the Soviet Union's fortunes had deteriorated so sharply from the 1950s, when the USSR seemed to be the major ascendant power in the world with a chance of eclipsing the United States, to the early 1990s, when Gorbachev's efforts to prevent the Soviet Union from falling into a steep decline proved counterproductive and hastened the final crisis and disintegration of the Soviet system.

Even though some aspects of Brzezinski's writings about the USSR were not borne out in the end, his assessments of Soviet history and politics were (and are) convincing on many key points. Brzezinski nowadays is well known mostly for his governmental service and public commentary on U.S. foreign policy and international affairs, and his appraisals of the Soviet political system in the 1960s and early 1970s have been largely forgotten. That is a shame because anyone who takes the time to re-read (or read for the first time) Brzezinski's analyses of the Soviet system will find them a rich, provocative, stimulating source.

## NOTES

1  Zbigniew Brzezinski, "The Soviet Political System: Transformation or Degeneration," *Problems of Communism* 15, no. 1 (January–February 1966): 1–15.

2  Zbigniew Brzezinski, ed., *Dilemmas of Change in Soviet Politics* (New York: Columbia University Press, 1969).

3  All quotations here are from Brzezinski's essays in ibid.

4  Brzezinski, "Concluding Reflections," in *Dilemmas of Change*, 160–61.

5  Myron Rush, *Political Succession in the USSR* (New York: Columbia University Press, 1965); Rush, *How Communist States Change Their Rulers* (Ithaca, NY: Cornell University Press, 1974); and Rush, "The Soviet Military Buildup and the Coming Succession," *International Security* 5, no. 4 (Spring 1981): 169–85.

6  Richard Löwenthal, "Development vs. Utopia in Communist Policy," in *Change in Communist Systems*, ed. Chalmers A. Johnson (Stanford: Stanford University Press, 1970), 33–116.

7  Robert C. Tucker, "The Dictator and Totalitarianism," *World Politics* 17, no. 4 (July 1965): 555–83.

8  Zbigniew Brzezinski, "Soviet Politics: From the Future to the Past," in *The Dynamics of Soviet Politics*, ed. Paul Cocks, Robert V. Daniels, and Nancy Whittier Heer (Cambridge, MA: Harvard University Press, 1976), 341.

9  Ibid., 341–42.

10  Zbigniew Brzezinski, *Between Two Ages: America's Role in the Technetronic Era* (New York: Viking, 1970). For the earlier article, see Zbigniew Brzezinski, "America in the Technetronic Age," *Encounter* 30, no. 1 (January 1968): 16–26.

11  Unless otherwise indicated, quotations here are from Brzezinski, *Between Two Ages*.

12  Ibid., 164–66.

13  Stephen Kotkin, *Armageddon Averted: The Soviet Collapse, 1970–2000* (New York: Oxford University Press, 2001), 27.

14  Jerry F. Hough and Merle Fainsod, *How the Soviet Union Is Governed* (Cambridge, MA: Harvard University Press, 1979).

15  Zbigniew Brzezinski, *The Grand Failure: The Birth and Death of Communism in the Twentieth Century* (New York: Charles Scribner's Sons, 1989).

16  Zbigniew Brzezinski, *The Soviet Bloc: Unity and Conflict* (Cambridge, MA: Harvard University Press, 1960). The revised and expanded edition was published in 1967.

17  Unless otherwise indicated, all quotations here are from Brzezinski, *The Grand Failure*.

18  Zbigniew Brzezinski, "From Eastern Europe Back to Central Europe," in Centre for Policy Studies, *A Year in the Life of Glasnost: The Hugh Seton-Watson Memorial Lecture and Other Essays*, Policy Study No. 94 (London: CPS, 1988), 6–18.

19  Brzezinski, *Grand Failure*, 105.

20  Brzezinski, "From Eastern Europe Back to Central Europe," 14.

21  Ibid., 15.

22  Ibid., 15–16.

23  On this episode, see Mark Kramer, "The Demise of the Soviet Bloc," *Journal of Modern History* 83, no. 4 (December 2011): 816–17.

24  All quotations here are from Brzezinski, *Grand Failure*.

# PART II

To the National Security Council

# CHAPTER 4

# Setting the Stage for the Current Era

DAVID J. ROTHKOPF

Governor Jimmy Carter of Georgia met his future national security advisor when Zbigniew Brzezinski was serving, in addition to his teaching post at Columbia University, as executive director of the North American branch of the Trilateral Commission. The commission brought together senior business, government, and academic representatives from Europe, the United States, and Japan to help address issues they faced as leaders of the developed world as well as potential challenges from the developing world. Brzezinski had been introduced to this club of influential individuals when he came to the attention of David Rockefeller, chairman of Chase Manhattan Bank, after the publication of Brzezinski's book *Between Two Ages*, in which he highlighted many of the difficulties confronting the world's developed, Communist, and less developed countries.

The Trilateral Commission was one of those clubs of Establishment insiders that provoke in conspiracy theorists visions of men in gray suits gathering to run the world. The Council on Foreign Relations, the Bilderberg Conference, the Pugwash Conference, the Bohemian Grove, and the annual meeting of the World Economic Forum in Davos, Switzerland, are all such gatherings. As anyone who has ever participated in any of these events will tell you, they are at best excellent networking opportunities and forums for the exchange of interesting ideas—and they seldom offer much more than that. Indeed, it stands to reason that a good conspiracy would require a much smaller group of people operating much farther from the limelight. That said, in the 1970s, the Trilateral Commission was in its prime, and many who ended up playing important roles in the Carter administration were drawn from its ranks. The list includes Vice President Walter Mondale, Secretary of State Cyrus Vance, and Secretary of Defense Harold Brown—which means that with Brzezinski and Carter, every member of the inner circle of that administration's foreign policy apparatus had been associated with the commission. Others who were important to the administration, such as Deputy Secretary of State Warren Christopher (later Bill Clinton's first secretary of state), Carter arms control chief Paul Warnke, State Department head of policy planning Tony Lake, Assistant Secretary of State for East Asian Affairs Richard Holbrooke, and director of the Political Military Bureau at State (and future head of the Council on Foreign Relations) Leslie Gelb, were also members of the Trilateral Commission or had worked with the group as authors. That's how conspiracy theories get started; the fact that over time various members of this group would be at each other's throats would no doubt be discounted by committed conspiracy theorists as a clever distraction.

In 1973, Brzezinski recommended Carter as a potential member of the group, seeing him as a promising, high-profile politician interested in broadening his horizons and deepening his knowledge about international issues. Brzezinski helped Carter join the group and was quickly impressed by him as a rising star. Brzezinski also understood well that merit alone does not bring advisors to the attention of prospective patrons or would-be presidents. You need to work the system—getting involved in networking groups, getting published, going to cocktail parties, developing connections, sending encouraging notes to those on the rise, offering to help.

In 1974, when Brzezinski learned that Carter was considering running for president, he dropped him a line offering his services. Carter accepted the offer, and during the course of 1975, Brzezinski and Carter communicated periodically. Brzezinski offered memos, articles, ideas, and suggestions, and Carter found them useful. Eventually, after Brzezinski had told his wife how struck he was with Carter's performance at a Trilateral meeting in Japan where he made the case for a balanced approach to achieving peace in the Middle East, Muska Brzezinski suggested that he play a more active role in Carter's campaign. "Put your money where your mouth is," she said. "If you like him and believe in him, don't wait for developments, come out and support him."[1] Brzezinski made a donation to Carter's campaign and started "more systematically" writing papers for Carter—even though at the time the Georgia governor barely showed up on the national political radar, with poll ratings down around 2 percent. Brzezinski, who was known well to all the candidates in the race and could no doubt have worked with most of them, had placed his bet on the longest shot in the race. Soon he was Carter's top foreign policy advisor, his resident "professor" on issues that were of much greater importance to Carter as a presidential candidate than they had ever been when he was dealing with local issues in the Peach State.

Carter's campaign was as much a watershed in American politics as the foreign policies he and Brzezinski and the other members of the administration promulgated would be. The nation was numb in the aftermath of both Watergate and Vietnam. While few in the street would consider or articulate questions about American decline as academics might, people knew in their gut that something was deeply wrong, that this was not the America they had been raised believing in, and that much of the blame lay inside Washington, inside the Establishment—and in the Oval Office itself. To many, Nixon was a discredited villain. Gerald Ford, who had pardoned Nixon, knew that he would have to run at a distance from the man who had appointed him to the vice presidency. By contrast, Jimmy Carter was something altogether different. He spoke softly and simply of giving the American people a government as good as its people. He was an unknown, and he seemed very different from most professional politicians. He was a born-again Christian from the Deep South who taught Sunday school and actually seemed to believe in it. He was the anti-Nixon, perhaps honorable to a fault. He was straight out of the populist traditions of American politics, and yet he was something new—and he signaled something new.

One of the themes of Carter's campaign was to differentiate himself from Ford and Nixon, and one of the few things that these two very different men had in common was Henry Kissinger. On the campaign trail, Carter decried the Lone Ranger diplomacy of the previous administrations. He didn't beat around the bush on this point. "As far as foreign policy goes," he stated, "Mr. Kissinger has been the president of this country."[2] After the election, there was a concerted effort to ensure that the foreign policy formation process during the Carter years would contrast substantially with those that preceded it.

❖ Carter made Brzezinski his national security lead during his transition and discussed a variety of different combinations of personalities and structures with him. In his memoirs, Brzezinski writes,

> I started off by saying that he ought to think of appointments within the context of three alternative types of foreign policy leadership: there was direct and dominant Presidential leadership, in which a strong President (like Nixon) is assisted by a dominant White House (Kissinger) overshadowing a weak Secretary of State; there was, secondly, the model of a predominant Secretary of State, as with Dulles under Eisenhower or Kissinger under Ford, with a relatively passive President and

a non-obtrusive White House; and thirdly, there could be a more balanced "team" arrangement, combining a strong President (like Kennedy) with a relatively secure and strong Secretary of State (Rusk) with an equally confident and energetic White House (Bundy). I said that I assumed that Carter would strive for the third model. In the back of my mind I did have the feeling that although he might naturally gravitate toward the first model, in view of the Kissinger legacy he would find it awkward to admit it. . . . Moreover, at this stage, I did genuinely believe that the team approach would work.[3]

During the same conversation, Brzezinski explored with Carter the strengths and weaknesses of various secretary of state candidates, including George Ball, whom Brzezinski saw as a flawed candidate because of his tough stance with regard to Israel; Cyrus Vance, who, Brzezinski noted, "would fit well into my third model of a balanced leadership in the area of foreign affairs"; and Paul Warnke, whom he saw as a bit soft on the Soviet Union. They also discussed various candidates for the national security advisor position, and Brzezinski noted a number of others, including Harold Brown, a former secretary of the air force and president of the California Institute of Technology.

Later, after the appointment of Vance as secretary of state, Carter and Brzezinski discussed what role Brzezinski might play, and Brzezinski proposed either deputy secretary of state to Vance or assistant to the president for national security, expressing a preference for the latter. One week after that, Carter called Brzezinski while he was at a party in New York City. According to Brzezinski, Carter's tone was light, and it was clear he enjoyed toying with Brzezinski in a friendly way:

"Zbig, I want you to do me a favor—I would like you to be my National Security Advisor."

"That's no favor—that is an honor. And I hope and feel confident that you won't regret your decision," Brzezinski replied.

"Actually, I knew as of some months ago that you were my choice but I had to go through these processes of selection. But I knew all along," Carter then noted.[4]

Because of Carter's presumed preference for a more balanced, team-driven approach than that of the Kissinger years, Brzezinski collaborated on a plan with the man who had been designated to be his deputy, David Aaron, a former Kissinger National Security Council (NSC) staffer who had been an advisor to the new vice president, Walter Mondale, when Mondale was in the Senate. The plan they proposed to Carter would have seven different committees, a majority of which would be chaired by cabinet secretaries, such as Vance at State; Brown at Defense; Michael Blumenthal, the incoming treasury secretary; or Admiral Stansfield Turner, the incoming CIA director. Only three of the committees would report to Brzezinski in this scheme: those pertaining to arms control, sensitive intelligence, and crisis management, matters that demanded the president's personal involvement or attention.

Carter rejected the proposal when it was presented to him during a planning session on St. Simon Island, off the Georgia coast. "Too many committees," the president-elect said; "I want a simple, cleaner structure." So, sitting in a cottage on St. Simon, Brzezinski and Carter worked out a different scheme, this one with only two committees. The Policy Review Committee (PRC) was to deal with foreign policy issues, defense policy issues, and international economic issues. It would be chaired by whichever cabinet secretary was closest to the issues being discussed (in practice, in all but a handful of instances, this turned out to be the secretary of state). Twice a year it would be chaired by the CIA director when intelligence budgets were being discussed. The second committee, the Special Coordination Committee (SCC), would deal with intelligence policy issues that had to do with covert and otherwise sensitive operations, arms control, and crisis management. This group would be chaired by Brzezinski. Whenever possible, the meetings would be attended by the cabinet members themselves, not by subcabinet officials, as was the case with many of Kissinger's committees. To enhance the functioning of this structure, Carter informed his team at the first cabinet meeting that he was elevating the national security advisor to cabinet status. It was a first and sent an unmistakable message.

The message was equally clear when Carter surprised the other members of the cabinet with the new structure during another meeting on St. Simon. Since it was a fait accompli, all they could do was accept it—or appear to. Brzezinski translated the structure into two presidential directives, which were submitted to Carter a few days before his inauguration. Aaron collaborated on these, as did Brzezinski's special assistant, Karl "Rick" Inderfurth, both of whom would, like so many of the Carter team, serve in senior capacities during the next Democratic administration, that of Bill Clinton, over a decade later.

The first of these memos completed the now predictable if vaguely absurd task of renaming presidential memoranda. What were once National Security Study Memoranda (NSSMs) became Presidential Review Memoranda (PRMs), and what were National Security Decision Memoranda (NSDMs) became Presidential Directives (PDs). The second PD outlined the new structure of committees and processes that would be implemented under Carter. These documents were signed on the eve of Carter's inauguration and were distributed to the cabinet immediately after the president was sworn in. Not surprisingly, there was some discomfort with the system. It was a bureaucratic first strike of the first order. The system essentially gave responsibility for the most important and sensitive issues to Brzezinski, and the vague definition of what constituted crisis management essentially ensured that if anything came up that was important it could be claimed by the White House.

Vance was unhappy and asserted that he had not been consulted, even though the plan had been brought up at the island retreat. He and Brzezinski met to discuss the issues, and ultimately Vance came to accept the new approach. Over more than three decades later, Vance supporters from the State Department still smart from this first "Brzezinski" move and assert that with this step he did precisely what the president had said he was not going to do, and that is "become another Kissinger." Indeed, the divisions that began with this issue spread into one of the bitterest rivalries in executive branch history, and it ultimately resulted in Vance's resignation over differences about the appropriate response to the Iran hostage crisis that would dominate the last years of the Carter administration and reverberate for years.

The tension was due to not simply turf rivalries between the State Department and the White House and NSC staff but also the tug-of-war over who would serve as the president's principal foreign policy spokesperson on key issues. The patrician Vance did not embrace the media spotlight in the way that a modern foreign policy leader must (since so much of diplomacy was already being conducted by the late 1970s via television), and as a result, Brzezinski says, he was forced—and asked by Carter—to step up into this role. Vance "wasn't very good at selling the policy," says Brzezinski. "That's why I ended up on television even though the original intent was for me to be practically invisible. Then, when the Secretary of State complained about that and said that I'm propagandizing myself by being on television, the President told him quite explicitly, 'I told him to do it.' And that was true. I never appeared on television without an explicit request from the President."[5]

Vance protégés argue that this analysis ignores Brzezinski's own formidable drive to be the president's principal policy collaborator, but the reality is that, as ambitious as Brzezinski was and as direct and aggressive as he could be in his bureaucratic style, this structure could not have evolved without the support or direction of the president—who in fact embraced and largely shaped it. Indeed, although Jimmy Carter came into the office amid sniping that as governor of Georgia he was ill prepared for the foreign policy challenges he would face in the presidency (Bill Clinton and George W. Bush would face the same kind of criticism), it is clear from his early actions that international affairs was important to him and that he was going to take a very hands-on approach in that area. The evidence that he did is expressed best by the fact that 80 percent or more of his book *Keeping Faith: Memoirs of a President* is about international issues—they were in many respects his passion, his legacy, and his undoing (although skyrocketing inflation and a lousy economy sure didn't help).

Although Carter dominated the team he gathered around him as he conducted the affairs of state, its members were not relegated to the kind of secondary roles on foreign policy that all but Kissinger had for most of the Nixon years. Indeed, although the rows between Vance and Brzezinski that were to break out over issues of policy and primacy were cited as a sign of dysfunction in the Carter administration, they are also clear testimony to the fact that both strong personalities were given prominent roles and that Carter valued them as much for their differences as for their individual contributions.

But, beyond the traditional roles for traditional players around the heart of the NSC, there were some new players in the mix in Carter's inner circle. Vice President Mondale was surely one of them. It was, Mondale said, Carter's commitment to the idea from the start that made it happen, made it more than some of the promises of "partnership" other vice presidents have received and which then were ignored. "I really did have an open invitation to attend all meetings. Saturday discussions and on. If Deng Xiaoping comes to town, I'm there with Carter and that sort of thing. I also had any number of private discussions with him. It was understood that whenever I wanted access I would have it."[6]

Carter's team met informally more often than formally. Friday morning breakfast meetings were attended by Carter, Mondale, Vance, Brown, and Brzezinski, and later Chief of Staff Hamilton Jordan and occasionally others. As in past administrations, it was in meetings like these where much of the real work for major decisions was done. Vance, Brown, and Brzezinski also had their own weekly lunch, and Carter and Mondale typically had a private lunch each week. So did Carter and his wife, First Lady Rosalynn Carter, each Thursday, to discuss management issues associated with the White House, their schedules, and any other issues that were important. Says Brzezinski, "Smaller groups obviously generate more discussion and give the President the opportunity to engage in a much more intimate view of the issues. You can't make policy through informal procedures, but you can crystallize directions and then supervise both the implementation and coordination via the formal process."[7]

❖ As in most administrations, Brzezinski and Carter kicked off their operation with a series of PRMs that dealt with what they determined would be front-
burner issues or issues that would arise in the near term. These included memoranda looking at what U.S. policy should be concerning the Panama Canal and
how to manage the handover to the government of Panama; one on the Strategic
Arms Limitation Talks (SALT); one on the Middle East; one on South Africa and
Rhodesia; one on Cyprus; one on mutual and balanced force reductions (MB-
FRs); one on an upcoming economic summit and trilateral (U.S.-Europe-Japan)
policies; one on North-South strategy; one on European policy; one on military
force positions; one on intelligence community structure and mission; one on
Korea; one on Philippine base negotiations; and one on nuclear proliferation.

As part of this policy framing process, Brzezinski and his team also drafted a
list of ten goals that included strengthening trilateral relations, expanding political and economic relations with emerging powers, enhancing North-South
relations by stimulating greater economic stability in the developing world,
moving from strategic arms limitation talks to strategic arms reduction talks,
normalizing U.S.-Chinese relations, obtaining a comprehensive Middle East
settlement, promoting peaceful transformation in South Africa and rebuffing a
Soviet-Cuban presence in southern Africa, restricting the level of global arma-
ments, promoting human rights, and maintaining a strong defense. Given that
Carter ended up serving only one term, the degree to which many of these goals
were achieved or advanced is remarkable, although evaluations of his administration over the years have been lukewarm at best, with some of the crises Carter
and his team faced overshadowing their considerable achievements.

Brzezinski's team at the NSC included a few holdovers from the Ford years,
such as Bob Hormats, who handled international economics (and today serves in
the Obama administration as under secretary of state for economic affairs), and
Roger Molander, who handled SALT issues. Brzezinski's military aide was Colonel William Odom (promoted to general while serving on the NSC staff), who
had worked with Brzezinski at Columbia. Another former academic colleague,
Samuel Huntington, came in to assess the state of relations between the United
States and the Soviet Union. Also in the group were regional specialists such as
Robert Pastor, who joined the NSC fresh from defending his doctoral dissertation to handle Latin America; Robert Hunter, who handled Western Europe; William Quandt, who handled the Middle East; and some, like 31-year-old Jessica
Tuchman, formerly of the staff of Congressman Morris Udall, who handled clusters of global issues, including human rights. Among Brzezinski's special assistants was Bob Gates, who would later be deputy national security advisor, then

head of the CIA and most recently secretary of defense for both George W. Bush and Barack Obama. His congressional liaison work was handled by a former young staffer of Senator Edmund Muskie's named Madeleine Albright. Brzezinski established another precedent by hiring a dedicated press staffer to the team, Jerrold Schecter, formerly of *Time* magazine. This worried some who saw it as a play for more exposure for Brzezinski, but it also provided important expertise when it came to handling foreign policy–related press issues. The practice was adopted again in later years by the Clinton administration and the second Bush administration; in the latter, the press lead for the NSC gained the title of deputy national security advisor. Overall, Brzezinski tried to trim the NSC staff from its large size under Kissinger, and he began with about twenty-five professionals on the team.

Before her sudden call to the NSC, Madeleine Albright had been working for Senator Muskie, of Maine. She described her initial experience this way:

> I worked for Muskie until a particular Friday before moving over to the NSC/White House. Muskie was on the Law of the Sea Advisory Committee and, of course, Maine has a long coastline. So, on behalf of Muskie, I wrote a letter to President Carter saying how very important the Law of the Sea was but asked him to understand that we have all these fishermen in the state and we should not stop them from earning a living. We put the autopen signature on the letter and sent it over to the White House. A few days later I left my job and went to the NSC. Upon arrival, I found this bloody letter I sent the week before. So, I did what a staffer should do: I wrote back—to myself, so to speak—and I explained on behalf of the President that I was very sorry about the fishermen but the national interest was really much more important. We signed it "Jimmy Carter" and off it went. This was proof of the Washington adage "Where you sit is where you stand."[8]

The Panama Canal Treaty was an early triumph for Carter, especially considering how unpopular giving up the canal was. Carter and his team knew long before his inauguration that they would have to deal with what promised to be a tough issue. They recognized that negotiations with the Panamanians were necessary, that ultimately our control of the canal would have to be phased out, and that Panamanian sovereignty would have to be recognized. What is more, they knew that the year before, thirty-eight senators—more than the number needed to kill a treaty—had supported a resolution opposing a new treaty. Those senators also enjoyed broad support among the American people, according to the polls.

The negotiations turned on several key issues, described in two treaties. One covered joint operation of the canal for the remainder of the twentieth century, after which the Panamanians would assume full responsibility for the canal. The second guaranteed the neutrality of the canal and the right of the United States to defend its interests there. The negotiations were tricky, and they stalled around demands for huge U.S. payments to the Panamanians. Ultimately, it took the direct intercession of Carter via a letter to Panamanian president Omar Torrijos to resolve the issue, and by early August it was done. Although it had taken longer than the Carter team had hoped, they had achieved in eight months what had not been accomplished in fourteen years of negotiations before that point.

By February 1978—a congressional election year—public support for the treaties finally turned positive, with 45 percent favoring them and 42 percent opposed. But then—and possibly because of this surge—a new wave of opposition was mounted by Senators Robert Dole, Richard Helms, and others, who made charges ranging from accusing Torrijos's family of drug trafficking to suggesting bribery of high U.S. officials. Although all the charges ultimately proved untrue, it was Washington politics at its nastiest—and it can serve as a reminder to all present-day Americans that politics in the United States has been a dirty business, going back to the lies and lie-driven scandals that swirled around Alexander Hamilton, Thomas Jefferson, and other members of Washington's administration. Every generation says that it's worse than ever and yearns for the civility of yesteryear. There was no civil yesteryear. As one former high official in the Carter administration said to me, "The stakes are too high for these guys to play clean—especially when they can't win on the merits."[9]

∴ Another early focus of the Carter administration bears out the difficulties of working in the modern political environment equally well, but the outcome for the Carter team in this case was less satisfying. It concerned arms control.

Jimmy Carter, a former nuclear engineer, had expressed interest in eliminating nuclear weapons and soon after becoming president requested a study by the Pentagon on the possibility of reverting to a "minimum deterrence" capability limited to 200–250 nuclear delivery vehicles. The president-elect and his incoming national security team received briefings on the U.S. strategic nuclear war plans before entering office, and the NSC issued a series of PRMs that reviewed the U.S. defense posture soon after Carter's inauguration. A reappraisal of the Nixon-Ford position resulted from PRM-10, "Comprehensive Net Assessment and Military Force Posture Review," and a subsequent five-month interagency study, supervised by Samuel Huntington, the NSC staffer responsible for national security planning.

Brzezinski had intended that these reviews would "spur within the Defense Department a broader review of our strategic doctrine and also interest the President himself in this difficult and complicated issue."[10] But frustrated with the Pentagon's slow response, Brzezinski himself promoted efforts by the administration to craft a new nuclear doctrine and began by "strengthening" the NSC cluster dealing with military issues. His senior military aide, William Odom, recalled that "for the next two years, based on the kind of analyses we had done in PRM-10, we had to work slowly to try to bring the realities to the eyes of the President, the eyes of the Secretary of Defense, Secretary of State and make them realize that we had to tackle some of those policies from very fundamentally different directions." Brzezinski adds, commenting on the dynamic behind this and other initiatives, "It wasn't the Defense Department running foreign policy, nor the State Department running foreign policy. It was the White House setting the pace and direction for both."

Despite Vance's skepticism, Carter signed the presidential directive in July 1980. "Nuclear Weapons Employment Policy," as it was called, modified U.S. nuclear strategy by shifting and expanding targeting priorities from those mandated by the Nixon administration (from 25,000 to 40,000 potential target installations).

❖ Simultaneously, the administration worked on a parallel initiative through the NSC's SCC, one that pertained to the U.S.-Soviet SALT negotiations. Carter attended the first session of this new entity on February 3, 1977. He opened the discussion with general motivational remarks about the team and the system he had put into place, but before leaving he emphasized his desire to engage in a SALT process with the Soviets that produced deep cuts. Brzezinski was to play a key role in the SCC sessions, as John Prados recounts in *Keepers of the Keys*: "Brzezinski deliberately tried to balance the hards and the softs by the order in which he called on them to speak. Zbig reserved the final say for Cy Vance, then summarized and reported the SCC deliberations to the President. Carter followed up directly at his breakfast with Vance, Mondale and Zbig. Harold Brown was only later admitted to the foreign policy breakfasts as were Hamilton Jordan, Jody Powell and special counsel Hedley Donovan."[11]

Brzezinski shepherded the process closely and even went so far as having William Hyland, working for the NSC, oversee the delivery of the negotiating instructions to ensure that they did not get into the hands of the State Department until the instant of their departure. The national security advisor also managed the key decision-making meetings involved in the process in a way that he thought would preserve the equities of the military and not cut too deeply into arms stockpiles they felt were essential. He did this by, for example, ensuring that Brown joined him in meetings with the president, Mondale, and Vance. As it happened, Mondale, who had a reputation as something of a dove, was a "pleasant surprise" to his less dovish colleagues, for he "regularly showed extremely sophisticated knowledge of military issues and a real commitment to protecting America's defense structure."[12]

The final set of proposals offered to the Soviets, as laid out in PD-7, did put forward the deeper cuts because of Carter's commitment to this approach. A slightly more moderate option was the fallback position. As the Soviets had not been prepared for such a proposal, their sclerotic and somewhat paranoid leadership could neither respond to it swiftly nor fully trust the motives behind the approach. Vance's talks with Brezhnev went very badly, and he felt uneasy doing what his predecessor Kissinger surely would have done, which was improvising, thinking on his feet, and exploring avenues by which the discussions might have been salvaged. Subsequently, in the press, Brzezinski took the line that the United States had made a good faith effort to make a constructive proposal and implied that the Russians were the ones who had dropped the ball. While this is true to some extent, it is also true that anticipating the expectations of one's negotiating partner is a key to success, and the U.S. team showed very little sensitivity to the likely reactions of the Soviets at that time. One former NSC staffer speculated that this might not have been entirely an accident on the part of Brzezinski, who "should have known and perhaps even did know" that Moscow, backing a "more moderate set of cuts," might not react well to the new proposal favored by the Carter team. But others deny that this was a calculated attempt to "show up the Soviets for what they were."[13]

The negotiations were rekindled and then went on for another nine months. Critical issues that became central included parameters for telemetry encryption, the Backfire bomber, and limits on the number of warheads allowable per long-range missile. The long-distance communications and differing positions about where to come out on encryption-related issues caused a considerable hiccup in the negotiating process. Vance got it back on track, and Carter and Brezhnev signed the SALT II Treaty at a summit meeting in Vienna in June 1979.

After that, the politics of Washington and Capitol Hill kicked back in, and the treaty became a hockey puck to be batted back and forth by the Left and the Right in the Senate. Once again the two-thirds majority required to ratify a treaty was needed. The problem was exacerbated when a controversy arose over the alleged presence of a brigade of two to three thousand Russian troops in Cuba.

Hawks saw this as further evidence of the Soviet Union's malevolent intentions. As Brzezinski was also frustrated with Vance's management of this set of events, he noted in one of his weekly memos to the president, "You may not want to hear this, but I think that the increasingly pervasive perception here and abroad is that in U.S.-Soviet relations, the Soviets are increasingly assertive and the U.S. more acquiescent. State's handling of the Soviet brigade negotiations is a case in point. I recommend that in the future we will have to work for greater White House control."[14] Carter responded in the margin (as he did in detail with most of the memos he got): "Good!"

Alas, one of the by-products of the controversy, and of the political divisions in Washington, was that the SALT II Treaty was never ratified.

⁛ One of the early areas in which the split between Brzezinski and Vance manifested itself had to do with the president's long-held desire to move toward normalization of relations with China. Of course, the seeds of discord were brewing from the days before the administration, when Carter and Brzezinski arrived at a national security operational structure that ensured the centrality of the NSC and marginalized the State Department on key issues. Vance balked at this but accepted it, either because of the arguments for it offered by Brzezinski and Carter or because he had no choice. Nonetheless, Richard Holbrooke, Tony Lake, and Peter Tarnoff, Vance's chief of staff, had tried to alert Secretary Vance that Brzezinski was trying to put the NSC at the center of the foreign policy making process at the State Department's expense. When you speak to them about this period, they argue, as do many of Vance's supporters, that Vance simply didn't play ball the way Brzezinski did, that he had too much character and dignity. Brzezinski staffers to this day say the Vance-Brzezinski split was overstated, that the system worked pretty well, and that Vance's role diminished because of the bureaucratic inertia and lack of creativity of the State Department (a refrain heard from administration to administration).[15]

The tension between these men—and from time to time between their staffs—may have stemmed from traditional State-NSC rivalries, differences between their character types (the patrician Vance and the hard-charging, "confrontational" Brzezinski), or differences in worldview over how to approach the Soviet Union, as is often suggested. Harold Brown commented:

Brzezinski had, I think, a much more apocalyptic view of the world and especially a different attitude toward the Soviets. And he is also a more confrontational individual. He is not necessarily abrasive—but more willing to push things hard on a

personal basis. That is not to say he used his position as the last person to talk to the
president improperly. At least, in formal terms, my belief is that he always correctly
reflected other people's views, gave his own, but didn't try to force a compromise.

Nonetheless, I think his was a more confrontational personality. And he had
a very fundamental difference with Vance in that he believed that concessions to
the Russians merely encouraged them to press further, and he was willing to use
almost any device or any other relationship with other countries to contain them.
He saw relations with other countries in those terms.

That was the big difference on China. Clearly, Vance was willing to play down
U.S. relations with China in order to get better relations with the Russians. Brzezinski's view was that we should use China as a weapon against the Soviets. And
inevitably, I think we did to some degree, and I played a part in that. My own position was more in between. I felt that we should not avoid improving relations with
China in order to make life easier in dealing with the Soviets. In any event, it was a
very fundamental clash both in policies and in styles between those groups. And it
really damaged the administration badly.[16]

During the Carter years, China policy primarily revolved around the issue of
the full normalization of relations with the People's Republic of China, which
emerged soon after President Carter took office. Vance and Brzezinski articulated dissimilar opinions on the impact of China on the U.S. geopolitical competition with the Soviet Union, with Brzezinski hoping to utilize the "China card"
in order to help curb the Soviets. In contrast, the secretary of state viewed an
evolving U.S.-China security relationship as detrimental to the détente relationship and "pos[ing] substantial risks for our relations with Moscow and for our
relations with Tokyo and other Asian allies."[17]

Given the centrality of the China policy and Brzezinski's role in framing that
policy, chapter 5 deals with this issue separately. It can be said, however, that the
China normalization—guided by Carter and implemented largely by Brzezinski—ended up as a success, as had Panama and the negotiating process around
SALT II.

❖ Yet the biggest and most celebrated success of the Carter era, the one for
which he is most remembered, centered on a thirteen-day marathon negotiating
session in the Maryland woods at Camp David. The effort, the capstone of Carter's early commitment to achieving a breakthrough in the Arab-Israeli conflict,
was one case in which the State Department and the NSC teams worked together
in very close harmony. But it also illustrated the extraordinary degree to which

Carter's diplomacy was conducted by Carter. Here, the fact that he was a hands-on manager made a significant difference for the better. He took the process very personally, was well prepared for it by his staff, and tackled the big problems in closing the epochs-old rift between Israel and Egypt.

His relationship with Anwar Sadat, the president of Egypt, is encapsulated well in his memoirs, in which he writes, "On April 4, 1977, a shining light burst on the Middle East scene for me. I had my first meetings with President Anwar Sadat of Egypt, a man who would change history and whom I would come to admire more than any other leader." The bond between the two was mutual, and it enabled Carter to keep Sadat in the negotiations at several key junctures when they were breaking down, often as a result of the tough stance of Israel's prime minister, former underground fighter Menachem Begin. Carter and Begin could not be described as close. Nonetheless, it was often personal diplomacy, including the kind of very direct conversations that could only take place between two leaders in private, that produced the breakthroughs and communicated the leverage needed to achieve the deal.

So much has been written about the Camp David process that it would be hard to shed much light on it here. However, in the context of the operations of the NSC and the high-level interagency process, it should be noted that unusually close collaboration existed between the two in the extensive preparations for Camp David peace talks. For instance, a secret planning group with Vice President Mondale, Vance, Brzezinski, Deputy National Security Advisor David Aaron, NSC Middle East specialist William Quandt, and several other State Department officials was formed in May to coordinate the administration's strategy. One author concluded that the "cooperation of State Department and NSC officials enabled Carter and Vance, as the principal negotiators, to be ahead of the Israelis and Egyptians on technical and negotiating issues and thus to keep the initiative."[18] Brzezinski and Quandt were present at the talks at Camp David, but the national security advisor expressly acknowledges that Vance had a pivotal role during the difficult negotiations.

Meanwhile, however, not only did the unraveling of the shah's regime in Iran shatter the uneasy interagency peace, but, more importantly, the consequences of the shah's fall embroiled the Carter administration for the rest of its term and seriously damaged its record of foreign policy achievements. The question facing the national security team was now as complex as it was agonizing: what could be done—diplomatically or militarily—about the new Khomeini regime? Initially, President Carter was unable to decide whether to heed the counsel of Brzezinski, who wanted to encourage the shah to suppress the revolution (or, if the shah was unable to do so, encourage a military dictatorship that could), or that of Vance's more cautious State Department, which suggested that the administration reach out to opposition elements in order to smooth the inevitable transition to a new government. No wonder Carter observed in his diary at this time that "Zbig is a little too competitive and incisive. Cy is too easy on his subordinates. And the news media constantly aggravate the inevitable differences and competition between the two groups. I hardly know the desk officers and others in State but work very closely with the NSC people. When we have consulted closely, like in the Mideast area, at Camp David, and otherwise, we've never had any problems between the two groups."

However, things were clearly changing. On the morning of Sunday, November 4, 1979, the White House Situation Room received an emergency call from the U.S. embassy in Tehran. The embassy had been overrun. Elizabeth Anne Swift, one of the embassy staff, began to give a nonstop commentary of the situation from inside the embassy over an open line connected to a speaker on the table. From another speaker, Kathryn Koob and her staff some miles away in the American Cultural Center in Iran spoke for a record day and a half until she, too, was discovered (the revolutionary authorities would later present the phone bill to her in captivity). At the end of the day, sixty-six U.S. citizens were held hostage.

At the time, the United States was involved in delicate, highly classified negotiations with Tehran to arrange safe passage for a group of U.S. officials stuck in northern Iran. Washington was also worried about security threats from U.S.-based pro-Khomeini factions and possible legal action against the shah and was trying to secure the safety of Americans threatened by local "revolutionary committees" roaming Iran. Brzezinski decided that the invitation should be retracted and the shah should postpone his arrival in the United States. Moreover, Carter did not want the shah "playing tennis" in the United States while Americans ran the risk of being kidnapped. As David Aaron suggested to the president, if the shah moved to the United States, a "guerrilla group could retaliate against the remaining Americans, possibly taking one or more Americans hostage and refusing to release them until the shah was extradited."

The 444-day hostage ordeal began.

On November 5, Brzezinski chaired the first of the SCC meetings that would work toward the release of the hostages. The meetings would occur every morning, sometimes seven days a week, with no agenda circulated in advance to maintain operational security. By the next day, the problem had become more complicated. The entire religious revolutionary leadership had thrown its support behind the students barricading the embassy. That morning at 8:00, Carter met in the Oval Office with the principals—Brzezinski, Vance, Under Secretary Newsom, Secretary of Defense Harold Brown, Chief of Staff Hamilton Jordan, Press Secretary Jody Powell, and Gary Sick from the NSC taking notes. Carter asked the State Department to do everything possible to get any remaining U.S. citizens out of Iran. Brzezinski suggested that a veiled public threat or a private threat to bomb Qom or Iran's oil fields should be given in case they killed hostages. Carter was not so convinced: "They have us by the balls." However, Carter did ask his staff to examine the possibility of expelling students (something Walter Mondale later opposed—why would a great nation respond by "kicking out a few sad-ass students"?), freezing Iranian assets, and stopping the supply of military spare parts: "Get our people out of Iran and break relations. Fuck 'em!"[19]

At 4:30 that afternoon Carter summoned the full NSC in the Cabinet Room. He opened by asking the group to fill out policy options: What punitive options should be used if Iran began killing hostages? Should U.S. forces be sent to Iran, or would this lead to them getting bogged down? After Carter was finished, Brzezinski noted that NBC had found out about U.S. emissaries being dispatched to the Middle East and was going to publicize the fact that evening (when the news reached Khomeini, he gave the order that no one was to meet with the emissaries). On November 10, Carter wrote in his diary, "I asked Cy for his opinion on punitive action to be launched against Iran. His recommendations were exactly what I had already decided tentatively with our military people. We want it to be quick, incisive, surgical, no loss of American lives, not involve any other country, minimal suffering of the Iranian people themselves, to increase their reliance on imports, sure of success, and unpredictable. No one will know what I've decided—except Fritz [Mondale], Zbig, Harold, David [Jones, chairman Joint Chiefs] and Cy."

On November 17 the administration's secret initiative to the Palestine Liberation Organization (PLO) bore fruit. Thirteen African American embassy officials and women were released and subsequently debriefed on November 20 in Germany. The principals now learned that many of the embassy's files had been captured (prompting Carter to task Anthony Lake with a complete review of the documents) and that the conditions inside the embassy were poor: those suspected of spying were being threatened with torture and show trials. On the same day, Khomeini also threatened that "if Carter does not send the shah, it is possible that the hostages may be tried, and if they are tried, Carter knows what will happen." The United States replied that Iran "would bear full responsibility for any ensuing consequences, [and that] other remedies [were available to the United States]."

On November 28 a meeting that later on would be seen as one of the most contentious of the crisis was held. Until then, Vance had managed to keep the diplomatic track from being overtaken by the military track. That day Carter asked the SCC, chaired by Brzezinski, to comment on the possible mining of Iran ports to escalate military pressure on Iran. Vance was opposed, arguing that it would threaten the hostages. Brzezinski, on the other hand, suggested that it would force the Europeans to act more forcefully. Vance won the argument. As a consequence, diplomatic action continued for another two months. However, the military track began to assume greater importance. Meanwhile, the shah left the United States for Panama, the PLO initiative ended, and the NSC was deadlocked: all the reasons that Vance was using to avoid use of force were passing.

On December 27, when the Soviets invaded Afghanistan, the crisis grew even more complex. Now, not only was Iran in turmoil, but American hostages were in captivity, oil markets were unsteady, and the Soviet Union was making an unabashed play for a country in a critical and deeply troubled region. Although the Soviets insisted they had been "invited" into Afghanistan by the local government, it was clear that this was a strategic ploy. Carter noted in his diary, "The Soviets have begun to move their forces in to overthrow the existing government. 215 flights in the last 24 hours or so. They've moved in a couple of regiments and now have maybe a total of 8,000 or 10,000 people in Afghanistan—both advisers and military. We consider this to be an extremely serious development."

Via the hotline to Brezhnev, Carter stated that the invasion "could mark a fundamental and long-lasting turning point in our relations.... Unless you draw back from your present course of action, this will inevitably jeopardize the course of United States–Soviet relations throughout the world." He could not have known how prophetic he was. Thanks in large part to U.S. support of the anti-Soviet forces in Afghanistan—an approach devised and recommended by Brzezinski—that country turned into a quagmire for the Soviets, and their inability to defeat the ragtag but fierce and determined mujahedeen fighters became a great embarrassment to the Soviet leadership and a source of real dissent in that society. Indeed, some trace the early impetus for glasnost, Gorbachev's policy of openness in the mid-1980s, to, among other things, the pressure among many in Russia for the truth about the Afghanistan fiasco.

After the Soviet invasion, the NSC weighed many other options, and the president ultimately enacted a number of policies that were not politically popular. These included a grain embargo, which was not embraced by farmers in the key state of Iowa, home to important party caucuses during the presidential primary season of 1980. Carter was being challenged by Senator Edward Kennedy, among others, and this was risky. But it was not his only risky political stance during this period. The boycott of the Olympics was also unpopular with some groups. And, more important, Carter's decision in late 1979 not to leave the White House to campaign, so that he could manage the hostage crisis (and not appear to be insensitive to it while pursuing his own political gains), is now cited by many as a source of his ultimate defeat in 1980. This "Rose Garden strategy," where he stayed close to home, may have been a tactical blunder, but there is no doubt that it was yet another example of political courage.

The next key meeting in the hostage crisis began at 10:45 a.m. on March 22, 1980, at Camp David. Carter met with Mondale, Vance, Brzezinski, Defense's Brown, CIA's Turner, Joint Chiefs chairman Jones, David Aaron, and Jody Powell. Jones began by briefing the group on the likely success of a rescue mission. The actual attack on the embassy would be easy; it was getting there without the Iranians' knowledge (which could prompt them to move some of the hostages) and exiting Iran that would be hard. Brzezinski was highly pessimistic about the operation remaining undiscovered along the way, given its logistical complexity. Initial preparations for a rescue mission were authorized.

On April 9 Brzezinski sent a memorandum (originally drafted by Gary Sick) to Carter making the case for a military rescue of the hostages. There were essentially two choices left, the memorandum stated: an escalation of pressure on Iran that ended with the mining of harbors, or a rescue that would swipe the hostages out from underneath Khomeini and make him look weak. The memorandum ended with the following line: "In my view, a carefully planned and boldly executed rescue operation represents the only realistic prospect that the hostages—any of them—will be freed in the foreseeable future. Our policy of restraint has won us a well-deserved understanding throughout the world, but it has run out. It is time for us to act. Now."[20]

On April 11, Carter convened a meeting of the NSC with the same participants as at Camp David, except that Vance was notably absent. He had gone on vacation a day earlier and was not informed of the meeting's results until he returned. General Jones gave an update of the preparations of the rescue mission. Everyone agreed that the negotiation track was dead, apart from Warren Christopher, Vance's deputy. At this point, however, Carter's mind was already made up: the rescue operation would go ahead, as it was preferable to running the risk of uncontrollable escalation by mining Iran's harbors. By the time Vance returned and objected—saying that "our only realistic course was to keep up the pressure on

Iran while we waited for Khomeini to determine that the revolution had accomplished its purpose, and that the hostages were of no further value"—the die had been cast.

In the early evening of April 24, eight helicopters took off from the USS *Nimitz* in the Arabian Sea. While traversing the desert, one of the helicopters' warning lights went off, signaling a technical malfunction. The helicopter was abandoned on the ground, and the Delta team on board was picked up and carried on to the mission. Two hours into the operation, another helicopter, while flying through the dust clouds in the desert, decided to turn around and return to the ship (even though there were only sixty minutes to go to the desert refueling pad outside Tehran). At the same time, another helicopter developed hydraulic problems and had to be abandoned in the desert at the refueling pad. The mission was canceled—six helicopters constituted the minimum required for a successful assault. To add to the failure of the mission, while the helicopters were being refueled for the way back, one of them collided with a refueling plane and both burst into flames. Carter called it the worst day of his life.

After the failure of the mission, the public learned that Secretary of State Cyrus Vance had resigned. Vance effectively resigned when, during a meeting with the president, Brzezinski, and Brown, they were discussing how to handle Congress and other groups regarding the rescue mission and how to handle the period after the operation in general. The president mentioned that a group opposed to the administration's policy in Iran wanted to come in and see them and that he'd like Vance to handle the meeting. Vance said he could not. Carter notes that it was the first time in his presidency that anyone had refused to obey a direct order of his. But Carter was also sympathetic to Vance, knowing how deeply upset he was by the rescue mission.

Later that day, Vance submitted his resignation and graciously agreed to stay on and stay silent until after the operation. The president did not, however, try to talk him out of his resignation. The policy gulf had grown too wide, and all of the internal bickering, leaks, accusations, and counteraccusations had taken too great a toll. Senator Edmund Muskie would replace Vance in early May. Among the first things on the agenda was establishing that he would be the principal spokesperson for the administration on foreign policy matters—and that he would minimize the time he spent managing the department and the issues associated with it. From that point forward, Carter and Brzezinski played an even more dominant role in the management of the administration's foreign policy simply because Vance, the main counterweight to many of their efforts, was now gone.

Iran formally and finally accepted the U.S. demands after lengthy negotiations, which concluded on January 19, 1981—on the eve of Ronald Reagan's inauguration as president of the United States. Warren Christopher authorized the transfer of $7.97 billion (representing the net return of frozen assets) to the Bank of England, then on to the Algerian central bank, and finally to Tehran, possibly the biggest single private transfer of funds in history.

⋰⋱ As far as international accomplishments are concerned, then, few presidents have achieved more in four years than Jimmy Carter—from the signing of the Panama Canal Treaty to the agreement on SALT II, which was important even though un-ratified; from the normalization of relations with China to the breakthrough at Camp David; from new military and nuclear doctrines that enhanced America's strength and flexibility to effective challenges to our principal adversary. It was a period rife with achievements even though few appreciated it at the time and only gradually more in the years since. The Iran hostage crisis, while bad, was neither Vietnam nor Iran-Contra, and yet it made all earlier successes fade from memory.

With the perspective provided by the intervening three decades, the Carter administration and Brzezinski's tenure in office can be seen as something more than a success in terms of the momentary issues it faced. It also presaged many of the issues that would endure and shape U.S. policy throughout the intervening years. The issue of Israel's relations with her neighbors endures, and in retrospect, the Camp David Accords remain the most important breakthrough that has taken place on that complex diplomatic front. Carter and Brzezinski not only anticipated the decline of the Soviet Union but helped accelerate it with their tough stand in Afghanistan. Via the normalization of relations with China, they set the stage for shifting U.S. policy priorities that have coincided with the rise of emerging powers that has been perhaps the greatest global-affairs story of the period from then until now. They were the first to deal with the problem that Iran would become; indeed, they were among the first to deal with the rise of Islamic fundamentalism and its complex consequences. Their goals for nuclear weapons reductions are still the stated goal of the current U.S. administration. Their grappling with the centrality of energy policy and American foreign policy and with the consequences of economic weakness for our international position also track directly with issues in the second decade of the twenty-first century.

That most such events dominated their agenda is certainly not something for which they should receive credit. The world turns, and the team in the White House must respond to it. But some teams are led by individuals who have a unique capacity for foresight, and rarely can those individuals translate that foresight into coherent effective policy. Zbigniew Brzezinski stands in the forefront of such people. His role as one of America's most respected, incisive policy commentators since his time in the White House only underscores that fact.

NOTES

A longer version of this chapter appeared in David Rothkopf, *Running the World* (New York: Public Affairs, 2006). Used with permission.

1  Zbigniew Brzezinski, *Power and Principle: Memoirs of the National Security Adviser 1977–1981* (New York: Farrar, Straus, Giroux, 1983), 6.

2  "The Second Presidential Debate," October 6, 1976. Available at www.pbs.org/newshour/debatingourdestiny/76debates/2_a.html.

3  Brzezinski, *Power and Principle*, 10–11.

4  Ibid., 4.

5  Zbigniew Brzezinski, interview with author, May 21, 2004.

6  Walter Mondale, interview with author, May 19, 2004.

7  Brzezinski interview.

8  Madeleine Albright, interview with author, September 10, 2004.

9  Senior official, interview with author.

10  Brzezinski, *Power and Principle*, 456.

11  John Prados, *Keeper of the Keys: A History of the National Security Council from Truman to Bush* (New York: Morrow, 1991), 390.

12  Senior official interview.

13  Ibid.

14  Prados, *Keeper of the Keys*, 405.

15  For President Carter's account of the reasons why Brzezinski was authorized to pursue negotiations with China and why he did not want to share some information with State Department officials below the level of Secretary of State Cyrus Vance, see Jimmy Carter, *Foreign Affairs*, Letters to the Editor, November/December 1999, 164–65. See also Brzezinski's letter to the editor in the same issue, 165–66. See also his foreword to this book.

16  Harold Brown, interview with author, July 21, 2004.

17  Cyrus R. Vance, *Hard Choices: Critical Years in American Foreign Policy* (New York: Simon and Schuster, 1983), 78–79; Brzezinski, *Power and Principle*, 222.

18  Erwin Hargrove, *Jimmy Carter as President: Leadership and the Politics of the Public Good* (Baton Rouge: Louisiana University State Press, 1988), 104.

19  Gary Sick, *All Fall Down: America's Tragic Encounter with Iran* (New York: Random House, 1985), 246, 249.

20  Ibid., 290.

# CHAPTER 5

# Beijing's Friend, Moscow's Foe

WARREN I. COHEN AND NANCY BERNKOPF TUCKER

Zbigniew Brzezinski's encounter with China came after he had established himself as an influential foreign policy thinker and a specialist on Soviet affairs. At first, he approached China as a part of the Soviet Bloc, hostile to the United States. Concerned primarily by how it extended Moscow's influence, he is not known to have studied China's history, economy, culture, and society. China would, nevertheless, have a profound impact on his thinking, career, and reputation.

Brzezinski became the driving force, arguably the essential force, behind the Carter administration's "normalization" of relations with China. He perceived creating a quasi-alliance against the Soviet Union as a way to secure victory in the cold war and accordingly committed himself to establishing diplomatic relations with Beijing, a task that Richard Nixon's White House began in 1971–72 but left incomplete. He overrode opposition within the administration and objections from Congress and Taiwan. Criticism that he moved too quickly, neglecting consultation and ignoring problems, does not diminish this signal achievement.

In subsequent years, his success kept him focused on China, consistently stressing the importance of the relationship. Even after condemning the brutality of the Tiananmen Massacre of 1989 that soured Sino-American relations, he continued to make U.S.-China ties a high priority.[1] Ultimately, he would insist, it was the most significant bilateral relationship for the United States. Concerns about human rights abuses, threats to democratic Taiwan, and anxiety about rising Chinese power remained secondary; instead, he pressed for realization of a G-2—a Chinese-American condominium—to protect U.S. interests.[2]

❖ As Brzezinski became interested in China as an antagonistic state within the Soviet Bloc, he puzzled over the meaning of the Sino-Soviet split. He understood that China's status was unlike that of the East European Communist states, that Moscow had less control over Mao Zedong than it did over European Communist leaders. By 1960, he predicted ideological disputes between the Soviets and the Chinese, recognizing declining unity in the bloc. In 1961, however, he contended that journalists were exaggerating the rift. The bloc was not splitting and not likely to split. People who thought otherwise did not understand the nature of international communism. Further, he argued, Americans should not hope for the collapse of the bloc. A "dissident but lonely China" inside the Soviet orbit would be preferable to an independent China eager to lead a more militant branch of the movement.[3]

By late 1961, when it was no longer possible to minimize the split, Brzezinski began to focus on its meaning and the appropriate American response to it. He rejected the idea that the United States should do anything that might strengthen Soviet premier Nikita Khrushchev in his struggle with Mao, insisting that the Soviet Union remained an immediate threat. Moreover, concessions to Khrushchev risked further radicalizing Mao, who would see them as evidence of the weakness and indecisiveness of Western leaders. Concessions could even make Khrushchev more confrontational and unpredictable as he competed with Mao.

On the other hand, Brzezinski opposed any effort to court Beijing. It risked frightening the countries of Southeast Asia, leading them to abandon hope of U.S. support and accommodate to China's growing influence. In line with the consensus among American analysts after the Cuban Missile Crisis, Brzezinski perceived China as a greater long-term threat to world peace than the Soviet Union. He argued that it was essential to continue policies designed to isolate the People's Republic of China (PRC).

Brzezinski supported the Johnson administration's massive intervention in Vietnam, arguing that to do otherwise would mean a victory for China. He was concerned that a different course would reward Beijing's militancy, escalating its inflammatory and destructive behavior, as well as its dedication to inciting revolution. In 1966, the president named Brzezinski to the State Department Policy Planning Council, in which post he focused on Moscow but also proffered advice on China-related problems. In 1967, for instance, he warned that Beijing wanted the war in Vietnam to continue because it destabilized Southeast Asia, aggravated U.S.-Soviet frictions, and tied down American and Soviet resources.

Until 1968, Brzezinski opposed reaching out to Beijing. He was contemptuous of those who contended that China would change after Mao's death, that it would shift toward a more "evolutionary" policy, similar to Khrushchev's "revisionism." But he was running against the tide of elite opinion in the United States, epitomized by the Senate Foreign Relations Committee Hearings of 1966, in which his Columbia University colleague A. Doak Barnett argued for an end to efforts to isolate the PRC. Barnett, the country's leading analyst of contemporary Chinese affairs, advocated a policy that came to be called "containment without isolation." In fact, in 1968, the Johnson administration quietly sought to ease tensions with China, but—as Johnson was weakened by opposition to his policies toward Vietnam and the Chinese were caught up in the Cultural Revolution—the initiative went nowhere. Nonetheless, Brzezinski reversed himself and joined those who perceived a need to redefine policy toward China. He called existing efforts to isolate China an "anomaly" that hurt the United States in Asia and, worst of all, in its relations with the Soviet Union.

As a Democrat, Brzezinski was not, of course, in line for a position in the Richard M. Nixon administration that came to power in 1969. The powerful post of national security advisor went to Henry Kissinger, an appointment that soon revealed a Brzezinski-Kissinger rivalry that some of their colleagues believed had begun years earlier at Harvard.

Brzezinski was not opposed to the Nixon/Kissinger approach to China and was pleased by the impact it had on the Soviet Union. Nonetheless, he found much to criticize. In 1971, he suggested that the Nixon administration, by organizing opposition to China's admission to the UN, a foregone conclusion, had forfeited an opportunity to keep a seat for Chiang Kai-shek's Taipei regime. He complained that Nixon had violated the *spirit* of the principle of joint consultation with Japan by hiding his intention to normalize relations with China from Tokyo—and foresaw complications in Japanese-American relations that might lead to the two allies becoming adversaries. In a 1972 article he worried that Nixon and Kissinger were imagining that the Washington-Beijing-Moscow triangle would function like American relations with Europe and Japan, and that they were investing too much in relations with China and the Soviet Union to the detriment of relations with U.S. allies in Europe and Japan. He feared they were unrealistic in their efforts to create a balance of power in Asia. And yet he gave them a passing grade, B, for their policies toward China: good on trade and travel, slow to manage the UN issue properly.[4]

Brzezinski firmly believed that the U.S- Europe-Japan triangle remained far more important to Washington. In 1971, supported by the Ford Foundation, he spent six months in Japan to assess its development, politics, and security and what the implications would be for the interests of the United States. His resulting study, published as *The Fragile Blossom*, urged greater American attention to, and realism about, the alliance with Japan, especially in light of Japanese interest in China and desire to exploit the China market.[5] In 1973, with his study as a springboard, he worked with financier David Rockefeller to launch the Trilateral Commission.

Not long afterward, he called for an expansion of relations with China. He wanted the United States to give the Chinese aid that they could use against the Soviet Union—such as sophisticated communications systems. Strengthening China, he argued, would help create more stable relations between the United States and the Soviet Union. Even when he gave the Nixon administration an A for improving policy toward China, Brzezinski implied that Nixon was holding back because of excessive concern for détente with the Soviets. And then it was his turn.

After his victory at the polls in 1976, Jimmy Carter appointed Brzezinski as his national security advisor. He had provided Carter with briefings on international relations during the campaign and won the president-elect's confidence. Carter appointed Cyrus Vance as his secretary of state. When asked whether Brzezinski might overshadow Vance and dominate the process of making foreign policy— as Kissinger had overshadowed William Rogers in the Nixon administration— William Bundy, then editing *Foreign Affairs* for the Council on Foreign Relations, assured friends that Cy would never let it happen.[6] He had underestimated Brzezinski.

Sitting in the White House, with easy access to the president, an ambitious national security advisor has tremendous advantages should he or she choose to compete with the secretary of state. Brzezinski was unquestionably ambitious, and he thought that Vance was on the wrong track, that he was too optimistic about the possibilities of strengthening détente with the Soviet Union, and that he was missing opportunities to increase pressure on Moscow.[7] Vance argued for giving relations with the Soviets priority over those with the Chinese. Brzezinski believed the opposite: working with the Chinese would facilitate reaching agreements with the Soviets beneficial to the United States.

Initially, Brzezinski hesitated, thinking that there could be strategic cooperation with China without diplomatic formalities. Once he realized that that would be impossible, he became eager to move ahead with Beijing. Not yet able to convince the president that China policy should originate in the National Security Council (NSC), Brzezinski could only observe Vance's August 1977 trip to Beijing. Vance's instructions required him to press for some form of official American relations with Taipei, perhaps a consulate. He had the authority to go further—and Assistant Secretary Richard Holbrooke urged him to do so—but he held back, probably out of concern that he would jeopardize ratification of the Panama Canal Treaties in the U.S. Senate. The Chinese contended he was retreating from positions taken by Nixon and Kissinger. Vance's mission failed.

Eager for a personal triumph and a coup in his anti-Soviet strategy, Brzezinski thereupon persuaded Carter to allow him to deal with the Chinese. One asset Brzezinski was quick to exploit was his principal staffer for Chinese affairs, Michel Oksenberg, a protégé of Barnett and one of the leading China analysts of his time. Oksenberg was not only a brilliant analyst but also a superb bureaucratic infighter, having honed his skills in the academy. Holbrooke, his counterpart in the Department of State, no less skilled and determined, did not know China as well and did not have Oksenberg's access to Chinese officials. Oksenberg constantly outmaneuvered him, frequently denying him essential information. Brzezinski used Oksenberg to open up his own channel to the Chinese, specifically to solicit an invitation for Brzezinski to visit Beijing. The invitation, in turn, gave him leverage. "I pressed the [U.S.] bureaucracy for . . . a more favorable attitude toward the transfer of militarily sensitive technology to China," he would later write. "On my own authority, I also arranged for the Chinese to obtain a NATO briefing on the global strategic problem, thereby initiating a tacit security relationship with them."[8] The Chinese, well aware of his attitude toward the Soviet Union, were happy to encourage him.[9]

Once the Chinese had indicated their willingness to receive him, Brzezinski won Carter's permission to go. He told Leonard Woodcock, heading the liaison office in Beijing, that he had no desire to engage in negotiations and intended only to discuss the administration's global policies, its strategy toward the Soviet Union, and related issues. He acknowledged that bilateral relations and normalization fell within the purview of Vance and Woodcock, but there was widespread suspicion that Brzezinski was trying to emulate Kissinger. Advisors had warned president-elect Carter that Brzezinski would be aggressive, contentious, and outspoken as national security advisor, and China policy unleashed his competitiveness, activism, and exuberance. Harvard's Stanley Hoffmann—a sharp critic of foreign policy as conducted by both Kissinger and Brzezinski, his former colleagues—complained also of the Carter/Brzezinski tendency toward activism, a tendency to "talk now, think later."[10] Increasingly, Vance was troubled by Brzezinski's freelancing—and opposed allowing him to go to China.

Brzezinski lobbied hard and eventually won the support of Vice President Walter Mondale and Secretary of Defense Harold Brown. He was convinced that he was the one senior official in whom the Chinese had confidence and whose strategic perspective they shared. His staff assured him he was the right person to undertake the mission to Beijing and worked assiduously to hide public awareness of Vance's opposition. But Elizabeth Drew in the *New Yorker* and Don Oberdorfer in the *Washington Post* recognized the differences between Brzezinski and Vance and wrote about Brzezinski's aspiration at least to equal Kissinger's role.[11] Others noted that Brzezinski wanted to use relations with the PRC to unnerve Soviet leaders. Brzezinski later wrote of having to make "pious noises" that normalization had nothing to do with the Soviet-American rivalry, but he left no doubt that this was central to his thinking.[12] In the end, Brzezinski won the power play and gained Carter's authorization to travel to Beijing. Much as Kissinger had done in 1971, Brzezinski succeeded in wresting control of policy toward China from the Department of State with Oksenberg's skillful denial of information about the mission to Holbrooke and Vance. William Gleysteen, the senior deputy assistant secretary of state for East Asia, declared in his 1997 oral history interview that Brzezinski's delight in humiliating Vance and Holbrooke had been "a national disgrace."[13]

As approved by Carter, Brzezinski's instructions stated that he was to stress to Chinese leaders the resolve of the United States to respond to the Soviet military buildup and its use of proxies, specifically Cuba, to expand its influence. He met with the key figures in the country's hierarchy in Beijing in May 1978: Huang Hua, foreign minister; Hua Guofeng, Mao's successor as Communist Party chairman; and Deng Xiaoping, vice premier and the most powerful figure in the government of the PRC. The Chinese were pleased that he chose to arrive on the very day that Chiang Ching-kuo was being inaugurated in Taipei as president of the Republic of China—presumably a signal of his indifference to Taiwan.

The Chinese were well prepared to receive Brzezinski. Huang Hua immediately informed him that he had read his books. For two and a half hours Huang harangued him on the failings of the United States, insisting that the Americans, by their actions in Cambodia, had forfeited the right to question China on human rights, a key Carter concern. After a spirited defense of North Korea, Huang demanded that the United States withdraw its forces from South Korea. His central point, however, was a call for Americans to take a "strategic point of view" on the Taiwan issue—a line that Huang had every reason to assume would resonate with his interlocutor. Brzezinski tried to assure Huang that Carter had made up his mind to proceed with normalization, that he recognized that "there is only one China," but there were "complexities"—domestic politics created obstacles to abandoning Taiwan. The United States would continue to withdraw its military from the island, but he warned of a future "historically transitional relationship" to the people of Taiwan. In his reply to Huang, he rejected charges that Washington sought hegemony or was appeasing the Soviet Union. He also left no doubt that the United States intended to stay in South Korea. An American Foreign Service officer present for this discussion, a man generally critical of Brzezinski, credited him with being more assertive in refuting Chinese complaints than Kissinger had been.[14]

On the issue of human rights in Cambodia, where Pol Pot and the Khmer Rouge had emptied their country's cities, driving people into the countryside, Brzezinski faced a difficult problem. On the one hand, the United States had moral concerns about the massive and brutal killings perpetrated by the Khmer Rouge. On the other, it hoped for effective Cambodian resistance to Soviet-supported Vietnamese aggression. To this end, according to journalist and author Elizabeth Becker, Brzezinski boasted of having encouraged the Chinese to support Pol Pot, a charge Brzezinski categorically denied.[15] Replying to Brzezinski, Huang conceded that China liked the American use of the human rights issue against Moscow but insisted that it was irrelevant to people fighting for independence and unity. For them the major human rights issue was their struggle against imperialism, colonialism, and hegemonism. For these people, China's friends, normalization of U.S.-China relations would improve the image of Americans—and, he added, prove that the United States was not weak.[16]

In his meeting with Hua Guofeng, Brzezinski once again declared that Carter had made up his mind to proceed with normalization. The United States was prepared to begin serious negotiations the following month. He insisted that Washington was not acting, as had Nixon and Kissinger, with a sense of America's decline and a need for Chinese cooperation against the Soviet Union. The Carter administration did not want normalization as merely a "tactical anti-Soviet expedient." It perceived an enduring relationship of long-term strategic importance no matter whether the Soviets were friendly or aggressive. Hua reserved judgment, apparently unconvinced by Brzezinski's earnest assurance of Carter's intentions.[17]

And then came a fascinating meeting with Deng, who had been briefed, of course, on everything Brzezinski had said to Huang and Hua. Brzezinski repeated his basic line: the United States was ready to move toward normalization of relations with the PRC and was acting out of long-term strategic interest—not a tactical expedient. Deng's immediate response was blunt: if the United States was ready to move, it should dump Taiwan and China would be ready to proceed. Brzezinski had no choice but to temporize. He confirmed American acceptance of China's basic points regarding Taiwan, but he stated in his reply that for domestic political reasons Washington would have to express the hope and expectation of a peaceful unification of Taiwan with the mainland. Deng had no objection to anyone expressing "hope" for a peaceful resolution of the issue. China, however, would never agree to a promise of peaceful resolution as a precondition for normalization. Brzezinski stressed the need for a "historically transitional period" in U.S. relations with Taiwan, presumably to cover the continuation of arms sales to Taipei. He said nothing, however, to discourage Deng's assumption that unification would be the ultimate result of recognition. Deng brushed aside Brzezinski's suggestion that an insecure Taiwan might turn to the Soviets.

Pretending he was not persuaded that the Americans were ready to act, Deng repeated that he would be ready "when President Carter makes up his mind." Brzezinski once again declared Carter's readiness and was quick to dismiss any notion that the administration feared the Soviets. He stressed that the United States had more experience opposing them than did China—and that he was less popular in Moscow than Deng.[18]

In addition to conversations with China's leaders, Brzezinski and Oksenberg gave the Chinese what the *New York Times* called an unprecedented and detailed briefing on SALT talks with the Soviet Union and shared secret White House memoranda on the subject. Both men promised Beijing a "substantial security relationship." They wanted to learn more about the Chinese military and encouraged the Department of Defense to consider placing more intelligence facilities in China, to use the PRC as a base of electronic intelligence against the Soviet Union. Not surprisingly, the Chinese media praised Brzezinski's strategic vision while denigrating Vance. One senior Chinese official told *Newsweek* that "we know where Brzezinski stands on the Soviet Union, China, and Japan. With Vance we never knew."[19] James Lilley, the CIA's man in Beijing, later ambassador to China, described the Chinese as "subtle and sophisticated" in moving negotiations from the lawyerly Vance to Brzezinski. They "wanted to deal with a Polish-American who was anti-Soviet."[20]

Indeed, according to Richard Solomon, who served on Kissinger's NSC, the Chinese believed they could more easily manipulate Brzezinski. Feigning disbelief in his assurances about Carter's decision to move ahead with the establishment of diplomatic relations, they forced him to repeat himself in every meeting. As James Mann has noted in *About Face*, Brzezinski repeated secret promises Nixon had also offered about Taiwan. Beijing pushed the Americans to relinquish support for the Republic of China, which the unresolved Chinese civil war of the 1940s had left beyond PRC control ninety miles across the Taiwan Strait. Washington had supported Taiwan with military and economic assistance as part of the anti-Communist cold war struggle, championing it as "Free China." Nixon's pledges, reiterated by Brzezinski, stated that Taiwan was part of China and the U.S. would not support Taiwan's independence; Washington would prevent Japan from taking its place on the island and would accept any peaceful resolution of the struggle between Taipei and Beijing. And he went further, informing his interlocutors that the United States would withdraw any government presence on the island. Holbrooke, who agreed fully with the goal of normalizing relations with Beijing and with the need to break relations with Taiwan, and who admitted he didn't care much about Taiwan, nonetheless thought that Brzezinski was consistently brutal in his handling of Taiwan, that "Zbig just didn't give a god damn about Taiwan."[21]

Deng, delighted by Brzezinski's repeated insistence that Carter was ready to act—and by his exuberant Russophobia as illustrated by his anti-Soviet antics on the Great Wall—authorized Huang Hua to undertake secret talks with Woodcock.[22] They began meeting in July, with Woodcock assisted by J. Stapleton Roy (later ambassador to China). Brzezinski also held intensive talks with Chai Zemin, head of China's liaison office in Washington, meeting him at least once a month. In late October, he told Chai that if agreement on normalization could not be reached quickly, it would have to be postponed until autumn 1979 when Congress was in session and focused on Soviet-American relations. Chai reported the conversation to Beijing, creating a sense of urgency. After reading Chai's report, Deng told the Politburo that it appeared that the United States wanted to accelerate talks: "We should seize the opportunity."

Throughout, Brzezinski fought successfully to control the process—eventually with Carter's full support. Brzezinski kept information on the progress of negotiations in the White House and would reach agreement with Beijing while Vance traveled to Jerusalem, believing that an accord was still two weeks away.[23] Vance and Holbrooke, while approving of the plan to normalize relations, differed with Brzezinski on several points, including consultation with Congress and Soviet policy. Vance's principal advisor on Soviet affairs, Brzezinski's Columbia colleague Marshall Shulman, consistently warned that concessions to China would hurt Soviet-American relations.[24] Brzezinski, as always, was eager to use relations with China against the Soviets, to prod Moscow.

But the major differences between the NSC and the Department of State in the closing weeks of negotiations between the United States and the PRC related to Taiwan. All of the participants in the discussions understood that for many reasons, not least domestic political exigencies, the island could not be abandoned, that some sort of informal relationship would have to be maintained, and, most importantly, that arms sales to Taiwan would have to continue. Brzezinski had hinted at this to Deng, and Oksenberg told friends that this would be a highly contentious issue after normalization with Beijing.[25] Holbrooke proposed selling FX fighters to Taiwan before normalization, "as a big fat farewell kiss." He argued that such a sale would create fewer problems before than after normalization, but Brzezinski and Oksenberg—outraged by the proposal—were not willing to take the risk. The lesser issue was the matter of when to inform Chiang Ching-kuo that the United States had shifted recognition from Taipei to Beijing. It was evident that Chiang and his government were in denial, that they were ignoring all signs that the Americans were distancing themselves. Holbrooke and his colleagues wanted to give Chiang twenty-four hours notice before the change, but Brzezinski and Oksenberg refused. Holbrooke contended that they "deliberately jerked" Chiang around—and gave momentum to Congressional Taiwan supporters who contended that the Carter administration had stabbed Chiang in the back.[26]

In January 1979, Deng came to the United States to meet Carter, discuss joint strategies, and see some of the country. It was a glorious time for Brzezinski. He had managed the normalization process and was credited by Carter, Vance, and even the media for its success. He requested permission to stand in the receiving line for Deng's arrival at the White House, and Carter agreed, without objection by Vance. The next extraordinary event was dinner for Deng at Brzezinski's home in Virginia, Deng's acceptance of an invitation Brzezinski had extended in May. These days were the acme of Brzezinski's career.

Deng's widely celebrated visit was not without complications. In a gala party in his honor at the National Gallery in Washington, he shocked his audience by eschewing niceties about the wonders of the new Chinese-American relationship and gave a ferocious anti-Soviet speech. At the White House, he informed his new friend, Jimmy Carter, of his intention to punish Vietnam for its invasion of Cambodia. Deng perceived normalization with the United States as a signal to Moscow that he had American support for his endeavors—expecting that to deter Soviet intervention when China attacked a Soviet ally. Brzezinski persuaded Carter not to express "any excessive U.S. alarm over possible Chinese actions."[27] Carter was troubled and warned Deng that an attack on Vietnam might be destabilizing, urging restraint. Brzezinski developed a formula that he later concluded had worked: the United States would criticize Chinese military action and simultaneously condemn Vietnam's occupation of Cambodia—and demand that both sides withdraw their forces. He knew that the Vietnamese would reject the demand and thus give China a bit of diplomatic cover, allowing the United States "a slight tilt" in favor of the Chinese. He arranged to have the Soviets warned that any military response by them would drive the Americans closer to China. Brzezinski called his approach "formally critical but substantively helpful," a signal to the Chinese that they had a reliable friend.

That friendship was soon tested by Congress's passage of the Taiwan Relations Act (TRA) in April 1979.[28] In severing official relations with Taiwan, the Carter administration had declared to Chiang Ching-kuo, Deng, and the American public that it would maintain unofficial economic and cultural ties with Taiwan. Taiwan would be treated in these areas as a sovereign nation, even if it was not recognized as such. The administration had also left no doubt that it intended to continue selling arms to Taiwan. Deng, although unhappy about arms sales, finally decided not to let the issue block normalization. He assumed from his conversations with Brzezinski and other Americans involved in the process that the arms sales would gradually diminish into insignificance and the United States ultimately would abandon the island. Congress had other ideas.

The process of working with Taipei after de-recognition was novel, to be developed slowly and with difficulty. The Carter administration submitted a draft law to Congress, fully expecting Congress to strengthen it, but Carter, Brzezinski, and others who oversaw the drafting were shaken by the extent to which it was changed. Vance had argued for the need to consult Congress as agreement with Beijing crystallized, but Brzezinski and Oksenberg persuaded Carter not to, presumably out of fear of leaks or of enabling opponents of normalization to prevent it. Holbrooke and others have surmised that key members of Congress were angered by the administration's brusque treatment of Taiwan generally and Chiang in particular. Most significantly, they wanted to be certain that the islanders would be able to protect themselves should Beijing decide to resort to force in its quest for unification. Specifically, the TRA required the American government to provide Taiwan with whatever military equipment it required to defend itself, to keep U.S. forces in the Pacific strong enough to help Taiwan if Washington opted to, and to warn China against using force. Deng was outraged, and even

Carter's secret assurances that arms sales would be limited did not make the issue go away. Every transfer of military equipment to Taiwan ever since has elicited furious howls from Beijing.

In his remaining months in the White House, Brzezinski sought to deepen the security relationship between the United States and China. He succeeded in having more dual-use equipment, unavailable to the Soviets, sold to the Chinese. With unintentional help from Moscow—the Soviet invasion of Afghanistan—he had little trouble persuading the Department of State to liberalize the regulation of exports to China, including items such as electronic countermeasures (ECM) equipment and air defense radar, which were of obvious military use. Whatever the long-term value of the Chinese-American relationship, he was convinced that, at least for the duration of the cold war, China was useful for diverting hundreds of thousands of Soviet troops from military bases at home and in Eastern Europe to East Asia, to China's borders. In May 1980, Brzezinski met the head of Beijing's Military Commission in Washington and explained that the Soviet Union was pursuing a two-pronged offensive strategy: through Afghanistan to the Persian Gulf and through Cambodia to the Strait of Malacca. However questionable the analysis, the Chinese liked it, adopted it as their own, and Deng repeated it to Brzezinski when he visited Beijing in 1981.

⋯ Brzezinski's successful management of the normalization process was enormously important for the very reason he offered again and again: it greatly enhanced the American position in East Asia in particular and in the contest with the Soviet Union generally. It is unlikely that Vance or Carter would have performed as well without Brzezinski. Not least, he had done what Kissinger had been unable to do. Early in his career, Brzezinski's colleagues in Soviet studies judged him brilliant and erratic—brilliant all the time, right about half the time. On establishing relations with China he was surely right. On the other hand, there were significant trade-offs. Brzezinski was too ready to reduce U.S. commitments to Taiwan, he was indifferent to violations of human rights in Cambodia and in China itself, he did not cultivate Congress effectively, and his treatment of Vance in pursuit of normalization was harsh.

Toward the end of the Carter administration, Brzezinski came under increasing fire from the media, largely for issues on which he prevailed over Vance. Leslie Gelb, who had served under Vance, distinguished between the two men for readers of the *New York Times*: Vance fought fairly; Brzezinski was a street fighter. He claimed that Brzezinski misrepresented Vance to Carter. *New York Times* syndicated columnist Anthony Lewis went so far as to ask why Carter kept

Brzezinski on; he thought Brzezinski was a man with a "record of folly, distrusted abroad and divisive at home." But for at least one of the Carter administration's major foreign policy successes—the establishment of diplomatic relations with China— credit must go to Brzezinski.[29]

❖ Out of office after the election of Ronald Reagan, Brzezinski still had ready access to the media for his views. He supported the Reagan administration's decision to supply arms to China, arguing that the PRC was part of a new global coalition opposing Soviet expansionism. Beijing's rhetoric, which lumped the United States and the Soviet Union together as hegemonic powers to be opposed, brought his argument into question. But Brzezinski, dismissing the rhetoric, contended that it was inconsistent with China's actual policies and actions. At the same time, however, Reagan's affinity for Taiwan troubled him. There were indications that the administration might sell planes to Taipei, which he had blocked in the Carter years. Were Reagan and his advisors signaling a return to a two China policy? Surely that would be Deng's perception. When Secretary of State George Shultz demonstrated that the PRC was not as important to him as it had been to Brzezinski and Kissinger by confronting Beijing on textile exports and policy toward Taiwan, Brzezinski was critical. He argued that China should be treated as a partner. He warned against letting the Soviet Union drive a wedge between Beijing and Washington.

In 1988, Reagan and Mikhail Gorbachev worked together to ease tensions between the United States and the Soviet Union. There was widespread acknowledgment that Gorbachev was a new type of Soviet leader, determined to end the cold war. Historians would later credit Reagan for his openness to Gorbachev's overtures. To Brzezinski, however, it was the relationship with China that was bringing peace and stability, allowing Americans to see the Soviet Union as less ominous.

The Tiananmen massacre in 1989 shook Brzezinski. While he still believed that China had to be integrated into the community of nations, he called upon the administration of George H. W. Bush to indicate that it would only help a Chinese government that respected its people. There would be no assistance to a repressive regime. He expressed hope that the tragedy would pass, and that Chinese leaders would understand that a despotic government would bring about a socioeconomic disaster. By the spring of 1990, Brzezinski joined those who urged the United States to revoke most-favored-nation (MFN) treatment for Chinese imports. He affirmed that Beijing had to be punished for its repressive, authoritarian policies. When the Democrats regained control of the White

House in 1993, Brzezinski, without hiding his conviction of the importance of relations with Beijing, toed the Clinton campaign line by criticizing the Chinese government for its brutal response to the Tiananmen protest and similar protests elsewhere in the country. He demanded that Washington refrain from assisting China if the regime remained oppressive. With the end of the cold war and the collapse of the Soviet Union, he found it easier to back away from his earlier insistence on strengthening China, and he expressed some concern about human rights in the PRC.

Once in office, the Clinton administration quickly realized that the Chinese would be intransigent on human rights issues in general and in its response to political dissent in particular. Threats to deny China MFN treatment proved to be in vain. Desperate to find a course between the "realist" position of Brzezinski and Kissinger, who stressed the importance of good relations with China, and campaign promises to stop coddling the "Butchers of Beijing," Secretary of State Warren Christopher asked Brzezinski and Kissinger, as "friends of China," to tell their contacts that there had to be more progress on human rights.[30] Confident that American business interests would force the administration to yield on the MFN question, the Chinese held firm, eventually humiliating Christopher when he traveled to Beijing to argue for more respect for human rights. In the end, the administration caved and the Chinese continued to receive MFN privileges.

During Clinton's presidency, Brzezinski became outspoken in his demand for better relations with China, especially when he compared China to Russia. He argued that the PRC, a major military power and an economic success, was more entitled to be at the G-7 meetings than was Russia. He insisted that China was not the enemy, not a threat to U.S. interests, and that America's most important bilateral relationship was with the PRC. To the delight of Jiang Zemin, China's president, Brzezinski contended that the Chinese were trying harder than Americans to find a common vision, to stop the growing acrimony between them. He reported that increased American military collaboration with Japan worried Beijing. In 1999, Brzezinski damned Taiwan president Lee Teng-hui's "two states theory" as an attempt to legitimate the permanent division of China. He never swerved from his view that Taiwan's interests had to be subordinated to the American need for good relations with Beijing.[31]

Brzezinski's partiality toward China and hostility to Russia were evident in his 1997 book *The Grand Chessboard*. Later on, after the rise of Vladimir Putin, Brzezinski criticized Clinton for seeking a "spectacular accommodation" with the Russian leader on the issue of national missile defense (NMD). He wanted to know why Clinton was passive on Putin's brutal war on Chechnya while charging

China with human rights violations. And he warned that if anti-ballistic missiles (ABMs) were deployed in Alaska against "non-existent" North Korean missiles, tensions between the United States and China would increase. In his book, he was even willing to brush aside the foreign policy elite's mantra, and his own earlier position, that Japan was the lynchpin of American security in Asia; he argued that China rather than Japan should be Washington's principal Asian partner.[32]

In 2000, Brzezinski published an essay in the *National Interest* on "Living with China." He was gentler with the Russians, including them along with China, Europe, and Japan among the four most important relationships of the United States. He noted that there was no realistic consensus on China in Congress or among the American people. He found the Clinton administration inconsistent in its policies toward China. Among his suggestions for improvement were exclusion of Taiwan from theater missile defense (TMD), a three-way strategic dialogue with Japan and China, admitting China into the World Trade Organization, and bringing Beijing into the G-8 (making it 9). It was time to stop complaining about China's international behavior—it was probably better than India's.[33]

And yet Brzezinski also angered the Chinese leaders by defending Under Secretary of State Tom Pickering's report, which claimed that when American planes bombed the Chinese embassy in Belgrade in 1999, it had been an accident. The Chinese accused Brzezinski and others holding that view of being hypocrites, blathering about human rights until their own country killed innocent people. They think like a "hegemon." It was evident that the Chinese did not want their friends to deviate from their line.

With the election of George W. Bush in 2000, Brzezinski settled back into the role of a public intellectual. He perceived the relationship between the United States and China to be deteriorating rapidly, for which he found the Chinese to be more responsible. He judged the Chinese press, especially publications of the People's Liberation Army (PLA), to be very hostile. He argued that China had overplayed its hand in the incident in which a Chinese interceptor crashed into the South China Sea after a midair collision with an EP-3, an American reconnaissance plane. In its handling of the American aircraft and its crew, China had acted like an unfriendly state. He also warned Beijing that unification with Taiwan would have to be peaceful. As for the Bush administration's policies, Brzezinski was critical, repeating the point that the relationship with China was the most important bilateral relationship the United States had. He rejected the administration's view that China was a strategic *competitor*.

Indeed, Brzezinski argued that a collision with China would not occur. In a published debate with John Mearsheimer, a prominent political scientist at the

University of Chicago who contended that a Chinese-American conflict was likely if not inevitable, Brzezinski spelled out his convictions. He insisted that China was focused on its economic development and its acceptance as a great power. He assumed that it would pursue a cautious foreign policy through the 2008 Beijing Olympics and the 2010 Shanghai Expo. Conceding there would be frictions in the future, he argued there would be no clash. The Chinese military was not strong enough to challenge the United States, and Chinese leaders understood that the impact of a confrontation on their economy would be intolerable. He also suggested that the negative consequences, which had often accompanied the rise of a new power in the past, could be avoided because of the existence of nuclear weapons—an argument frequently used to explain why direct military action between the United States and the Soviet Union did not occur during the cold war. Furthermore, he asserted that China could not push the United States out of Asia and would be deterred from seizing Taiwan by the likelihood of American intervention.

Growing cooperation between the United States and China that reached beyond bilateral issues delighted Brzezinski. Cooperation on coping with North Korea's possession of nuclear weapons should, he thought, be extended to dealing with the Iranian nuclear program. More strategic dialogue between Beijing and Washington, he imagined, might help avoid a crisis in the Persian Gulf and would have the extra benefit of upsetting Moscow.[34]

Thus, prior to Barack Obama's inauguration in 2009, Brzezinski called for regular meetings between Chinese and American leaders, for a comprehensive, global partnership—a version of what became his "G-2" proposal. Together, he suggested, China and the United States could manage many of the world's problems. In March, he offered a "laundry list" of issues with which the PRC could help: the global financial crisis, climate change, Iran's nuclear program, India-Pakistan problems, and even Israeli-Palestinian relations.

In 2011, when Hu Jintao, China's leader, came to Washington, Brzezinski wrote about "How to Stay Friends with China." He worried about uncertainties in the relationship and the persistence of mutual mistrust, and he feared escalating reciprocal demonization. But it was essential that Obama and Hu remember that their countries needed each other. As the months passed, he gave predictable advice to his fellow Americans: don't demonize China—we have to work with it. He claimed the Chinese were toning down their aggressive rhetoric, hinting that they were responding to his suggestions. He rejected concern about China's building an oceanic or "blue water" navy, to which he insisted it, as a rising power, was entitled. He argued that the challenge to American leadership was posed by the political and economic mess in the United States, not by China. Ever the realist, Brzezinski advised playing down China's human rights abuses and concentrating on shared strategic interests. In an October 2011 speech, he reiterated his call for a Chinese-American condominium—a Group of Two that would collaborate in solving global problems—but, having recognized the alarm the prospect triggered among U.S. friends and allies, he recommended not calling it that.

❖ Looking back, surely the greatest achievement of Brzezinski's career was the normalization of relations with the PRC, unquestionably a major turning point in the history of the cold war. Many others had worked to that end and failed. He understood, circa 1978, that the interests of the United States would be best served by cooperating with the Chinese against the Soviet Union. Unsurprisingly, his success with the management of Chinese affairs in 1978 has made the maintenance and strengthening of Chinese-American relations a focal point for the remainder of his career. Many other analysts, not least his one-time rival Henry Kissinger, share that view. Others have developed doubts, especially after the end of the cold war. Brzezinski himself briefly questioned aspects of the relationship in the immediate aftermath of the Tiananmen massacre.

Brzezinski's call today for a G-2—in fact if not in name a Chinese-American condominium—suggests he has moved beyond his reservations. His optimism exceeds China's own assessment of its strength and is a cause for dismay among many U.S. friends abroad.[35] But if Brzezinski's vision of the future is rejected by many, they willingly give him credit for his 1978 efforts to normalize relations with the PRC. His management of the Carter administration's policy was brilliant—and certainly more than half right.

## NOTES

1 Brzezinski believed the Chinese government might disintegrate. "Chinese Rulers' Fall Predicted," *Wall Street Journal*, May 30, 1990, A9.

2 Zhang Haizhou, "Leaders Must 'Meet More Often,'" *China Daily*, January 13, 2009, 2.

3 Zbigniew Brzezinski, "The Challenge of Change in the Soviet Bloc," *Foreign Affairs* 39 (April 1961): 430–43; Zbigniew Brzezinski, Letter to the Editor, *New York Times*, July 11, 1961.

4 Zbigniew Brzezinski, "The Balance of Power Delusion," *Foreign Policy*, no. 7 (Summer 1972): 54–59; Zbigniew Brzezinski, "Half Past Nixon," *Foreign Policy*, no. 3 (Summer 1971): 3–21.

5 Zbigniew Brzezinski, *The Fragile Blossom: Crisis and Change in Japan* (New York: Harper and Row, 1972).

6  Warren I. Cohen's conversation with William Bundy, December 1976.

7  Zbigniew Brzezinski, *Power and Principle: Memoirs of the National Security Adviser 1977–1981* (New York: Farrar, Straus, Giroux, 1985), 37, 172–73.

8  Ibid., 203.

9  William H. Gleysteen Jr. in his oral history interview asserts that the Chinese used Vance and Brzezinski against each other. Association for Diplomatic Studies and Training, Library of Congress Foreign Affairs Oral History Project, June 10, 1997 (hereafter ADST).

10  Stanley Hoffmann, "The Hell of Good Intentions," *Foreign Policy*, no. 29 (Winter 1977–78): 14.

11  Elizabeth Drew, "Brzezinski," *New Yorker*, May 1, 1978, 90; Don Oberdorfer, "Brzezinski Plans to Visit China, Despite Reported Opposition from Vance," *Washington Post*, April 27, 1978, A18.

12  Brzezinski, *Power and Principle*, 196.

13  Gleysteen Oral History, ADST. Gleysteen had been detailed to the NSC prior to Carter's inauguration, returned to the State Department briefly, and then later in 1978 was appointed ambassador to South Korea.

14  Memorandum of Conversation, Zbigniew Brzezinski with Foreign Minister Huang Hua, May 21, 1978, Vertical File/China, MR-NLC-98–215, Jimmy Carter Library, Atlanta, GA (hereafter Carter Library).

15  Elizabeth Becker's book *When the War Was Over: Cambodia and the Khmer Rouge Revolution* (New York: Simon and Schuster, 1986), based on her coverage of the Khmer Rouge for the *Washington Post*, won the Robert F. Kennedy Book Award. She said that in an interview Brzezinski asserted, "I encouraged the Chinese to support Pol Pot. . . . Pol Pot was an abomination. We could not support him but China could" (435). When the book was republished in 1998 by Public Affairs, Brzezinski in a letter to the editor of the *New York Times* (April 22, 1998, A26) firmly denied having arranged Chinese aid to Pol Pot.

16  Memorandum of Conversation, Brzezinski with Huang, May 21, 1978.

17  Memorandum of Conversation, Zbigniew Brzezinski with Chairman Hua Kuofeng, May 22, 1978, Vertical File/China, Carter Library.

18  Memorandum of Conversation, Zbigniew Brzezinski with Vice Premier Deng Xiaoping, May 21, 1978, Vertical File/China, Carter Library.

19  Bernard Gwertzman, *New York Times*, May 28, 1978, A1; Holger Jensen with Sydney Liu, "Polar-Bear Tamer," *Newsweek*, June 5, 1978, 61.

20  James R. Lilley, Oral History Interview, ADST, May 21, 1998.

21  Richard Holbrooke, interview with Nancy Bernkopf Tucker, March 13, 2001; Richard H. Solomon, *Chinese Negotiating Behavior: Pursuing Interests through "Old Friends"* (Washington, DC: United States Institute of Peace, 2005), 40; James Mann, *About Face* (New York: Knopf, 1999), 86–89.

22  Brzezinski proclaimed to his Chinese companions that the last one to the top of the Wall would have to fight the Russians in Ethiopia. He made so many jokes about the Soviets that the Chinese called him the "Polar Bear Tamer." Nancy Bernkopf Tucker, *China Confidential: American Diplomats and Sino-American Relations, 1945–1996* (New York: Columbia University Press, 2001), 324; Jensen with Liu, "Polar-Bear Tamer," 61.

23  Cyrus Vance, *Hard Choices: Critical Years in American Foreign Policy* (New York: Simon and Schuster, 1983), 118–19.

24  Holbrooke interview, March 13, 2001.

25  Warren I. Cohen's conversation with Michel Oksenberg, January 30, 1979.

26  Holbrooke interview, March 13, 2001.

27  Brzezinski, *Power and Principle*, 409.

28  The following discussion of the TRA is based on Nancy Bernkopf Tucker, *Strait Talk: United States–Taiwan Relations and the Crisis with China* (Cambridge, MA: Harvard University Press, 2009), 116–26.

29  Leslie Gelb, "Muskie and Brzezinski," *New York Times*, July 20, 1980, sec. 6, 26; Anthony Lewis, "The Brzezinski Puzzle," *New York Times*, August 18, 1980, A23; Sally Quinn, "Zbigniew Brzezinski, Insights, Infights, Kissinger and Competition," *Washington Post*, December 21, 1979, C1.

30  Ann Devroy and Daniel Williams, "Top Clinton Advisers Are Said to Support China Trade Breaks," *Washington Post*, May 20, 1994, A30.

31  Liu Jiang and Yuan Binzhong, "Li Zhaoxing Urges US Adherence to 'One China' Policy," Beijing Xinhua Domestic Service, September 15, 1999, FTS19990915000260.

32  Zbigniew Brzezinski, *The Grand Chessboard: American Primacy and Its Geostrategic Imperatives* (New York: Basic Books, 1997).

33  Zbigniew Brzezinski, "Living with China," *National Interest*, Spring 2000.

34  Zbigniew Brzezinski and John J. Mearsheimer, "The Clash of the Titans," *Foreign Policy*, January 5, 2005, www.foreignpolicy.com/articles/2005/01/05/clash_of_the_titans.

35  Zbigniew Brzezinski, "How to Stay Friends with China," *New York Times*, January 2, 2011, www.nytimes.com/2011/01/03/opinion/03brzezinski.html; Edward Wong, "Former Carter Adviser Calls for a 'G-2' between U.S. and China," *New York Times*, January 2, 2009, www.nytimes.com/2009/01/12/world/asia/12iht-beijing.3.19283773.html?_r=1; "China Wary of 'G-2' with US," *Defencetalk*, April 8, 2009, www.defencetalk.com/china-wary-of-g2-with-us-analysts-17430/.

CHAPTER 6

# The Caricature
# and the Man

ROBERT A. PASTOR

To some scholars and journalists, Zbigniew Brzezinski was a classic, hard-line cold warrior, who was shaped by a Polish heritage that fused his hatred of Russia with disgust for communism. Like any stereotype, this stick-figure definition of the man shaped predictions on his foreign policy positions, his personal and managerial style, and his Machiavellian manipulation of an unschooled new president. This view of Brzezinski has been tempered as cold war passions have dissipated, and as his strategic vision has become appreciated by a wider audience, but the old view is still evident in histories of the Carter administration, most recently in Betty Glad's *An Outsider in the White House: Jimmy Carter, His Advisors, and the Making of American Foreign Policy*.[1]

There are shards of truth in this caricature, but if one really tried to understand the man or his impact on foreign policy in the Carter years, one could not find it by assembling those shards. His worldview was not conservative; it was liberal and, in some ways, revolutionary. He saw human rights not just as a weapon against communism, but against all dictatorships and as a compelling idea—and one that the United States had a special obligation to promote. He considered the Monroe Doctrine obsolete, and he sought to identify the United States with Third World aspirations for autonomy and for racial and social justice. He could be caustic in debate, but he was always respectful and collegial in his personal relations and the management of his staff. Contrary to the stereotype of a man fixed on the Soviet menace, he was always open to new ideas and initiatives, and he could absorb and articulate them with ease and remarkable speed.

A direct but complex man, Brzezinski was instinctively hard in his approach to

America's rivals, but sophisticated in trying to navigate awkward transitions or multileveled negotiations. He had an almost unique ability to capture succinctly a strategic problem in a crisp phrase. Indeed, the title of his memoir, *Power and Principle*, not only summarized the singular challenge of American foreign policy but also pointed to his own personal compass for using the former to achieve the latter.

⁙ As it evolved since John F. Kennedy's presidency, the position of national security advisor (NSA) was a combination of advisor to the president, coordinator of foreign policy and national security agencies, long-term planner and strategist, and manager of a team that ranged from ten to nearly three hundred experts in all the regions and functions of national security. The precise character of the National Security Council (NSC) and the particular role of the NSA depended partly on the individual but mostly on the president and the degree to which he wanted to make decisions. A president like Ronald Reagan preferred to delegate decisions, and so the NSA was not as influential as he was under a president like Richard Nixon, who wanted to manage foreign policy from the White House. President Kennedy wanted his advisor McGeorge Bundy, a brilliant academic, not just to coordinate policy but to provide him with fresh ideas.

President Jimmy Carter selected Brzezinski for similar reasons. Supremely confident in his abilities if not his knowledge of foreign policy, Carter liked Brzezinski because of his knowledge and creativity. He was pleased that both Brzezinski and Secretary of State Cyrus Vance recommended each other for the two positions,[2] but he recognized their differences in temperament and priorities, and he chose them both because of their differences and because they recommended each other.

The role of the coordinator is quite different from that of an advocate. The coordinator needs to present all the positions fairly without any bias, while the advocate makes a case for just one position. Brzezinski coordinated foreign policy, as was required, but he was never content with that role. He preferred to advocate a particular policy, and while he endeavored to present alternative options fairly, his strong views raised questions, particularly within the State Department, about the degree to which he was an honest broker.

Brzezinski assembled a staff that spanned the ideological spectrum of the Democratic Party—from liberal to conservative. All of them were recognized experts in their field, but some were just beginning their careers while others were well established. He would conduct weekly staff meetings as if they were seminars, posing the issue of the day and eliciting comments. He was a superb manager who read quickly, remembered details, but always placed the information in a strategic framework or a historical context. He had a playful side, too, which he would occasionally allow to show, but mostly he was serious. Brzezinski had zero tolerance, however, for one mistake—misspelling his name.

❖ To understand Brzezinski as NSA, however, requires an understanding of the Carter administration's foreign policy. The conventional wisdom is that Carter's foreign policy was ultimately the product of a clash between Vance, a wise and liberal patrician-statesman, and Brzezinski, a brilliant but manipulative strategist who used his proximity to Jimmy Carter to tilt U.S. foreign policy toward a new cold war. This is simplistic and misleading; it does not do justice either to the individuals or to the complexity of the foreign policy agenda faced by the Carter administration. That agenda was a formidable one, and Carter did not shy away from any of it. He went where his predecessors had feared to tread, and in the process he secured ratification of the Panama Canal Treaties and of Protocol I of the Tlatelolco Treaty (which made the Latin American and Caribbean regions free of nuclear weapons), strengthened inter-American institutions on human rights and democracy, normalized relations with China, mediated the Camp David Peace Accord between Egypt and Israel, moved human rights to the center of American foreign policy, negotiated and signed the SALT II nuclear arms agreement, negotiated the end of white rule in Rhodesia and adopted a new approach to Africa, forged a comprehensive energy policy, and developed new policies on conventional arms control and nuclear non-proliferation.

The conventional wisdom on Carter's foreign policy is flawed in four ways:

*First*, it views Carter as a passive leader mediating between Vance and Brzezinski or being manipulated by the latter, when in fact Carter was *the* policy maker.

It is true of course that Carter arrived in the White House with little foreign policy experience and that he was an eager student and Brzezinski was a persuasive professor. It is also true that Brzezinski occasionally tried to game the system, and this irritated Vance. It is also true that Carter preferred to deal more with paper than with briefings because paper was more efficient, and he could accomplish more by reading than attending meetings. Some thought this made it easier for Brzezinski to manipulate the process since all the foreign policy papers and the summaries of NSC meetings were either generated by or passed through him.

But Carter built a check in the system to keep the process honest. He insisted that the memos going to him should always include the views of the State Department and other interested agencies, and when there were differences he would often call Vance or other departmental secretaries directly. Therefore, Brzezinski's credibility with Carter depended in part on the fairness in which he summarized other views. No evidence has been found by historians searching through the archives that Brzezinski abused his position to mischaracterize Vance's views.

The principal point, however, was that Carter wasn't a cipher. Nor did he simply integrate the divergent views of his advisors. Like every adept politician, Carter had a sense of America that was refined during intensive years of campaigning across the nation, and he integrated his insights with his advisors' views of the world and policy recommendations. Indeed, the Carter administration's foreign policy was fundamentally *his* policy—more than any of his advisors. True, he did not arrive with a complete policy or a well-considered strategy anymore than Franklin D. Roosevelt or John F. Kennedy did. But he arrived with several themes and objectives in mind, such as the promotion of human rights, the pursuit of peace despite skepticism and political cost, the recognition of the importance of power combined with the imperative of morality, and a desire to assist the developing world. He also had an agenda, which combined challenges that his predecessors hadn't addressed (Panama, Cuba, Rhodesia) or hadn't finished (SALT, China, and the Middle East) or policy themes he considered important, such as human rights, nonproliferation, and arms control. Hence, Carter, entering the White House, knew his goals, but his specific policies emerged from the advice and background papers that he received primarily from Brzezinski and his staff. Note, too, that there was no difference among his advisors about the importance of pursuing this agenda.

There were differences—especially between Vance and Brzezinski—about the priority that should be given to individual items on the agenda, and there was one major difference between Carter and all of his advisors. While they all urged him to take on just a few of the issues and postpone the tough ones for a second term, Carter was determined to tackle the entire agenda and do it as soon as possible. And it turned out that he achieved more than anyone—except Carter himself—considered possible. In any case, the debates were wide-ranging, and Carter sought them so that he could consider divergent views before reaching a decision. In this process Brzezinski had one major advantage and one disadvantage. He had the capacity that neither Carter nor Vance had of placing international events in a strategic and a historical context that gave meaning to the importance of a particular decision; doing so, Brzezinski also gave Carter a sense of how individual decisions related to one another. The disadvantage was that Vance, like Carter, was a man of calmer and more liberal temperament and preferred to work through one issue at a time.

Though Carter was occasionally bothered by the gossip about the Vance-Brzezinski skirmishes, he was so sure he was in charge that he did not bother to take the public perception seriously or to try to correct it. This proved to be a political error.

*Second*, and contrary to conventional wisdom, the administration's setbacks—for example, the delay in the completion of SALT II, or the fall of the shah in Iran, or the rise of the Sandinistas in Nicaragua—were not the result of a failure of foresight or bickering officials but of stubborn Soviet opposition to deep cuts in nuclear weapons and of internal quagmires in Iran and Nicaragua.

Unfairly, Brzezinski was blamed for the breakdown in U.S.-Soviet relations due to the administration's rejection of Kissinger's Vladivostok proposal on SALT II in favor of a more ambitious arms control policy and for the administration's public criticism of Soviet repression and intervention in Africa. Actually, Brzezinski originally recommended more modest cuts; it was Carter who sought the deeper cuts. After all, Carter had campaigned not just against President Gerald Ford but also against Henry Kissinger's overly cautious diplomacy, promising instead a more ambitious policy aimed at the elimination of nuclear weapons. Therefore, it should not have come as a surprise to the Soviets that during the course of negotiations Carter would propose deeper cuts on each country's nuclear arsenal. Nonetheless, Leonid Brezhnev, the Soviet leader, was apparently surprised, or pretended to be surprised, and rejected the proposal, slowing the negotiating process. (Panama, on the other hand, embraced Carter's initiative, and the Canal Treaties were therefore the first on the Senate's agenda.) It may be that Brezhnev and his colleagues mistakenly assumed that Soviet rejection of Carter's initial proposal would prompt the United States to lower its ambitious objectives and accept Moscow's approach.

*Third*, the most important foreign policy changes in the second half of Carter's term were not because of the rise in Brzezinski's relative influence but due to changes in events abroad sparked by Soviet-Cuban interventions and the collapse of several Third World regimes. For sure, the Carter administration responded to a new global challenge—notably Moscow's apparent decision to test America's resolve—that required firm countermeasures. Some have criticized Brzezinski for goading Carter to make critical statements about Soviet-Cuban interventions,[3] for example, but national security documents show President Carter himself to have initiated these statements. Immensely frustrated by the

State Department's failure to implement his instructions to speak out on the subject, it was Carter who actually encouraged Brzezinski to do so. Of course, Brzezinski did not need a lot of encouragement.

On the issue of Soviet-Cuban involvement in the Horn of Africa, the three principal policy makers had different perspectives. Like Vance, Carter wanted the United States to play a key role in Africa, negotiating peace and political transitions in Zimbabwe, Rhodesia, and South Africa; like Brzezinski, however, Carter thought that Soviet-Cuban military intervention undermined such efforts. Brzezinski was much more concerned with the geopolitical implications: if the Soviet Union did not pay a price for military intervention, he argued, it might be tempted to move into other areas. Accordingly, in Brzezinski's eyes the Soviet invasion of Afghanistan occurred, in part, because the United States had not found an effective way to restrain the Soviets during the Ogaden War of 1977–78 between Somalia and Ethiopia. Carter favored the idea of raising the cost to the Soviets, but he did not think sending an aircraft carrier to the Horn of Africa, as Brzezinski recommended, would be effective; Carter feared it could raise expectations of possible military involvement that the United States had no intention of undertaking at the time.

Like Vance, Carter wanted to conclude a SALT agreement and sought good relations with the Soviet Union. Like Brzezinski, however, Carter also understood that selling a SALT agreement to the Senate would require that America's attentive public and the Senate in particular view him as ready to stand up to the Soviets. To achieve this, he would need to scold them publicly on violations of human rights and interventionism abroad. (Over time, Brzezinski developed a better sense of what was needed and what was possible politically; several White House political advisors, notably Hamilton Jordan, were his tutors.) In any case, Carter's policy incorporated elements of both perspectives, but it had logic of its own.

Looking back, then, the Soviet Union in the late 1970s was feeling as if it were on an upward trajectory and could begin to play the kind of global role that the United States had played before Vietnam. In the face of Soviet interventionism and rigidity, Americans were justifiably concerned, if not enraged, by Soviet-Cuban assertiveness in Africa, Vietnamese intervention in Cambodia, and the Soviet missile buildup in Eastern Europe. This uneasiness exacerbated the division between Vance and Brzezinski during the artificial crisis following the "discovery" of a Soviet brigade in Cuba in September 1979. The crisis was artificial because the brigade had been in Cuba since the 1962 Missile Crisis, and it represented a threat only to the supposedly non-aligned status of Cuba. But before the administration could clarify the issue, the information was leaked to the press, and Senators Frank Church and Henry "Scoop" Jackson—representing the spectrum of the Democratic Party—said that SALT could not be ratified unless the brigade was withdrawn from Cuba. Of course, the Soviets had no intention of withdrawing soldiers that had been there for seventeen years, and so the administration found itself trapped. Both Vance and Brzezinski wanted to save SALT, but Vance thought that this was more likely if the incident were downplayed, while Brzezinski thought that the administration would be in a stronger position if it pushed back against the Soviet Union. While Carter accepted some of Brzezinski's recommendations and concurrently tried to move the treaty forward, the Soviets, assuming that the treaty would not be ratified, felt unrestrained to intervene in Afghanistan. That, more than anything else, made the new cold war colder.

*Fourth,* the cold war was obviously not a consequence of the deterioration in the Vance-Brzezinski relationship. In fact, during the first two years of the administration, there were few serious disagreements because Vance and Brzezinski by and large agreed on most of the foreign policy agenda. The differences became pronounced as cold war tensions rose—beginning in Africa and peaking with the discovery of the Soviet brigade in Cuba and then the invasion of Afghanistan. U.S. foreign policy pivoted not because Brzezinski had outmaneuvered Vance, but because Carter needed to adapt to a changing world and be more forceful. Indeed, the time for negotiations with the Soviet Union passed by the time of the Soviet invasion of Afghanistan. While Vance had tried to keep it alive, Soviet foreign minister Andrei Gromyko wouldn't even meet with him.

President Carter understood that there was both a strategic and a political reason for the United States to pursue a more vigorous approach toward the Soviet Union. Strategically, the invasion of Afghanistan raised questions as to whether the Soviet Union would expand into the Persian Gulf—and the administration responded with the Carter Doctrine, which drew a clear line. Politically, as most Americans understood the dangers of Soviet expansion, Carter—having already been painted as soft—needed to respond in a strong enough way to recapture public support. This is why Carter swung toward the more determined policy promoted now by Brzezinski. Vance, a person with great confidence in American superiority, believed that a more conciliatory approach was needed. He was isolated not by Brzezinski, but by new developments on the world stage.

✥ In the final analysis, then, the return of a more hawkish America in the late 1970s was because of Soviet assertiveness and not because of Brzezinski's worldview. President Carter adapted to substantial changes in the world and not to the whispers of his NSA. Ironically, while Carter was attacked earlier by Republicans as weak and indecisive, Brzezinski was criticized by Democrats as an unrepentant cold warrior. In both cases, the gap between truth and invention—between reality and caricature—was chasmic.

## NOTES

1 Betty Glad, *An Outsider in the White House: Jimmy Carter, His Advisors, and the Making of American Foreign Policy* (Ithaca, NY: Cornell University Press, 2009).

2 Jimmy Carter, *Keeping Faith: Memoirs of a President* (New York: Bantam Books, 1982), 52.

3 Wayne S. Smith, *The Closest of Enemies: A Personal and Diplomatic Account of U.S.-Cuban Relations since 1957* (New York: W. W. Norton, 1987), 125.

Brzezinski's father, Tadeusz Brzezinski (shown with cane), served as Polish Consul General in Lille, France, in the 1930s, shown here with a Polish delegation (circa 1930). Tadeusz Brzezinski was posted to Canada in 1938. Zbigniew Brzezinski moved to the United States in 1950. He became a U.S. citizen in 1958. *Photo courtesy of Zbigniew Brzezinski.*

Brzezinski debates foreign policy issues, notably the Vietnam War, on *Meet the Press* with
Hans J. Morgenthau, the founding father of the realist school of international politics in the
United States. Lawrence E. Spivak was the program's founder and long-time moderator.
*Photo courtesy of NBC's* Meet the Press.

Brzezinski played chess with Israeli Prime Minister Menachem Begin during
Camp David Talks in 1978. *Photo courtesy of Zbigniew Brzezinski.*

Brzezinski hosted a dinner party at his home in Virginia for Deng Xiaoping, Vice Premier of the People's Republic of China, in 1979. *Photo courtesy of Zbigniew Brzezinski.*

Brzezinski greeting Pope John Paul II at the White House in 1979.
*Photo courtesy of Zbigniew Brzezinski.*

Brzezinski with Jimmy Carter, at the White House.
*Photo courtesy of the Library of Congress.*

A meeting of Brzezinski's biweekly Current Issues seminar, which he conducted for several years while teaching at Johns Hopkins University's School for Advanced International Studies in Washington, D.C. (circa 2000). *Photo courtesy of Johns Hopkins University–SAIS.*

Lifelong colleagues, Brzezinski with Henry Kissinger at the Center for Strategic and International Studies (circa 2010). *Photo courtesy of Zbigniew Brzezinski.*

Brzezinski participating in a foreign policy meeting focusing on Middle East policy with President Barack Obama at the White House Situation Room (2010).
*Photo courtesy of Zbigniew Brzezinski.*

# CHAPTER 7

# Dealing with the Middle East

## WILLIAM B. QUANDT

I first met Zbigniew Brzezinski in mid-1974. We were both members of a study group on how the United States should address the Arab-Israeli conflict in the years ahead. He and I were pretty much on the same wavelength. We thought that Henry Kissinger's step-by-step diplomacy had run its course; that a more ambitious American approach was needed; and that it would have to address the Palestinian issue in political terms, not just as a humanitarian problem involving refugees. Just as now, these were all contentious issues, but there was far less acrimony and partisanship then as we discussed how to move ahead.

The result of these meetings was a short publication called "Toward Peace in the Middle East" or the "Brookings Report," which was published in December 1975. It called for a comprehensive approach to Arab-Israeli peacemaking and strong American leadership, and it raised the possibility of a Palestinian state as an outcome of negotiations. I cannot claim that Zbig and I bonded during this exercise, but I did see that he understood my part of the world—the Middle East— quite well, that he took nationalism seriously, that he was good at summarizing the gist of a discussion, and that he had a knack for setting out a clear set of points that seemed to represent the consensus of the group.

About a year later, I received a call from Zbig out of the blue. He asked if I would like to work for him on the National Security Council (NSC) staff with responsibility for the Middle East. (I had been the deputy in that office under Kissinger from 1972 to 1974.) I asked for a bit of time to consider. In his typically abrupt style, he said OK, but began asking me what I thought of other candidates for the job. Not a very subtle form of pressure, but it worked. A week later I was on board. At this point I had never met president-elect Jimmy Carter and had no idea if he was going to be interested in the Arab-Israeli conflict at all.

My first day on the job, January 21, 1977, was memorable for me, and was also the day when I realized that Zbig was someone worth working for. At some point during the day I received a call from him. He said that Senator Richard Stone (D-FL) was in his office and would like to talk to me. I immediately walked to the office where the senator was waiting. Brzezinski excused himself, saying that he had to go see the president, leaving me alone with Stone and totally in the dark about what was going on. Quite simply, Stone had asked Zbig to fire me because of my "controversial" views on the Arab-Israeli conflict. Zbig had said that perhaps Stone should talk to me, so here I was.

Stone was armed with a sheaf of papers, and he began to interrogate me about what I had meant in 1975 when I had said that the "Palestinian issue should be resolved in negotiations," in addition to other strange notions. It was pretty clear that he had been fed a lot of material that was supposed to disqualify me from the job. But as we talked, he seemed to relax, and he finally said that he thought he "could work with me." Then he went on to say, "I have a list of other people in the administration whose views on Israel are unacceptable. I want you and Brzezinski to do something about them!" With that, he left, and almost immediately Brzezinski reappeared.

"What was that all about?" he asked. I explained and asked him what I should do with the long list of names Stone had given me. "Throw it in the trash," Zbig said. That was when I knew I had made a good decision in coming to work with him.

The story had one more angle worth recounting. A few months later, a front-page story appeared in the *Washington Post* with the title "Senator Stone's Hit List." It was a pretty accurate account of what had happened, and it portrayed Stone as a McCarthyite. Stone, furious, called Brzezinski and asked him to issue a denial. Zbig said something to the effect that he would be glad to deny the story except for one problem: it was true. We heard little more from Senator Stone.

As for substance, Zbig was deeply interested in the Arab-Israeli conflict, as was Carter. They were both avid consumers of analysis and intelligence, and each day I would send them memos and reports. Carter preferred to get his information in writing, whereas Zbig read rapidly and broadly but also wanted to talk things through on occasions. He was businesslike, quick to come to conclusions, but open to alternative views. In some issue areas, he and Secretary of State Cyrus Vance were at loggerheads, but not in my area. After helping to shape Carter's initial strategy for the region, Zbig left the day-to-day diplomacy to Vance. But whenever we hit a roadblock—which we often did—Zbig was there to help figure out a way to get around it.

By the time we all went to the Camp David Summit in September 1978, we knew the stakes were very high. Carter wanted to go for broke; Vance was a bit more cautious. I think it is fair to say that Israeli prime minister Menachem Begin was worried that we were going to spring some sort of trap on him at Camp David. In any event, he had heard plenty of negative things about Brzezinski and me. Ever since the Brookings Report, we had been viewed as pro-Palestinian by many Israelis. And I suspect that some Israelis thought that Zbig's Polish background meant that he was an anti-Semite, which was not at all the case. But Begin was an old-style gentleman and was always polite. In the midst of the tense negotiations, he and Zbig played a game of chess. Begin pretended to be an amateur but in fact was quite skilled, and there is a memorable image I have of these two strong-minded men of Polish origin staring at the chessboard and wishing deeply that they could defeat the other. I can't remember who won the match, but I do recall feeling that Begin, for all his complaining that we were biased and had pressured him unfairly, had done very well for himself and for Israel at Camp David.

Shortly after our breakthrough at Camp David, the situation in Iran began to fall apart. Fortunately for me, Iran was being handled by my friend and colleague Gary Sick. But the Iranian Revolution was making it much harder for us to bring the Egyptian-Israeli deal to a conclusion.

In March 1979, Carter decided to go to the Middle East to clinch the deal. Before doing so, he sent Zbig on his own to see Sadat. Vance was not too happy. While I did not accompany Zbig on this trip, I know that he helped set things up so that when Carter arrived in Egypt a few days later Sadat would go along with our final proposals. The same was not true when we went to Israel a few days later. Begin seemed to have no intention at all of signing an agreement with Egypt, or at least not any time soon. Those were tense, weird days, as we argued endlessly over words and side agreements. Zbig and I were convinced that Begin wanted Carter to fail, and that may have been true. But others in Begin's cabinet—especially Moshe Dayan and Ezer Weizman—were not prepared to see us leave empty-handed, and in the end we got what we needed from a reluctant Begin. It was a dramatic process, and Zbig was one of the key players in getting us to the point where finally Begin and Sadat signed a peace treaty.

A few months later I decided to leave the NSC. It was clear that reelection considerations were coming to the fore and the administration could not follow through to a Camp David deal on the Palestinian front. Vance had been taken off the case, and the veteran politician Robert Strauss was now in charge of the Palestinian dossier. I did not relish spending the next year and a half on the sidelines. Zbig tried to convince me to stay, but I think he also knew that we had accomplished pretty much all we could in the first term. Two or three other NSC staffers were planning to leave at about the same time. The inimitable Bill Safire of the *New York Times* announced this to the world in a column titled "Rats Leaving a Sinking Ship."

When I worked for Zbig, I almost always felt that his judgments on Arab-Israeli issues were clear and based on a sense of the American national interest. I never sensed a hint of bias against Israel, although Begin's policies and pedantic manner often drove all of us to distraction. On the whole, I think that in 1978–79 Carter, Vance, Brzezinski, and the rest of our little team had a pretty good sense of why it was important to try to resolve the Arab-Israeli conflict. We managed to do quite well at Camp David, but we all regretted deeply that we could not have achieved more. Had we succeeded then on the Palestinian-Israeli front, the region would have been a very different place and American interests would have been well served. As for Zbig, he has continued to speak out on this issue since then as a private citizen, and he has done so with remarkable clarity and courage.

# CHAPTER 8

# Working Hard, Having Fun at the NSC

## ROBERT HUNTER

*Council on Foreign Relations, talk by ex-President Jimmy Carter, 1981*

(Hostile questioner): "Mr. President, why did you always show preference to Dr. Brzezinski over Secretary of State Vance?"

(President Carter): "Because Zbig sent me 10 ideas a night, and I was lucky to get a single idea a month out of the State Department."

These quotations bookend a milestone in the history—or the histrionics—of the struggle between the National Security Council (NSC) staff led by Zbigniew Brzezinski and the State Department led by Cyrus Vance, perhaps forever unresolved and unreconciled. I am not impartial in this contest. I witnessed Zbig during our ill-fated effort to make Hubert H. Humphrey president in 1968, and also as one of his NSC staffers dealing with Western Europe and then the Middle East for all but two hours and twenty minutes of the Carter administration. True, I later worked closely with Cy Vance, whom I also greatly admired.

Jimmy Carter's summary comment, above, is a major reason for my partiality: Zbig valued and actively sought out talent, wherever it was to be found, in and out of government (while disdaining ignorance and suffering no fools). We were thus, perhaps, the most eclectic lot in NSC history. Over many years, Zbig had built up his mental Rolodex of people who might, one day, help him serve the nation at a president's right hand—as opposed to the motley that since those days has so often dominated the NSC staff. Indeed, the standard judgment is that Brzezinski's NSC team was rivaled only by Kissinger's—each team very small, very professional, very committed and competitive, and each adept at long-term, strategic thinking. They were the class acts of the White House national security apparatus throughout America's top days as superpower.

Equally important, Brzezinski respected others' opinions and judgments, once tested in the crucible of his pointed, often withering cross-examination. The surest test of his fair-minded approach to issues and ideas was found in the results of a staff member's debate with Zbig, in which he had to win not only the argument but every point in it, producing great frustration and a shaking of the head on leaving his office. Then a day or so later, insight set in for us, when Zbig would play back, even word for word, the colleague's "tested-to-destruction" analysis for the benefit of the president, a senator, or a foreign statesman—imitation as the highest compliment! Over time, he also developed enough confidence in us to forward our memos directly to the president with little blue-penciling—and this was a president who read every sentence, every word put in front of him (and who was as merciless on punctuation as on logical error).

Each night we had to report to Zbig by memo (no e-mail then!) our day's activities, along with ideas that he might use with the president. We had to report in detail all of our foreign contacts and our talks with journalists, but we were never told "don't talk with thus and so; don't do that again." We had license and his trust; he gained whatever insights we had to share with him and thus broadened his own reach, and this was another part of the building of mutual confidence with his staff. He also, from time to time, brought us with him to small meetings with the president, not just the grand and formal powwows in the Cabinet Room, and, at times, even sent us in alone to meet with him.

Everyone knows—or thinks that she or he knows—about Zbig's titanic struggles with State over Soviet policy. The common vision, fostered by too many midlevel officials in the "other building" (but never by Vance), was that of Angels versus Lucifer. I even suggested once that Zbig and Cy swap their respective drafts of speeches each was about to give on Soviet policy, to see whether Cy's words (in Zbig's mouth) would still earn the opprobrium of the State-partial and State-cultivated media. This bureaucratic gambit was too much to hope for, but it remains an interesting thought experiment.

A classic story involved the incomparable Robert Strauss, presidential emissary for Arab-Israeli negotiations. Zbig drafted instructions for Strauss, got them signed by the president, and had me transmit them just before Strauss's Air Force jet departed for the Middle East. Strauss was furious at the thought that he could be "instructed" and made his point clear to all as only Strauss could. Just before our next foray to the region, I was called to Zbig's office and handed a sealed envelope, bearing every classification stamp known to the United States or any other government. "Give this to Strauss only after 'wheels up,'" I was instructed, and I did as I was told. Strauss went red and rushed to his private stateroom to rip open the envelope. "Dear Bob," Zbig's message read, "Have a nice trip!"

Brzezinski also had a puckish, even wicked, sense of humor; some thought it was a wee bit "over the top." Remember "Bye, bye, PLO" (which still did not win him friends with the pro-Israel community); or his firing a Kalashnikov from Pakistan into Soviet-occupied Afghanistan; or his searing criticism of one staff member for supposedly inferior efforts regarding the Indian subcontinent, with the staffer's "punishment" being the assignment of additional responsibilities for the Southern Cone of South America. This provoked my colleague's jest: "Ah, I'm now in charge of downward-pointing triangles." And then there was Zbig publicly posing a riddle to the Polish prime minister in Warsaw: "If you had to fight both Russia and Germany, which would you do first? Germany, of course: business before pleasure." After Carter and a handful of us met with German chancellor Helmut Schmidt at the U.S. ambassador's residence in London, Zbig said sotto voce to the president, "Did you see that Schmidt was wearing elevator shoes?" "I noticed," Carter dryly replied. Later that day, Margaret Thatcher, freshly minted leader of the British Conservative Party, came to call: "Oh, Dr. Brzezinski, I spent this afternoon reading *all* of your books." Zbig was pleased.

Away from the office, Zbig was determined to beat the president at tennis, competitive for every point (and Carter would have had it no other way). He also had a proprietary relationship with the Pope, a fellow Pole, which included his having His Holiness's private Vatican phone number. And I had the honor to draft Carter's letters to the Pope, with the president adding at the end, "Yours in Christ."

The personal side of the working relationships at Brzezinski's NSC was that no one on his staff had a problem too big or too small for Zbig to take a personal interest in it. As a staff, with Zbig in the lead, we partied a lot, on any possible excuse, to break the tension of the highest-tension jobs just about anywhere. We picnicked at his home in Virginia. He was also a man of impeccable, Old World manners. The day after a dinner in his honor at my home, he himself placed a thank-you call to the hostess, now my wife of thirty-two years. Her office colleagues were agog that such a senior person would lift the phone to say "thank-you." And for so many years after we were all ousted by the Reagan crowd, Zbig would convene the staff for lunch and discussion of pressing issues, as well as at his home on New Year's Day.

Accomplishments? Here's a short list: new departures in China policy made at the NSC, though credit was taken by the usual credit takers elsewhere; the Carter Doctrine; the Panama Canal Treaty; NATO summits; the substance of Camp David; giant steps forward in relations with the European community; the Group of Seven summits; and on and on. All of this was done by Zbig and his team, arranged in our egalitarian clusters that were made up of a small handful of people assigned for each geographic and functional area; thus overburdened, we each had more work to do, but collectively we produced more ideas of "presidential quality."

Disappointments? The worst was the inability to get the U.S. hostages in Iran released until after Carter left office. And it had a bizarre side, as the United States scoured the world for a solution: Zbig once tasked me to find private funds to buy an original letter written by the Prophet Mohammed, to try giving to the ayatollah in exchange for the American hostages (the letter proved a forgery).

I remember Zbigniew Brzezinski at the NSC as a patriot, a consummate master of the art of turning ideas into policy, an innovator who also recognized others' contributions, a magnificent boss, and a wonderful friend. In paying its highest compliment, the U.S. Navy would say, "BZ, ZB!" (*BZ = Bravo Zulu or "Well done."*)

# CHAPTER 9

# The Evening Report

### JAMES THOMSON

When Zbigniew Brzezinski and his deputy, David Aaron, hired me in early 1977, I was an analyst at the Pentagon on defense policies and programs related to Europe. It seemed they wanted someone familiar with the nuts and bolts of policies and knowledgeable of ongoing bureaucratic wars. It was a surprise and an honor, and I got right down to work.

After a couple of weeks, I remembered that I was a registered Republican. I had earlier been a Democrat, but I had switched parties in order to vote in a Republican primary in 1976. No matter, I was a Republican and confessed to Zbig at the end of a group meeting with him. "The less said about that, the better," he advised me and moved on. It was a different time. No one had checked my registration before hiring me, and, at least in the national security area, no one really cared.

Washington is full of intellectual bullies who shout at colleagues and staff. I had seen plenty of them in the Pentagon. Zbig was definitely not one of them. He was respectful and courteous. But his sharp mind and quick tongue made him scary and made me reluctant, at first, to question his views. But one day, after I suggested to him that the United States might propose a nuclear weapons reduction in Europe in exchange for the withdrawal of a Soviet tank army from East Germany, he snapped: "Tanks are vague," he said, using an expression not normally associated with main battle tanks. A colleague suggested that it would be hard to change his mind in a meeting unless it was one-on-one and that I should write him a memo, which I did. It came back the next day with check marks throughout, indicating that he had read it and accepted the points.

One morning, probably in late 1978, I was called to see Zbig immediately. I found him seated in David Aaron's office looking shaken. He had just had an argument with the president about the president's commitment to NATO for 3 percent real growth in the defense budget. Zbig had told him that he, the president, had agreed to this. Disbelieving, the president replied, "If you can prove that, Zbig, I'll kiss your ass." Zbig wanted me to get the material together. Unfortunately, the president was technically, if not politically, correct. Defense Secretary Harold Brown had agreed to the commitment, not the president, who had never spoken of it or signed a communiqué containing it. Zbig didn't like that and told me to go back to my office and get the material. I said I would send him a memo, which came back with a check mark. I never heard more about ass kissing, but I assume it didn't happen.

Zbig's mind had an amazing ability to absorb great quantities of written material. All of us on the staff (we numbered in the low thirties) got back our "evening report" from the previous day with his marks, usually just checks, but occasionally a question or an invitation to call or see him. Later in life, when I led a large management team myself, I recognized that the evening report was an essential part of his management philosophy.

For example, I had given the green light to the Pentagon and State to negotiate a rotational basing arrangement for USAF KC-135s at a Royal Air Forces (RAF) base in Greenham Common, a town not too far from London. I knew that these tankers were loud and that the base was right in the middle of town. Thus, there was a real potential for controversy. But U.S. and UK diplomats said that the RAF had the politics in hand. Wrong! The politics blew up, and a contingent of citizens from Greenham Commons was on its way to the White House to protest. The president's political advisors wanted to know who had approved this deployment. Zbig's answer: "We did it," not "my staff did." In other words, he pointed at himself, not at me or the anonymous "staff." This is the kind of manager he was. He understood well that the most important action a leader takes is to appoint people and delegate authority to them. But it's a bargain: in return for the authority, the staff has the duty to keep the boss up to date. If they keep him or her informed (as I did via the daily evening reports), the staff has kept its part of the bargain. The leader's part of the bargain is to back the staff no matter what.

It was a great honor to work for a person of high integrity and great intellect. It was an exciting and challenging four years. The hours were long, but no one worked more than Zbig. As I told him in our last days in office, I was grateful because he had given me a chance to serve my country.

# PART III

# The Policy Advocate

# CHAPTER 10

# Brzezinski, the Pope, and the "Plot" to Free Poland

## PATRICK VAUGHAN

It was a cold and snowy morning in January 1978. Zbigniew Brzezinski arrived at the White House before sunrise. He looked over the overnight intelligence cables and foreign newspapers before jotting down the items he would cover during the president's daily foreign policy briefing. This particular morning he wanted to review Carter's recent trip to Poland. The trip had gone well. Poland was undergoing a quiet revolution, and America's support for human rights had encouraged an increasingly emboldened opposition.

Brzezinski had prepared Carter's tour of Warsaw to demonstrate that the president was visiting Polish society as well as the Communist government. The president laid a wreath at the Tomb of Poland's Unknown Soldier and the monument to the Home Army—both testaments to Polish national pride. There were clear signs that younger Poles regarded the American president as a symbol of human rights. One group of Poles broke through police barricades shouting "Carter! Carter! Save us!" Meanwhile, Brzezinski had arranged his own meeting at the residence of Cardinal Stefan Wyszynski, the Roman Catholic primate of Poland who after the war became a symbol of Polish national self-identity and resistance to Soviet imperialism. During the visit, he also learned more about Poland's "Flying Universities." This was an unofficial network of underground lectures dealing with issues forbidden in the official curriculum—including Poland's historic struggles under Russian domination and against Soviet occupation after World War II.

Such demonstrations of civil disobedience presented an especially vexing problem for the Communist authorities. That very week, for example, the crowd at a lecture by dissident Adam Michnik was brutally dispersed by club-wielding policemen. But then, within a few hours, a tape of the lecture was broadcast to a far larger audience over the airwaves of Radio Free Europe (RFE).

Brzezinski considered RFE very useful. In the White House, he had pushed for a vast increase in the transmitter strength of the five-station network broadcasting to the countries of the Eastern Bloc in their native languages. Brzezinski advised Carter that the radios were an invaluable weapon in a cold war that was as much about ideas as ballistic missiles and fighter jets. He did so despite the fact that in the early 1970s American senators, among others, had dismissed RFE as a "cold war relic."

❖ Karol Cardinal Wojtyla, then archbishop of Krakow, was one of the millions of Poles who listened to RFE each morning. When, at an event in West Germany many years later, an announcer from the radio's Polish desk introduced himself to Wojtyla, the cardinal replied, "There is no need. I recognize your voice. I listen to you every morning as I shave."

Wojtyla spent World War II hiding in an archbishop's palace during the Nazi occupation of Poland. After the end of the war, with Poland under Soviet occupation by then, he became a popular figure within the Roman Catholic Church. He enjoyed skiing and mountain climbing, and he socialized with poets and intellectuals within the Catholic intelligentsia. In August 1976 Wojtyla traveled to the United States for the International Eucharistic Congress. With Brzezinski in attendance, Wojtyla lectured his audience about the materialistic quality of both Marxism and capitalism, arguing that only Christian spirituality could cope with the alienation of the modern world. At a reception following the lecture, Brzezinski talked briefly with Wojtyla and came away impressed with his intelligence and quiet strength.

Two years later—in October 1978—Brzezinski was already President Carter's national security advisor when his long-time assistant, Trudy Werner, walked into his office. "Have you heard?" she asked. "They elected a new pope! And he's a Pole!" A few hours earlier, in St. Peter's Square, the Roman Catholic College of Cardinals elected Karol Cardinal Wojtyla, the archbishop of Krakow, as Pope John Paul II. The news seemed puzzling to the thousands waiting for the announcement. Was this possible? The new Bishop of Rome was *un Polacco*— a Pole? It was true: John Paul II was the first non-Italian pope in 455 years and the first from a Communist country. In Poland citizens flocked to city centers and sang patriotic songs and religious hymns. And there was little doubt that the appointment of a Polish pope would make a difference in the politics in Poland

and probably in several neighboring countries too. After all, not only was the new pope a Pole, but he was also a man keenly aware of the weaknesses of totalitarian systems—and how to fight them. "Here is a man who knows what lack of freedom really means," remarked a diplomat in Rome after hearing the news. "Our Italian cardinals are very nice people, but none of them has seen the inside of a prison.[1]

The Soviet leadership was of course deeply concerned. Long gone was the time when Stalin, with a degree of contemptuous jest, had asked, "How many divisions does the Pope have?" Now the answer, in the idiom of the 1970s, was blowing in the wind. The aging men in the Kremlin, sitting uneasily atop a restless empire, understood that they were suddenly facing a new and unwelcome reality; after all, control over Poland had been a Russian priority since the later Middle Ages. More recently, the Soviet Union regarded a tranquil Poland as the vital link to assure the security of the 350,000 Soviet troops that sat on its East German satellite.

Yuri Andropov, head of the KGB, placed an angry call to his agents in Warsaw, wanting to know what had just happened. He asked, "How could you possibly allow the election of a citizen of a socialist country as pope?" The agents were presumably very sorry, but even they could not control matters in the Vatican. Andropov ordered an analysis of the election from Section 1 (Reports) of the KGB's First Chief Directorate. The report concluded that John Paul II had been elected as part of a conspiracy. Specifically, the report said, Brzezinski (together with Cardinal John Krol, the Polish American archbishop of Philadelphia) had engineered a backdoor plot in the Vatican with the aim of destabilizing Poland and the Warsaw Pact alliance.[2]

The KGB could provide no evidence of such a conspiracy. But, in fact, Brzezinski had spent much of the previous two decades looking for ways to penetrate and undermine the closed systems that made up the Soviet empire. Was this the opportunity to advance his cause? The Communist systems were burdened with inefficiency. The public was demoralized, although the working class was beginning to express its opposition to Communist rule. And now Poles had a spiritual leader. "Zbig's got the president excited about this," David Aaron, Brzezinski's deputy, told an aide. "They sensed an enormous sea change in East-West relations." In a memo to President Carter, Brzezinski said that "the Pope's election can be viewed as part of a new era of human rights. The worldwide demand for human rights is a growing political force, and you should reaffirm the U.S. commitment."

Brzezinski was part of the U.S. delegation traveling to Rome for the papal ceremony. He waved at the thousands of happy Poles proudly waving white and red Polish flags as a statement of national pride. He met with Cardinal Agostino Casaroli, the Vatican's secretary of state, who was widely known as "Kissinger in a cassock." The two men sat beneath an Andy Warhol silk-screen portrait of Jimmy Carter and discussed the implications of the pope's election. They established the groundwork for a private channel between the White House and the Holy See. Over the next two years President Carter and John Paul II used the "Vatican hot line" to discuss matters of faith and continued support of human rights around the world.[3]

Brzezinski was also thinking of the geopolitical implications of what had just transpired. Decades earlier, when he was in his first year at McGill University in Montreal, Winston Churchill had famously declared that an "iron curtain" had fallen across Eastern Europe. Could it be that the election of a Polish pope was a confirmation of Poland's westward-looking or "Roman" tradition—and the end of the iron curtain? Back in the 1950s, Brzezinski wrote a thesis entitled "Russo-Soviet Nationalism." He noted that the single red mass shown on school maps across America gave an illusion of stability to the Soviet Union. He argued that the Soviet Union was not a single entity but a cauldron of conquered nationalities brutally consolidated over centuries of Russian expansion. With the Polish pope in the Vatican, it no longer seemed impossible that a more vibrant and autonomous Poland could shake Soviet control over Lithuania and the Ukraine, where Polish religious and historical ties were firm and deeply rooted.

∴ In the same year, the Soviet Union supported Ethiopia in expelling Somalia from the Ogaden region of the Horn of Africa. Brzezinski saw a broader implication: that the Soviet Union was attempting to gain control of the strategic choke points around the Persian Gulf. Closer to home, however, the new pope was presenting Moscow with a new challenge: in June 1979, he was getting ready to visit his homeland. Polish Party leader Edward Gierek had tried to break the news to Leonid Brezhnev, the Soviet leader, that he had little choice but to give John Paul a respectful reception. "Take my advice, don't give him any reception," snapped Leonid Brezhnev, "it will only cause trouble." Gierek insisted that it would be very difficult to overlook the pope's presence. Did Brezhnev expect the Polish government to simply ignore the pope's visit? Brezhnev replied, "Tell the Pope—he's a wise man—he can declare publicly that he can't come due to illness." Gierek insisted that that was only delaying the inevitable. "Well," Brezhnev concluded, "do as you wish. But be careful you don't regret it later."[4]

In June 1979 the pope made a triumphant return to Poland. Millions of Poles came to see him in person or heard his words on the radio. The visit was described as a "psychological earthquake." Pope John Paul II had become the source of moral and national inspiration in Poland's struggle against Soviet imperialism.

After Poland, Pope John Paul II visited the United States. Arriving in September 1979, he spoke before millions of Americans and graced the cover of *Time* magazine under the caption "John Paul, Superstar." He preached to two hundred thousand on the Washington Mall with a message that coincided with the human rights message coming out of the White House. The visit culminated with a presidential reception on the north lawn of the White House. There, John Paul II surprised Brzezinski with a spontaneous invitation for him and his family to visit him later that day at the nuncio's house. To make that happen, Muska Brzezinski, Zbigniew's wife, engaged in a frantic attempt to track down their three teenaged children, who were scattered all over town. Ian, the oldest son, was in fact out of town returning on a school bus from a cross country meet in Charlottesville. "I had already planned to go to the football game that night," he would recall. "And as we arrived at the parking lot in the distance we saw this woman in high heels running after the bus. And to my chagrin it turned out to be my mother." After his mother informed him that he had just made a change of plans—and the issue was nonnegotiable—he cleaned the mud out of his hair and quickly put on a clean shirt and trousers behind a nearby hedge. Arriving late, Ian found himself sitting across the table from John Paul II. "By that time I realized how utterly stupid I had been," Ian said. "I was just sitting there feeling ashamed for having embarrassed my family." But then the pope gave him a quick wink—as if to say that he understood. "And that lifted my entire spirit," Ian said. "I physically felt that calming presence—that this was a real leader who had this gift to associate and empathize with everybody."[5]

Brzezinski and John Paul II conferred in private later that evening. They discussed—among other things—the Soviet Union and the evolving political situation in Poland. Later, as the pope was preparing to depart, he told Brzezinski that they—Brzezinski and his family—had an open invitation to visit him at the Vatican. The Soviet conspiracy theory had now become something of an inside joke. "You elected me," he said with a smile. "You come see me."[6] The irony of the evening was not lost on Brzezinski. When he spoke with President Carter, it often seemed as if he were talking to a religious leader. But when he talked with John Paul II, it was more like talking to a world statesman. "He really [talked in the long-term] perspective of a hundred years from now," Brzezinski would subsequently recall. "Even about communism: when I was talking about how to undermine [the system] soon, he was talking about a long-term trend. He always said it would come out okay, but it bothered me that he was talking in terms of a hundred years, longer than was important to me."[7]

❖ There was not much good news for the White House in the coming months. On November 4, 1979, the U.S. Embassy in Iran was seized by a mob and its staff was taken hostage. This was proving an enormous distraction when two months later Soviet troops invaded Afghanistan. Carter sent Brzezinski to Pakistan, where he was asked by a reporter if the United States would supply arms to the Afghan rebels. "Will the Pakistanis act like Poles or Czechs?" he replied. He explained that in World War II the Poles had formed an underground army against both the Soviet Union and Nazi Germany. The Czechs—betrayed at Munich—had largely capitulated. "It's a fact that people who are determined to fight for their own freedom end up winning respect and sympathy and [even] something more than that from the rest of the world," Brzezinski concluded. "That's a historical fact, not a statement of policy."[8]

As the spring wore on, eighty thousand Soviet troops were struggling in the rugged Afghan countryside against the insurgency by the fierce mujahedeen. During the Moscow Olympics that year, foreign reporters began to hear the first rumors of "thousands" of Soviet deaths in what was gradually turning into a quagmire.

❖ On July 1, 1980, the Polish government announced that the price of foodstuffs would rise. In response to that announcement, a wave of labor strikes spread throughout the country—coupled with rumors that Polish meat was being diverted to Moscow for the Olympics. That same month Romuald Spasowski, the Polish ambassador to the United States, received an official cable from Warsaw. The American Communist Party was searching for information on Brzezinski—anything incriminating—perhaps, incredibly, about "him and his family's exploiting peasants."

Spasowski was a lifelong Communist. But something had changed over the past few years. He now questioned the ideology that once seemed to promise so much. His devoutly Catholic wife, deeply impacted by the election of John Paul II, seemed to influence him. That week, for example, she insisted on taking her nonbelieving husband to Mass at St. Mathew's Cathedral in Washington.

In late July Spasowski arranged a private meeting with the American national security advisor. They met at Maison Blance, a restaurant near the White House.

Brzezinski arrived late in the company of Secret Service agents; he wanted to discuss the situation in Afghanistan. "Do you see any possibility of Warsaw helping to find an honest solution," Brzezinski asked, "one we'd be able to accept?" He also asked if Gierek might serve as a bridge to Moscow—to broker some form of negotiation. "On no!" replied the Polish ambassador. He added that such a suggestion from him "would produce the opposite result. My cable would be read in Moscow before it even arrived in Warsaw. And the Soviets would treat it as provocative. There can't be any cable or any letters." "They read everything?" asked Brzezinski. "Of course. They have direct access to our entire communications system." "So what do you intend to do?" Brzezinski asked. "I'll speak with Gierek the next chance I have," the ambassador replied. "The only question is how should it be presented?" "We want an honest solution," said Brzezinski. "They should be able to save face; that's very important to them. I'll give it some thought, too.... Now for Poland. How could we help Poland?" Brzezinski asked. The Polish ambassador said that the government was increasingly out of touch with the population.

Upon leaving, the ambassador mentioned something else of interest: "The American Communists have requested that our post provide information to be used against you.... I've told them we don't collect information against members of the American government." "This is a democracy," Brzezinski remarked with a dry smile. "Anything's possible here." Then the ambassador revealed another secret: "When I was in Warsaw I learned that they were aware of your telephone conversations with the Vatican. Apparently you're talking with the Vatican a great deal.... I don't know how they're listening in, but they are. I have it on good authority. Be careful. That's all." Soon enough, Ambassador Spasowski resigned his post and settled in the United States.[9]

❖ Meanwhile, the Polish strikes had spread to the shipyards along the Baltic Coast. On August 14, 1980, Lech Walesa scaled the wall of the sprawling Lenin Shipyards. The unemployed shipyard electrician proved a charismatic figure and was soon leading seventy thousand workers demanding the right to form their own independent trade unions. In Washington, State Department officials seemed eager to avoid another dispute with Moscow. "Should we take a side in the [French] fisherman's dispute in Cherbourg?" one State Department official asked. "Is the United States supposed to take the position in a British steel strike?" asked another. Brzezinski, however, wanted to avoid sending the Soviet Union even an implicit signal of indifference from the United States. He told Carter that this was no mere labor dispute—and the trade union's survival was vital.

In Poland, the two sides engaged in dramatic negotiations inside the Lenin Shipyards for two long weeks. The Polish government finally agreed to virtually all of the worker demands, including the sanctioning of the first independent trade union in the Communist world. The workers named it "Solidarity."

But the heroic Polish workers could not save Carter's campaign against a Republican opponent that promised a more vigorous stance against the Soviet Union. In November 1980, Ronald Reagan defeated Carter in an electoral landslide.

The concern in Washington was that the Soviet Union would use the presidential transition to crush the Polish revolt. Brzezinski was well informed of Soviet intentions. For ten years, Colonel Ryszard Kuklinski, a Polish officer who served as a liaison between the Soviet and the Polish militaries, had provided the CIA with an unprecedented amount of information about, and insights into, Soviet military capabilities. And during the presidential transition in the United States in early December 1980, Kuklinski indicated that the Soviets were preparing for an invasion of Poland. Brzezinski advised Carter to avoid all ambiguity and send a direct warning to Moscow to stay out of Poland. He composed a terse warning to Moscow that President Carter sent directly to Brezhnev via the White House hotline. "The United States is watching with growing concern the unprecedented buildup of Soviet forces along the Polish border," Carter announced. Concurrently, the national security advisor briefed the pope at the Vatican and warned Solidarity leaders to take all necessary precautions. The Soviet Union halted its troop movements on the Polish border. Moscow apparently decided to give the new Polish leader Stanislaw Kania a chance to stabilize the situation. Kania claimed years later that Carter's message played a role in deterring the Soviet invasion. The Soviet leaders were also reluctant to launch a military intervention into Poland at a time when Soviet troops were bogged down in Afghanistan.

✴ In 1981, Brzezinski returned to private life, teaching again at Columbia University and assuming a post at what was then the Georgetown Center for Strategic and International Studies (now just CSIS). He settled into a quieter life of occasional speaking engagements and working on his memoirs. "I felt my time in the White House was like winning the Irish Sweepstakes," he said. "I loved every minute of it, but it only happens once and then it's over." Each week he hosted an informal foreign policy seminar in his office. There he and former staffers would discuss the major issues of the day over a brown bag lunch.

As Ronald Reagan took office, Soviet-American relations were at their lowest point in two decades. Reagan's instincts were to confront the Soviet Union. He warned that it was not possible to have a stable relationship with a totalitarian empire. While Brzezinski supported Reagan's tough stance, he also noted that more was needed than increased defense budgets. "I don't feel they have a strategic framework for spending it," he said. "It's not enough just to toot loudly anti-Soviet slogans. You have to have a policy." The reality of the world required a more flexible approach—and that was especially true in the evolving situation in Poland.

Solidarity had spread from industrial shipyards to the countryside, growing to 10 million members. In March, millions of Polish industrial workers held a four-hour strike to protest the brutal beatings of union activists. Walesa supported the effort while cautioning that if the Soviet Union invaded Poland "we might lose everything." In May, John Paul II narrowly survived an assassination attempt in Vatican City. The gunman was a Turkish national said to be an agent working under the direction of the Bulgarian secret police. Brzezinski said that the plot almost certainly originated within the Soviet KGB. At the same time, he was concerned that Reagan staffers seemed to ignore Poland—or merely treat it as another vehicle to inflict propaganda points against the Soviet Union. He was miffed that Reagan officials were putting roadblocks in front of a Polish application for International Monetary Fund (IMF) membership. "This simple-minded anti-Communist perspective," wrote Brzezinski, "is both tragically wrong and blind to the long-range opportunities for a better East-West relationship inherent in the Polish evolution."

All of this was clouded by changes in the Polish leadership. In February 1981, General Wojciech Jaruzelski became Poland's prime minister. His solemn demeanor, dark glasses, and straight arched back made him an enigmatic figure to Western television viewers. Having known many of the leaders in the Polish Communist elite, Brzezinski took note that Jaruzelski was an anomaly among them. He was born into a very traditional aristocratic family and received a Jesuit education. His life changed when the Soviet Red Army invaded Poland in 1939. He ended up in Siberia. While there, he became a true believer in the Communist cause. He served as a young army officer in a Polish infantry division of the Red Army. He saw the Soviet Union as a new civilization—a muscular and secular force bringing a sense of industrial modernity and social justice to a backward and feudal Poland.

The Soviet Union rewarded Jaruzelski for his loyalty. In the 1950s, he advanced to the highest ranks of the Polish Army. This was unusual in an era when social origins played a large role in determining how much trust the Soviets would provide to their East European satrapies. "What would it take you, as an NKVD [People's Commissariat for Internal Affairs] general, to trust someone of that background?" Brzezinski would wonder later on. "What kind of test? It would take not just words, but deeds."[10] Jaruzelski was indeed a loyal foot soldier supporting the Soviet occupation of Poland. And he spent much of 1981 putting in place plans for martial law—and the crushing of the Solidarity movement.

At the same time, the Reagan administration was anticipating a massive Soviet invasion. Kuklinski was still sending his clandestine internal reports to the CIA. But the rise in high-tech intelligence tools had changed the way the CIA assessed its information. "The CIA had lost faith in its political indicators," said Richard Ned Lebow, a scholar-in-residence at the CIA. "It meant less credibility for people's senses," he said. "It meant that people involved in national technical means—people who didn't know politics—rose to more prominence." Another insider noted, "Any assessment was possibly inaccurate. . . . They had contradictory reports. So they would fall back on technical sources."[11]

The Reagan State Department also tended to deemphasize Kuklinski's reports. "The feeling at State was: 'Let's not do anything precipitous until we're sure,'" said a Senate Intelligence staffer. "A policy in anticipation of events is not what they're taught."[12]

On September 15, 1981, Jaruzelski chaired a top-secret meeting outlining plans to declare martial law. Kuklinski smuggled out the final plans for martial law before giving the signal that his cover had been blown and that he required immediate exfiltration. He arrived in Washington in the ensuing days and was debriefed at length. Jaruzelski was stunned by the betrayal. He assumed that the United States now had access to his martial law blueprints. He took note that the White House issued no protest—and gave no warnings to the Solidarity leadership. "We took the lack of reaction as a positive signal," Jaruzelski later argued. "Do something, but don't upset the stability in Europe."

⁙ On Sunday night, December 13, 1981, Jaruzelski unleashed a military takeover of Poland. Solidarity leaders were arrested, and all communication lines were severed. There was a nighttime curfew and a ban on assemblies. Tanks and armed vehicles patrolled the snowy streets and enforced martial law with an iron fist. Jaruzelski justified the internal crackdown as the "lesser evil"—to prevent a much harsher Soviet invasion and "progressing economic ruin."

Brzezinski watched the shadowy reports coming in over the wire services. He caustically referred to Jaruzelski as a "Polish Quisling" that had served the interests of the Soviet Union rather than Poland. He saw martial law as simply delaying the inevitable. The events in Poland, he cautioned, were a dark harbinger for the Soviet Union. The empire could implode before the decade was over—likely along nationalist lines. "The French and British colonial empires have been terminated," said Brzezinski in the days following martial law. "The Soviet empire eventually will have to be terminated as well. The key question is: Can it be done peacefully and gradually, or will it be violent and dangerous?" He added, "Movements such as Solidarity offer the hope of peaceful evolution. Soviet suppression makes eruptions and dangerous consequences more likely."[13]

The Reagan administration suspended economic assistance to Poland—including $100 million worth of American food and feed grains. It was soon clear that military control of the streets could not put people back to work or put food on empty shelves. Solidarity retained the hearts and minds of the vast majority of the Polish people. Meanwhile, Brzezinski's articles were read over RFE and copied and passed around on an increasingly vast underground publication network. On one occasion, he paid a visit to the Solidarity office in Brussels. He delighted the director by taking out his checkbook and providing a generous donation. But there seemed no end to the political stalemate.

In October 1984, the body of Father Jerzy Popieluszko, a courageous supporter of Solidarity, was found dead at the bottom of a reservoir. An autopsy revealed that the priest had been beaten to death before being thrown in the water. Jaruzelski sought to distance his regime from the grisly act. He ordered a public trial, and members of the Polish security police received long prison sentences. The accused claimed that their orders came from "a very high level"—which most Poles took as the Soviet KGB.

❖ On March 12, 1985, Radio Moscow interrupted its music program to announce the election of Mikhail Gorbachev as general secretary of the Communist Party. He was young and energetic and seemed eager to end stagnation and corruption in the Soviet Union. He belonged to a new generation that had no memories of Stalin's terror or World War II. He introduced two new Russian words that entered the cold war lexicon: *perestroika*, meaning restructuring, and *glasnost*, meaning openness. Brzezinski initially took a skeptical view of the new face in Moscow. He noted that Gorbachev may be a cordial individual but the problems of the Soviet Union were systemic—and deeply rooted in Leninist dogma and seven decades of a corrupt one-party dictatorship. "We shouldn't look so much at the suit, or the way he conducts himself, or at whether he waves to Western correspondents or his wife carries a Gucci handbag," said Brzezinski. "One has to look at what the man stands for, what his career was."[14]

But Gorbachev's more flexible thinking did present new opportunities in Poland. Brzezinski sent overtures for a meeting with Jaruzelski—to see where things stood within the Polish leadership. Jan Nowak, de facto director of the Polish American Congress and Brzezinski's friend, advised against the meeting. "I was not in favor of this meeting," Nowak recalled. "In fact I strongly advised against it. I was afraid Jaruzelski would try to use it as a tacit sign of approval for martial law." Nowak later had a change of heart. "This was not a social meeting. Brzezinski knew these systems better than anybody in the West—but he also knew the tragic history of failed uprisings in Eastern Europe. . . . So he was using Jaruzelski as a bridge to the Polish government. Not for appeasement—that was not his style—but to try to facilitate this bridge for the peaceful evolution of the system. . . . And he wanted to convey one major point: a violent explosion in Eastern Europe would set everything back—including the Gorbachev reforms—and this was in nobody's interest."[15]

❖ In September 1985 Jaruzelski arrived in New York for a speech before the United Nations. "I come to New York because we are members of the United Nations," he said upon arrival at JFK airport. "This time I come personally because Poland wants to participate in the main story of today—the preservation of peace." Jaruzelski also gave several interviews. He appeared cordial, though he allowed himself to be agitated by Defense Secretary Casper Weinberger's quip that he was a "Polish general in a Soviet uniform." Of course, most Polish Americans felt the same way about the hated figure that had crushed Solidarity on that cold dark morning four years earlier. Groups waving placards shadowed him throughout his visit, and in New York City angry groups picketed in front of the Soviet Mission at 67th Street and Lexington Avenue.

Brzezinski treated Jaruzelski with some caution. They had lunch at the Rainbow Room, the stylish art deco hideaway located on the sixty-fifth floor of Rockefeller Center. The group included David Rockefeller and Lawrence Eagleburger, a former Reagan official who held a relatively favorable opinion of the Polish general—at least before the declaration of martial law. Jaruzelski arrived without his familiar dark glasses. He admired the vast panoramic view of New York City. He told an aide that he expected to see more air pollution in the den of vice and capitalism. "It is fair enough to say that he was impressed," mused one aide in a backhanded compliment. "Certainly, from that elevation the city is positively not repulsive."[16] When they met, Jaruzelski handed Brzezinski a large packet. It contained letters and documents about his father's military service in the 1920 Russo-Polish War. "He said it was some 'family materials,'" recalled Brzezinski.

"And I rather stupidly said, 'How did you find these documents?' Then I immediately realized they were from my file."

They spent the rest of the meeting discussing the state of the Communist world. Brzezinski offered an unvarnished view of the situation in Poland. The Soviet Union was moving against the tide of history. Gorbachev was trying to reform through a top-down approach in what remained a one-party dictatorship. It could have unpredictable consequences. Solidarity, on the other hand, was a genuine and organic mass opposition movement. It had developed a parallel society that offered a real alternative to the Communist Party. If the Poles could reach a political compromise, it could provide hope to the other Eastern Europeans. And he should think about that. Because there was no guarantee Gorbachev—or his reforms—would be around forever.[17]

Years later Jaruzelski recalled the meeting with Brzezinski in New York: "Brzezinski was a lifetime foe. So in that respect our meeting was somewhat strange. But it was also helpful because there was a common interest in avoiding an uprising. He was born a Pole. And he knew our romantic history and the history of tragic uprisings. And he was concerned about this—and he saw negotiations as an alternative possibility."[18]

❖ In June 1986, the *Washington Post* published a front-page article on a significant development in Poland. For the first time the Polish government revealed Colonel Ryszard Kuklinski's role in providing Poland's military plans to the CIA. Jaruzelski's spokesman insisted that this was proof that the United States had betrayed Solidarity. He explained that a copy of the martial-law plans sat on Reagan's desk for weeks and yet the United States said nothing. "The U.S. administration could have publicly revealed these plans to the world and warned Solidarity," said the government spokesman. "Had it done so, the implementation of martial law would have been impossible."

Brzezinski, in turn, still regarded Kuklinski as a Polish national hero. The two men met at the Four Seasons in Georgetown. Brzezinski addressed Kuklinski with the phrase traditionally conferred when a Polish solider was decorated. "*Pan sie dobrze Polsce zasluzyl.* You have served Poland well."[19]

❖ In the summer of 1986, Vice President George H. W. Bush was in the early stages of his own run for the White House. A Bush aide contacted Brzezinski with a political question. How would Polish Americans react if Bush made a trip to Poland? There were obvious political risks. The Reagan State Department had advised against the trip. There were still sanctions on the Jaruzelski regime, and the Republican right wing had never fully warmed to Bush. For his part, Brzezinski cautioned Bush that an official visit could be productive—but only if it were modeled on what President Carter had done a decade earlier. He should make it clear that any economic aid was linked to a more tolerant approach to Polish opposition groups. Brzezinski then used his back channel to persuade Jaruzelski to permit Bush to meet with regular Polish citizens—in addition to official events and rather staid tours of television and lightbulb factories.

Vice President Bush took full advantage of the opportunity. In Warsaw, he mentioned Solidarity in a live television broadcast and shook hands as he made an emotional visit to the shrine of Father Jerzy Popieluszko. He then slipped out of sight before reappearing on the church balcony overlooking the street. The crowd erupted when Lech Walesa appeared at his side and Bush took a Solidarity banner out of his pocket and gave the triumphant "V" for victory sign. The security units could do little as the crowds joined in the chant: "Solidarity! Lech Walesa! Long live Bush! Long live Reagan! Solidarity! Lech Walesa . . . !" The American media treated this as a largely domestic event—American politics. Bush added to that impression, referring to his meeting with Walesa. "How many delegates has he got in Iowa?" he joked. "That's what I want to know."

But the visit had to do with Poland as well. And it was more than ceremonial. It reflected Brzezinski's advice and at the same time was in the idiom of the Reagan administration. "Reagan's rhetoric was always very sharp, and we appreciated that very much," recalled Solidarity member Adam Michnik. "But Brzezinski always had a calibrated strategy about how to actually impact change—how to use political symbolism and economic leverage. Bush gave . . . clear signs of support to the opposition. And that visit provided a clear psychological turning point for us."[20]

⁙ In January 1988, Brzezinski gave the Hugh Seton-Watson Memorial Lecture at the Center for Policy Studies in London. He predicted that 1988 might be another 1848—where European states rose in the famous "Springtime of Nations"—drawing an analogy when Central European nations stood up for independence. "It is not an exaggeration to affirm that there are five countries now in Eastern Europe, all of which are ripe for revolutionary explosion," Brzezinski noted. "Nor is it an exaggeration to say that this could happen in more than one simultaneously." Realizing that there were risks if the situation were to get out of control, Brzezinski ended his generally optimistic speech with an important caveat. "A massive revolutionary outbreak in the region," he cautioned, "is not in our interest."[21]

The Polish situation appeared to have reached a crisis point. There were a series of vocal strikes demanding the re-legalization of Solidarity. If the Jaruzelski regime had responded with military force, it could have had ripple effects throughout the Soviet world. "If there is a revolution there, there will be suppression," Brzezinski warned in May 1988. "If suppression fails, there will be Soviet intervention, [and] that's the end of perestroika."[22]

❖ The changing dynamics in international affairs added importance to the 1988 presidential election. That summer Brzezinski crossed party lines to endorse Bush over Democratic candidate Michael Dukakis. "I thought this [a Dukakis victory] would be extremely bad for the United States," Brzezinski said. "[His course] was simply the wrong course to pursue for the country and the Democratic Party."[23] In September, Vice President George Bush introduced Brzezinski as a member of his National Security Task Force. "George Bush is the one who can best fashion a bipartisan foreign policy," Brzezinski explained. "In saying so, I remain proud, very proud, of my national service under President Carter."[24] "I was never a fan of his," replied Dukakis. "I thought he was a lousy national security advisor, with an ego as big as a house." In the autumn, the Massachusetts Democrat lost his lead in the polls. And by the time the new Bush administration came to Washington, Brzezinski was discussing his most recent book. The title was in some ways a broad summation of his academic and political career: *The Grand Failure: The Birth and Death of Communism*. The *New York Times* excerpt ran under the provocative title "Will the Soviet Empire Self-Destruct?" Brzezinski cautioned that this was not hyperbole but an increasingly likely scenario. In the meantime, there were more remarkable signs that the cold war may in fact end.

Around the same time, Jaruzelski was getting ready to make a critically important change. He had spent ten years seeking to contain Solidarity. But facing the labor strikes of August 1988 and a rapidly deteriorating economy, Jaruzelski called for a "courageous turnaround" by the Polish Communist Party. He wanted to enter talks with the Solidarity opposition.

Brzezinski, who had spent the previous three years talking with Jaruzelski, had mixed feelings about him. He certainly had no sympathy for Jaruzelski's willingness to introduce martial law in 1981, but he did have a sense that Jaruzelski was cut from another cloth than most of the Communist leaders he had dealt with over the years. The ambiguity stemmed, in part, from a conversation the two of them had in the late 1980s. The Polish leader confided in Brzezinski that he had two major life-defining moments. The first came as a young man when he left feudal Poland and saw the Soviet Union as a force of modernity and social justice. The more painful revelation had to do with what was happening in the late 1980s—when the grand promises of Marxism-Leninism were exposed as a cruel illusion.[25]

With Jaruzelski's concurrence, the so-called Round Table negotiations began in early 1989 with the relatively modest goal of legalizing Solidarity within what was still a Communist-dominated system. The negotiations soon expanded to include elections and a grand reconciliation that saw Polish television viewers watching Lech Walesa shake hands with General Jaruzelski as they discussed the possibility of real elections. Brzezinski's role was unofficial; he operated behind the scenes. But his presence provided a unique link between the concerned parties. "I do not believe that the 'Round Table' talks would have been possible without Brzezinski's influence," recalled Jan Nowak. "He had influence within the Bush staff and the American diplomatic service and behind the scenes he convinced both sides of the importance of a peaceful negotiation. And he had great authority within Solidarity—and to some extent with Jaruzelski."[26]

The "Round Table" produced the first peaceful and eventually successful transition from communism to democracy—the first known case of the evolutionary termination of Communist totalitarianism. Still, in later years the Polish Round Table compromise was criticized by right wing critics as too limited and perhaps even a cynical collusion among elites. But in 1988–89 the political situation in the Soviet Bloc was still fluid. There was concern that if things got out of control Kremlin hard-liners could stage a coup and reverse the entire process. Brzezinski believed that elements in the Polish secret police and party apparatus were goading Soviet hard-liners into a last-minute political intervention. It would have been easy to convince hawks in the Kremlin that Poland still provided the lifeline to the 380,000 troops in East Germany. And it was still unclear how the Soviet Union would react to the vision of a reunited German state in the middle of Europe.

In May 1989 Brzezinski traveled to Warsaw at the invitation of the U.S. ambassador. He watched the elections in amazement as Solidarity won the overwhelming support of the Polish people—and with it the repudiation of the Communist government. In August 1989 President Jaruzelski appointed Tadeusz Mazowiecki, a respected Catholic intellectual and key Solidarity advisor, as Poland's new prime minister. "These changes are the most important upheavals in Eastern Europe and in the Soviet world since the death of Stalin," Brzezinski said. "And they have enormous implications for the future of communism and the East-West relations.... We are seeing the end of an entire era."[27]

The year continued to surprise. In October, Brzezinski traveled to Moscow, where he received a standing ovation for his speech in front of the Diplomatic Academy. Strobe Talbott conducted an interview with him for *Time* magazine. The title said it all: "The Vindication of a Hard-Liner." In the interview, Brzezinski was cautious: "Now is the time to ask ourselves, creatively and historically, how do we respond to the apparent collapse of the Soviet Union? We can either deliberately shape a new world or simply let the old disintegrate—with some of the wreckage possibly even endangering us."

Within weeks, the Communist regimes of Eastern Europe fell in a series of peaceful, "velvet" revolutions.

A month later, in November 1989, Lech Walesa came to Washington to speak before the Congress of the United States. "We did not smash a single window pane," Walesa said. "But we were stubborn, very stubborn, ready to suffer. We knew what we wanted. And our power prevailed in the end."[28] Zbigniew Brzezinski was in the audience. "I had known Brzezinski for many years," recalled one Solidarity member. "He is a very proud man who rarely displays his emotions. But that night I looked over at him and saw him wiping a tear of joy from his eye. It was a great moment."

## NOTES

1  "A Pope from Poland," *Newsweek*, October 30, 1978.

2  George Weigel, *Witness to Hope: The Biography of Pope John Paul II* (New York: Harper-Collins, 1999), 279.

3  James M. Rentschler, "Meanwhile: Hooking Up the Vatican Hot Line," *New York Times*, October 30, 1998.

4  Weigel, *Witness to Hope*, 301.

5  Ian Brzezinski, interview with author, June 16, 2005.

6  Jonathan Kwitny, *The Man of the Century: The Life and Times of Pope John Paul II* (New York: Henry Holt, 1997), 341–42.

7  Ibid.

8  "Brzezinski at the Pass: Bonhomie, Bullets," *New York Times*, February 4, 1980.

9  Romuald Spasowski, *The Liberation of One* (San Diego: Harcourt Brace Jovanovich, 1986), 622–25.

10  Tina Rosenberg, *The Haunted Land: Facing Europe's Ghosts after Communism* (New York: Vintage, 1996), 146.

11  Ibid., 207.

12  Ibid., 210.

13  "The Polish Crisis: Proof of an Empire's Failure: Brzezinski Sees Similar Tensions for Russia Too," *Washington Post*, December 20, 1981.

14  Norman D. Sandler, "New Younger Leader; Same Old Policies," *United Press International*, March 11, 1985.

15  Jan Nowak, interview with author, September 4, 2003.

16  Elaine Sciolino, "Polish Chief Is Caught Up in the Whirl," *New York Times*, September 26, 1985.

17  Zbigniew Brzezinski, interview with author, July 27, 2007.

18  Wojciech Jaruzelski, interview with author, April 27, 2003.

19  Benjamin Weiser, *A Secret Life: The Polish Officer, His Covert Mission, and the Price He Paid to Save His Country* (New York: Public Affairs, 2004), 290.

20  Adam Michnik, interview with author, March 26, 2003.

21  Richard Gwyn, "Eastern Bloc May Be Ready to Explode," *Toronto Star*, February 7, 1988.

22  "Gorbachev's Weakest Link," *Newsweek*, May 9, 1988, 26.

23  Zbigniew Brzezinski, interview with author, September 27, 2003.

24  Diane Alters, "Brzezinski Named to Top Position on Bush Task Force," *Boston Globe*, September 13, 1988.

25  Stephen Engelberg, "As Jaruzelski Leaves Office: A Traitor or a Patriot to Poles?," *New York Times*, December 22, 1990.

26  Jan Nowak, interview with author, September 4, 2003.

27  Bryan Brumley, "Bush Administration Hails Move toward Non-Communism in Poland," Associated Press, August 18, 1989.

28  Lawrence Knutson, "Walesa Charms the Senate: 'I Really Am an Electrician,'" Associated Press, November 15, 1989.

CHAPTER 11

# Witnessing the Grand Failure in Moscow, 1989

MARIN STRMECKI

In late fall of 1989, Zbigniew Brzezinski sat in an airliner bound for Moscow, where he would participate in a privately funded U.S.-Soviet conference about the future of Eastern Europe.[1] Out the window, as the aircraft dipped below the clouds of an overcast day, it was not long before the socioeconomic misery of the Soviet Union cried out for recognition. Even on the outskirts of Moscow, the poverty of the countryside could be seen to surpass even the dismal condition of Appalachia in the 1950s. The roads were unpaved. The houses were assembled of stray pieces of wood and topped with corrugated tin sheeting, with chimneys from wood stoves casting a pall of gray smoke over the immediate surroundings. After landing, Brzezinski and the rest of the American delegation traversed the concourse of Moscow's international airport, finding it not much better than a typical terminal in a Third World country. It was dirty, dusty, and designed in an out-of-date modernist style. The group moved quickly through the customs line for those with nothing to declare. Soviet citizens, who seized any opportunity to forage for consumer goods abroad because so few were available at home, clogged the other lines. These were the sights that greeted the Americans as they set foot in the superpower that for seventy years had devoted enormous resources to a military competition with the West and the pursuit of a global ideological revolution.

Brzezinski had just published a book, *The Grand Failure: The Birth and Death of Communism in the Twentieth Century*, in which he argued that the Communist world had entered a systemic crisis that would lead to the demise of its ideological experiment. In his office at the Center for Strategic and International Studies in Washington, where he was a senior scholar and counselor, he closely followed day-to-day events in the Communist world. He was an inveterate reader of key articles in the Soviet press translated and published on a daily basis by the Foreign Broadcast Information Service of the U.S. government. In a comfortable reading chair, he would methodically work through the beige-colored, soft-covered reports, tearing out specific articles and putting them in manila folders labeled with a set of discrete topics. He began drafting and revising his chapters in early 1988, finishing the manuscript in August. The thinking expressed in *The Grand Failure* represented the intellectual framework that Brzezinski brought to the meetings in Moscow, shaping the questions he pursued and the arguments he proffered.

Western experts had for the previous four years debated whether Gorbachev's reforms were a ruse, designed to lull the West into a false sense of security, or a genuine attempt to start a transition away from the totalitarian order built by Lenin and Stalin. This question sparked contentious debates in policy circles. Yet, by late 1989, too much had already happened to dismiss lightly the implications of the reforms for Soviet domestic and foreign policy. The independent trade union Solidarity had swept elections in Poland. Hungary's Communist Party had approved the holding of multiparty elections. Days before Brzezinski traveled to Moscow, Gorbachev himself had engineered a leadership transition in East Germany, putting in power a group of putative reformers. Political unrest, beneath the surface, roiled other Warsaw Pact states. Closer to home, greater political openness in the Soviet Union had produced sharp critiques of the Communist system in the press and had led to increasing self-assertion of the peoples in the non-Russian republics. These events loomed as a dramatic political backdrop to the conference in Moscow.

In his book, Brzezinski had already worked through a comprehensive analysis of the intellectual debates in political and intellectual circles in the Soviet Union. He distilled these contentious debates down to what he called "the ten dynamics of disunion":

1.  Economic reform: To overcome the "era of stagnation"—the economic decline of the Brezhnev years—did the Soviet Union need to move away from a centrally planned economy? How could the system transition to one composed of self-reliant firms that responded to demand and prices? How should the Soviet government manage the likely economic shocks involved in such a transition?

2. Social priorities: Should investing in heavy industry and the military be curtailed in order to raise the dismal standard of living of the Soviet public? Should the privileges of the *nomenklatura*—the high-ranking state and party officials—be scrutinized in public and reduced?

3. Political democratization: Can economic and social change be brought about without a willingness to listen to public demands and to encourage bottom-up political spontaneity? If not, should the Soviet system accept the possibility of ideological pluralism and political choice?

4. Role of the party: Should ideological debate and pluralism lead to democracy within the Communist Party or even to an end of its political monopoly? Should a multiparty system replace a system dominated by a "vanguard party" that controlled the state and oversaw the actions of all of its officials?

5. Ideology, religion, and culture: With glasnost opening the door to belief systems other than Marxism-Leninism, should the Communist Party cede its ideological control of society's value system and allow a restoration of religion and culture in the public mind?

6. History (Stalinism): Since the Soviet system was a legacy of the Stalinist period, should this period be reexamined from a moral point of view? Should responsibility for the crimes of Stalin be attributed to him alone, or should it be shared with Lenin and the nature of the ideology of Marxism-Leninism? And what was the legitimacy of a political system that enabled such crimes and oppression?

7. Internal national problems: As glasnost took hold in non-Russian areas of the Soviet Union, the façade of national unity broke down. Non-Russians started asking themselves whether they should revive their national identities and histories and whether they should challenge the legitimacy of ethnic Russian domination of the political system. They even broached the question of whether national self-determination for the non-Russian peoples should be placed on the agenda.

8. The war in Afghanistan: As casualties and costs mounted, commentators questioned the benefits of the intervention. Was the effort futile? Was the suffering of the war equitably distributed across society when little of the burden fell on the sons of the political elite?

9. Foreign and defense policy: Should the Soviet Union abandon the doctrine of peaceful coexistence—which allowed for temporary accommodations of the capitalist powers as a "breathing spell" in the quest for

world revolution—in light of the risk of nuclear war and increasing interdependence? If so, what did this mean for the massive investment in Soviet military capabilities?

10. The Soviet Bloc and the world Communist movement: Should the Communist Party of the Soviet Union abandon its leading role vis-à-vis parties in other countries? If so, what would this mean for the Brezhnev Doctrine?

It was late October 1989, a momentous time to be coming to the Soviet Union. The political debates identified in *The Grand Failure* were historic, for it was not the critics of the Soviet Union abroad but the members of the political elite who were raising these fundamental questions. The issue before Brzezinski and the rest of the American delegation was to try to discern where all of this would lead.

⁛ On the opening day of the conference, Brzezinski was to deliver the keynote address at the Diplomatic Academy of the Foreign Ministry, which until a few months before had been an institution closed to foreign visitors. In a display of continuing socialist vigilance, it still did not even post its name on the outside of the building. It was an imposing if nondescript edifice. As members of the two delegations entered, the Americans walked down the tile-covered hallways, lined with plaster walls painted in a faded avocado green. Glass cases enclosed exhibits on the great thoughts or achievements of Lenin and Gorbachev. A political message was implicit in the fact that no other leader made the cut.

He entered the main lecture hall, which for the event was configured like a giant law school classroom, with a series of long horseshoe-shaped tables creating a small amphitheater. Within the inner horseshoe were conference tables from which Brzezinski and the other principals addressed the audience. Behind them, on what looked like a red-felt altar, loomed a massive white bust of Lenin. The atmosphere in the hall was reminiscent of the scenes depicting revolutionary meetings in the movie *Reds*. The room itself was packed, with students lining the walls and peering through doorways, and the Soviet-era lighting creating a dimly lit, suspenseful setting. Since the 1960s, Brzezinski's criticism of Soviet ideology and foreign policy had given him a certain level of notoriety in the Soviet press. He was typically referred to as the "infamous" or "notorious" Brzezinski. Thus, when this prominent figure in the pantheon of the Kremlin's ideological foes rose to speak, the audience became perfectly still, with only the shutters of cameras breaking the silence.

Brzezinski began by observing that he had previously spoken publicly in

Communist countries on three occasions, in Czechoslovakia in 1968, Hungary in 1988, and Poland in 1989. He added that it was merely coincidence that his appearances were followed by the anti-Communist revolution in Prague, the fall of the long-time Hungarian leader János Kádár, and the sweeping electoral victory of Solidarity in Poland. He then noted that, in this spirit, he was happy on this day to be speaking before such a distinguished group in the Soviet Union. A wave of knowing laughter swept the audience.

Brzezinski quoted Gorbachev to begin his address. He recalled that Gorbachev described the goal of his European policy as the building of "a common European home," which was part of a broader effort to defuse East-West tensions. Many observers in the West at the time believed that this policy was designed to fracture transatlantic unity, for a common *European* home would by its nature exclude North American powers such as the United States. Instead of contesting Gorbachev's formulation, Brzezinski surprised the audience by endorsing it as a noble aspiration. This palpably intrigued the assembly. He then proceeded to ask what would be required to build the common European home. It needed a foundation of common values. He took note of the calls in the Soviet Union for fundamental economic and political change. He argued that these signaled a growing recognition within Soviet society that certain universal values were essential to success for all modern countries. He now had the rapt attention of the audience, with many listeners leaning forward to catch what would come next. Then, step by step, Brzezinski took the audience through the changes that would need to come in the Eastern Bloc to make the vision of a common home a reality. Moscow would need to accept freedom for East European countries to choose their own political systems, German unification (if this was desired by the German people), genuine democracy and freedom of choice in the Soviet Union, market-based economic systems throughout the socialist world, and a confederational structure for the Soviet Union.

These propositions, heretical even at the time, were offered as a sympathetic appeal for the Soviet side to achieve its own declared aspirations and as a road map for Soviet society to let go of ideological dogma and geopolitical positions that had separated its citizens from their European brethren. At the close of his remarks, the room erupted in thunderous applause, an early signal of how much change had already occurred in Soviet thinking. As the other principals made their remarks, and as Brzezinski sorted his notes, a buzz caused by several hundred people whispering to each other at the same time pervaded the room.

Now would come the tough part. Members of the audience submitted their questions on pieces of paper. It was natural to expect antagonistic or confrontational responses. However, the audience instead came back with questions grounded in intellectual curiosity and acceptance. One asked, somewhat sardonically, how Brzezinski felt making a major speech while standing in front of a bust of Lenin. Brzezinski coolly responded by saying that, as a major historical figure, Lenin had had something very interesting to say about the salient issues of a particular point in *past* history. His connotation, which was picked up by the audience, was that Lenin and his ideas had no relevance for today's world. At another point, Brzezinski observed that the Soviet Union spent 20 to 30 percent of its GNP on defense and that this was a major drag on the Soviet economy. A predictable defensive outburst came from the Soviet side. One of leaders of the Soviet delegation interjected that the right figure was at most 20 percent. Yet, even this statement stood in stark contrast to Gorbachev's public assertions that defense spending was no more than a third of that figure.

❖ After the address, Brzezinski and the rest of the American delegation moved to a threadbare meeting room for a conversation with Georgy Shakhnazarov, a senior official of the Central Committee of the Communist Party and a personal advisor to Gorbachev on Eastern Europe. It was a remarkable discussion, touching on the upheaval underway in Eastern Europe and the profound crisis of a political system based on the outmoded ideology of Marxism-Leninism. The Soviet side, while open and candid, at once accepted the need for transformational change but sought to put boundaries on such change in the false belief that the Communist system could be reformed and thus preserved.

After some introductory statements on both sides, Brzezinski got down to business. He asked about the meaning of recent statements by Gorbachev that intimated approval of the changes underway in Poland and Hungary, both of which had done away with the Communist Party's monopoly on political power and moved toward multiparty systems. He noted that Gorbachev had not intervened to stop these changes and asked at what point such events might begin to threaten Soviet interests.

Shakhnazarov replied, in a formal tone at first, that the Soviet Union wanted its security respected by other powers and friendly relations with its neighbors and that "we also have an interest in the political process now underway in Europe—the unification of Europe, the dismantling of the two blocs." Warming to the subject, he argued that the process of change in the relations between Eastern Europe and the Soviet Union should go forward in parallel with the transformation of the relationship between NATO and the Warsaw Pact. He expressed the view that the Soviet Union would "like to maintain the long-standing relationships with its allies on the level of economics, politics, and culture." Hinting at the scope of the ambitions of the Gorbachev government, he added, "This task is within reach, particularly as we ourselves change. The idea is that it will be not only Eastern Europe but also the Soviet Union that will be joining Europe."

Suspicious, Brzezinski inquired what Shakhnazarov meant by "friendly relations," a term that, he noted, Stalin also used to describe his goals vis-à-vis the countries of Eastern Europe. He added that Poland and Hungary were embarking on "truly comprehensive reforms of their political and economic systems" and were "very far ahead of what is being done in the Soviet Union." He drew the logical conclusion: "If the balance between the processes of reform in Eastern Europe and the Soviet Union is to be maintained, either Poland or Hungary will have to slow down or the Soviet Union will have to accelerate the pace of change."

Plaintively searching to support his position, Shakhnazarov said that the Polish prime minister had indicated that the Soviet Union was still needed as the "main guarantor" of Polish security, which would continue to be true for the ten to fifteen years required for the East-West relationship to lose its confrontational character. Leaning forward in an effort to impress his sincerity on his interlocutors, he pointedly stated, "We will not try to slow down change in Eastern Europe. These changes are going in the same direction as the reforms in the Soviet Union—reducing the role of ideology, increasing the influence of the market, enhancing legality, and decentralizing political power. These processes are generalized. The same things are taking place in the Soviet Union and Eastern Europe."

After taking in the Soviet statement, Brzezinski quizzically asked, "What would be your attitude if the Poles started to hang the communists from the light posts? Would you maintain this aloof attitude?" The head of the Soviet delegation, Oleg Bogomolov, answered without missing a beat: "That is an internal matter for the Poles to decide." Shakhnazarov restated his point with added emphasis: "As we have said many times, we will not interfere in the internal affairs of other countries." Gorbachev's leading advisor on Eastern Europe had in effect stated that the Soviet Union would not resist the anti-Communist upheaval that threatened to sweep away the governments of its Warsaw Pact allies. After reflecting a moment, Brzezinski observed with a wry smile, "Well, I can only say that I hope that the Poles don't hear about this because they might start to do just that if they think they could get away with it." The Soviet delegation responded with uneasy laughter.

The conversation turned to ideology. Shakhnazarov said that he found Brzezinski's book, *The Grand Failure*, to be most interesting. He added pedantically, "I don't think that it has the proper title, however. The failure has not been of the ideas of socialism and communism but simply of one model derived from those ideas."

Brzezinski calmly engaged the point, as if leading an academic seminar. He said that the only model for what we call communism was the Soviet Union after the end of the New Economic Policy in 1928. He explained, "That is the reality of communism. It does not exist theoretically. As it has been known in reality—that is, the experiences of the Soviet Union, Eastern Europe, and China—it has been a grand failure." He observed that judging the system in terms of social preferences, the human condition of those living under it, and the costs of progress would lead to the same conclusion. He continued, "You have paid a terrible price for the progress made under communism—and that progress has not been as extensive as that achieved under Western systems. Moreover, all examples of reform point in the direction of abandonment of the principal features of communism. You are in effect conceding that socialism is best represented by the ideas of social democracy, not communism. You are saying that the Mensheviks were right." He concluded by noting that "Gorbachev has already told Hungarian party leaders—who repeated his statement to me shortly thereafter—that everything done after 1928 was a mistake."

Shakhnazarov flashed an ironic smile. He retorted, "We are no longer afraid of being called Mensheviks. That is in the past." After a discussion of whether the political-economic systems of the West and East were converging, the two delegations debated the need for Soviet leaders to abandon ideological slogans and symbols. Shakhnazarov waved away the point, saying that this was a peripheral question. Symbols were changed by Stalin when he needed to mobilize patriotism in World War II, but the oppressive system persisted nevertheless. He explained that Gorbachev was seeking to elevate the importance of Leninism, which, he argued, was a moral framework of socialist ideas that Stalin subsequently distorted. Referring to the crimes of Stalin, he argued, "Lenin did not do those things. He created the party and state but would have democratized the system. He would have seen that life itself had shown that it was impossible to do things otherwise. It was a tragedy that he did not live long enough to carry out this vision."

Brzezinski took a moment to absorb this point and then moved the conversation to the philosophical plane: "I have been struck in listening to you, and in participating in our conference, by how different your processes of thinking are from those of the United States and the advanced countries of Europe. First, in advanced Western countries, practice precedes social theory. Here, social theory precedes practice. An intellectual construct—an abstract construct—literally determines policy. In the West, we make policy after the electorate expresses its preferences and by trying to figure out what will work to solve a particular problem." A note of urgency crept into his voice as he continued: "Second, I am struck by the preoccupation with Lenin. I am not saying that he was not an interesting man. But to keep referring to him, not only in the search for legitimacy, but also as a guide to policy is absurd. You make yourselves prisoners of the past. You cannot use Lenin as a basis for a comprehensive set of reforms. You need to find institutions that work and to stop worrying about whether or not Lenin would approve of them."

Shakhnazarov nodded hastily and conceded that much of this was true. He then countered that "you have not taken into account our political processes." Wistfully, he added, "The ideology has its roots in the system." A member of the American delegation, Mark Palmer, asked how Soviet leaders would distance themselves from ideology. Shakhnazarov, energized by the opportunity to speak of coming reforms, said that a central challenge was the question of private property. He explained, "Our central idea is that the idea of public property is good. Private property creates a great rift between people—the upper classes who own private property and the lower classes who do not. The Supreme Soviet is grappling with the problem of how to name property in the Soviet Union. There is opposition to the notion of private property. Some have suggested 'individual property.' There is already 'personal property,' but that refers to property not used for the pursuit of profit. We do not want to give up public property. We believe it is good. But if certain kinds of private property can be developed—forms that are well regulated and so on—then perhaps a mixed system will work." The group then briefly discussed the various forms of ownership in the West and what models might be drawn upon by the Soviet Union.

Surprisingly, it was Shakhnazarov who raised the link between economic and political change. "We need a more effective economic system," he said, "but the political system must come first. That is Gorbachev's main idea. He understands that perestroika can only succeed after a fundamental reform of the political system." He ticked off the laws that Gorbachev's government was developing to end censorship, authorize independent private organizations, protect freedom of conscience, liberalize emigration, and reform economic relations. American delegates asked whether the often-discussed plan to institute pluralism within the Communist Party was sufficient to enact this scale of change and whether these objectives could be achieved only by moving to a multiparty system. With excessive confidence in the public standing of the Communist Party, Shakhnaz-arov replied, "We have the ability to win the votes to maintain the right to keep power. This is a question of the nearest future. It will be tested in the next elec-tions of local governments. The issue of a multiparty system is a question for the future. In such conditions, it is a false issue. We are in a deep crisis. There can be a blow-up leading to chaos. The only institution that prevents this from happen-ing is the Communist Party. A multiparty system is a luxury. For us, it would be dangerous."

After a discussion of the future of censorship, a sensitive subject was raised. The head of the American delegation, Charles Gati, asked whether Moscow would reevaluate its position on the intervention to suppress the Prague Spring in 1968 or even issue an expression of regret, warning that, without such a step, an uprising in Czechoslovakia was inevitable. Looking down at the table, Shakh-nazarov deemed this to be "a very delicate issue" and argued that local leaders in Prague should initiate such a reevaluation. Raising his head to make eye contact with his American interlocutor, he added, "We all have a common opinion on this subject. The intervention badly influenced domestic and international events. We all understand this, but have not said so explicitly in public."

Another American, Strobe Talbott of *Time* magazine, observed that Foreign Minister Shevardnadze's willingness to say that the invasion of Afghanistan was "an illegal, immoral act" stood in striking contrast to the silence regarding 1968. Growing frustrated at the insistence of the Americans, the head of the Soviet delegation interjected, "Do you really expect us to destabilize Czechoslovakia?" Patiently seeking to ease tensions in the room, Shakhnazarov commented, "We as a country will not resolve this issue. We will not prevent others from changing, however."

After briefly discussing East Germany, the two sides returned to Czechoslo-vakia. Bogomolov said, "As far as Czechoslovakia is concerned, we have not ex-plicitly denounced the 1968 invasion because we do not want to create another Ceausescu. Such a move would lead the old conservatives to get together and try to remain in power by their own means." Somewhat exasperated at the un-willingness of some of the Americans to accept the sincerity of his statements, Shakhnazarov said, "Gorbachev has said he would not interfere in domestic change, and he has not done so. The Brezhnev Doctrine was never published, so it cannot be formally repealed. What further do you want us to do?"

❖ The next day, Americans and Soviets reconvened in an unexceptional con-ference room for alternately insightful and tedious discussions across a range of topics. After an extended back-and-forth on the future of Europe toward the end of the session, a concluding exchange drew a sharp point into focus.

A member of the Soviet delegation, in an extended but systemic presentation, portrayed the future evolution of Europe as a convergence of East and West. In his view, Europe had been the fulcrum of the cold war, triggered by fears on both sides of the divide. The resulting tensions produced the arms race and defensive reaction from Moscow, which sought to preserve its socialist model and position in Eastern Europe. Now, Moscow sought to find a way out of this confrontation, which had produced economic stagnation in the socialist world. Internal reforms were one vital line of action. Abroad, Moscow was abandoning its messianic policies and seeking to end the division of Europe. The speaker foresaw an evolution toward the creation of "military equilibrium at minimal levels" with both sides maintaining "non-offensive" forces. In this setting, nationalism might be accentuated, but even this would give way to economic integration and interdependence. He concluded by saying that Moscow foresaw a future in which the United States and the Soviet Union would both support "all-European cooperation."

Brzezinski challenged this rose-colored view of the future of the Soviet role in Europe. Specifically, he took issue with what he viewed to be "a superficial symmetry in supposing that the fading of the conflict in Europe will have the same effect on the relations of both superpowers in Europe." He saw as more likely that the United States would achieve a more pervasive presence, while the Soviet Union would be relegated to the periphery. He explained, "The present situation is based on the division of Europe, and the military presence of the superpowers is the key index of their relative positions. With the fading of the confrontation in Europe, the importance of their military presence will diminish. As a result, the importance of other factors—such as ideology, culture, communications, politics, and economics—will rise. In every one of these areas, the United States holds superiority—and a growing superiority—over the Soviet Union." He proceeded to assess the comparative position of the two superpowers in these non-military dimensions of influence and drew a stark conclusion: "The real question is whether the Soviet Union will *retain* a presence in Europe." Summing up the implications of his point, he said, "The only hope for your country in this respect is dramatic internal reform that enables you to take part in these global processes."

Those words had a visibly sobering effect on some members of the Soviet delegation, perhaps confirming their own worst-case assessments. The conference session drew to a close, with participants quietly shuffling out of the room and into the dining hall. Over lunch, Brzezinski was seated with three Soviet participants, all of whom were senior figures from the diplomatic academy or other institutes and had risen to their positions under the Communist system.

Transparently seeking to provoke his counterparts, Brzezinski commented that he continued to be struck by the contrast in the thought patterns of Soviets and Westerners: "The latter think pragmatically, and the former think ideologically. Soviets tend (a) to create slogans, such as perestroika or the 'common European home,' that have no content and then (b) to elaborate a theory about what the slogan means without reference to reality and finally (c) to impose this artificial ideological vision of what is desirable on society." He added that with this kind of thinking, the Soviet Union would never get to the point of solving its problems. "As I think about it," he went on, "it occurs to me that this pattern of thinking is probably partly a result of the fact that your system was founded by a propagandist and sloganeer. And for your country to move out of its present crisis, there really has to be a more explicit break with Leninism, though I understand that this poses serious problems for the legitimacy of the regime."

His gambit succeeded. The outburst from the Soviet side was immediate, and the emotional, and decibel, level of the conversation rose markedly. His tablemates defended Lenin and the merits of the October Revolution and condemned Stalin for distorting the revolution's "deep humanistic aspirations." Pleased with the controversy he had stirred, Brzezinski replied,

But Lenin created the preconditions for Stalin to emerge and, in fact, made it far less likely that someone different from Stalin would emerge to lead the Soviet Union. Leninism was based on three things—a dogmatic ideology, a totalitarian party, and terror. It is one thing to respect Lenin as a political analyst and activist and as a historical figure. But it is another when you ignore the fact that he was the founder of the gulag and that he killed thousands of people simply because they belonged to various ideologically defined classes. Until you renounce the legacy of Leninism, it will impede your reforms and will prevent you from making the necessary break with the past.

Unconsciously slipping into traditional Soviet formulas and rationalizations, one of his Soviet counterparts replied that the gulag existed for the "reeducation of these classes" and that repressive actions had "historically been necessary after revolutions." Another contended that the gulag was necessary "given the situation and political conditions at the time of the revolution." Raising his glass in a toast, the third said, "To perestroika and the gulag." This went too far for the others. Visibly disgusted, one of his compatriots said, "To perestroika but not to the gulag." Yet, even she still insisted, "It is my view that the contradictions within Soviet society required drastic measures to bring the situation under control and to create stability."

Brzezinski countered levelly, "You can make that argument if you want to. But Lenin's intolerance of dissent—even within the party—went far beyond what was necessary to prevent anarchy. And that intolerance made Stalin in some senses inevitable."

⁂ The struggle between official Soviet history and the actual record was most evident during a side trip that Brzezinski took to the site of the Katyn massacre, where the People's Commissariat for Internal Affairs (abbreviated from the Russian as NKVD), the predecessor of the KGB, put to death thousands of Polish officers captured as a result of Stalin and Hitler's division of Poland at the start of World War II. The official Soviet version of events pinned responsibility for the killings on the Nazi forces that captured the area when Germany turned on the Soviet Union in 1941. While glasnost had already led to revisions of official history on many issues, this was not yet the case on Katyn.

Brzezinski took this trip with a handful of members of the American delegation, as well as the U.S. ambassador to Moscow, Jack Matlock. In early evening, the group rode in the ambassador's car to a train station in Moscow, where they would embark for an overnight trip to Smolensk. In the muffled atmosphere of the limousine, Brzezinski recounted what was then known of the history of the Katyn massacre.

He said that the Soviets had captured Polish officers and put them into three camps, where they were interrogated about whether they would be willing to serve in the Soviet armed forces. Several hundred who expressed a willingness to do so survived, and they later reconstructed from memory a list of the others held in their camps. Those who refused enlistment were killed. About 4,500 were put to death at Katyn. The other two camps simply disappeared, though years later a Polish construction crew working in the western parts of the Soviet Union may have happened upon the mass grave of another camp, a discovery that prompted Soviet authorities to evict them from the country. A great deal of physical evidence implicating the Soviet Union in the atrocity came to light when the Red Cross examined the site after Germany exhumed the mass graves. There was even an eyewitness who had been pulled out of the group at the last moment. On the body of one officer, a diary was found, and it gave eloquent testimony to the fact that the Poles were in Soviet hands when they were killed. There was a moment of somber stillness at this point. Then, Brzezinski said that he remembered the last line of the diary, which had later been sent to the officer's daughter. It simply read, "What will become of us?"

When the group reached Smolensk, it was greeted by local Soviet officials. Much to their discomfort, Brzezinski spoke about the massacre and the various sites he wished to visit in a manner that plainly attributed culpability to the Soviet Union. Since the official history still blamed Hitler's forces for the killings, this placed his interlocutors in an ideological no-man's land, requiring them to defend the indefensible while attempting not to be wholly out of touch with reality. At times, members of the Soviet party earnestly plied members of the American group with the Soviet version of events, to little effect. At the site of the massacre was a black-marble monument with an inscription reading "In memory of the Polish officers murdered by the Nazis in 1941." Well away from the monument, Brzezinski laid down a basket of flowers with a signed card that read, "For the victims of Stalin and the NKVD." Other members of the American group added individual red carnations that had been provided by the Soviet hosts.

As the Americans moved on to other parts of the site, a group from Poland organized by a private association, Families of the Katyn Victims, began streaming in through the misty forest. It was All Saints Day or Remembrance Day, in the parlance of atheistic states. This was to be the first visit by a group of relatives of the victims that the Soviet government had ever permitted. It was the result of a high-level decision by Gorbachev's government. The several hundred members of the group were all wearing red-and-white pins embossed with the word *Katyn*. Most were carrying candles, some carrying signs, and a few bearing Polish flags. After touring other areas, the American group passed by the monument again. A memorial mass, organized by the Polish group, was underway. Hundreds of candles dotted the ground where symbolic graves were lined up. An improvised sign with the Polish letters signifying "NKVD" had been posted on top of the word *Nazis* on the monument, thereby correcting the attribution for the massacre.

In press interviews, Brzezinski held up a mirror for Soviet society to understand its own history. He openly discussed with a Soviet television reporter the reality that Stalin's forces carried out the atrocity. When this report was later broadcast, it constituted an unprecedented step forward in airing the historical record. In an interview with BBC, Brzezinski said, "It isn't a personal pain which has brought me here, as in the case of the majority of these people [in the Polish group], but rather recognition of the symbolic nature of Katyn. Russians and Poles, tortured to death, lie here together. It seems very important to me that the truth should be spoken about what took place, for only with the truth can the new Soviet leadership distance itself from the crimes of Stalin and the

NKVD." He later added, "The fact that the Soviet government has enabled me to be here—and the Soviets know my views—is symbolic of the breach with Stalinism that perestroika represents."

❖ It was not just in the struggle over official history that the drama of the end of communism was being played out. This was also happening in the lives of the individuals in the Soviet delegation and other officials whom Brzezinski met during the trip. The most striking was his conversation with a senior aide to Gorbachev who was a key proponent of glasnost. In a private meeting, he told Brzezinski that glasnost not only was changing the Soviet system but also was transforming individual Soviet citizens, himself included. He recounted how the process of abandoning the straightjacket of ideological dogma altered the way he thought about problems and even changed who he was as a person. He said that he and his colleagues noticed this change in themselves and that he, for one, liked much better the person he had become. He then added, "We will never go back."

This transformation also had its lighter side. Members of the Soviet delegation were comfortable openly sharing jokes about the Soviet system. In noting how glasnost had changed the way everyone thought and behaved, a Soviet delegate smiled broadly as he told a story about life under the old system. In the Brezhnev years, subordinates had to toe the line set by their superiors. At one point, Brezhnev had forcefully expressed an opinion on a foreign policy question. Then, turning to his aide, he said, "But we are democratic here. Do you have a different opinion?" After a pause, Brezhnev's assistant answered, "Yes, I have a different opinion, but I don't agree with it."

Another Soviet delegate, with mischievous delight, flaunted political proprieties by telling a joke about the failures of the economy even under glasnost and perestroika. A man was waiting in a long line for bread. When he finally reached the front, all the bread had been sold. Angry, he proceeded to denounce the Soviet system: "There is a shortage of bread. There is a shortage of sugar. There is a shortage of soap. There is a shortage of meat. The system does not work, and we should overthrow it." That night, the KGB knocked on his door, and he was taken downtown. A KGB officer told him that he was aware of his outburst that afternoon and that this kind of behavior was clearly unacceptable. The officer added, "In the old days, you would have been shot for saying those kinds of things." The man went home. "Things are worse than I thought," he said to his wife. "There is now even a shortage of bullets."

A younger member of the Soviet delegation, Vladimir Chernega, recounted how even in the darker days he and others sought the truth at substantial risk to themselves. He expressed an admiration for Brzezinski's scholarly writings, noting that he had snuck a copy of *The Soviet Bloc* out of the closed section of the library in order to read it at home. He said that he was young at the time but already understood that a wide gulf existed between what was written in the Soviet press and what was true in reality. He added that he had read Solzhenitsyn's classic book *The Gulag Archipelago* during the Brezhnev years. Some colleagues at the diplomatic academy had obtained a copy and furtively shared it with each other. He noted that if he had been caught with the book, it would have ended his career. When asked why he took the risk, he said that "a true intellectual must take risks if necessary to seek the truth" and that he would not have been true to his profession if he did not defy such censorship. He spoke with evident pride about the fact that glasnost had made the notion of banned works almost obsolete.

Members of the Soviet group powerfully felt the need to effect irreversible change. In one conversation over breakfast, Brzezinski returned to the theme that for perestroika to succeed Gorbachev needed to articulate more explicitly the type of system he sought to create. His Soviet counterpart responded that Gorbachev "clearly intended to create a market-based economic system and a pluralistic political system based on legality and respect for universal human values." Brzezinski countered that this was far from clear to him. His interlocutor came back with emotion in his voice: "But that *must* come about. The change must involve a radical transformation of the system. Anything less than that will mean the society will fall into the abyss."

⁙ Brzezinski and the other Americans were witnesses to the death throes of communism. What they had seen and experienced was remarkable, even startling at times. The Soviet establishment welcomed and forthrightly engaged a man always cast as an irreconcilable ideological adversary. Senior officials and scholars candidly described their new policies and characterized them as a fundamental break with the Soviet past. Some of these remarks—such as the statement by a senior advisor to Gorbachev that the Brezhnev Doctrine was dead— were such stark policy departures that many in the American delegation found them difficult to accept. At the same time, it was evident that the Soviet reformers were sailing headlong into uncharted waters, convinced of the need to act but unknowingly setting uncontrollable forces and unintended consequences into motion.

The discussions had a significant effect on Brzezinski's thinking. In a press interview touching on his trip about a month later, he said, "There was a breakthrough taking place in the thinking of people who for 70 years were artificially divorced from the intellectual and philosophical currents of the Western world. They are now in the process of restoring some of those connections, of rejoining that process." When asked whether there would be a Soviet Union in the year 2001, he replied without hesitation, "No. There will have to be something very different. The pace of change, the scale of change, and the drama of change are all such that we have to stop thinking in conventional terms."

In the subsequent weeks and months, the pace of historical events accelerated. In early November, the Berlin Wall fell, initiating a process that would lead to the reunification of Germany in 1990. The fall of the Communist regimes in Czechoslovakia, Romania, and Bulgaria soon followed. In February 1990, Gorbachev directed the Communist Party to cede its monopoly on political power. On April 13, 1990, the forty-seventh anniversary of the discovery of the mass graves at Katyn, the Soviet government officially acknowledged its responsibility for the massacre and expressed its "profound regret." In the non-Russian republics, new political forces organized parties and pressed for greater autonomy. Several non-Russian republics held multiparty elections, leading to sweeping defeats of the local Communist parties.

In Moscow, reactionary forces fought back in 1991. Some of the most ardent reformers around Gorbachev were dismissed and even expelled from the Communist Party. In August, hard-liners attempted a coup against Gorbachev. At that time, Shakhnazarov was at a resort in the Crimea, near Gorbachev's, where he was working with the Soviet leader on the draft of a "union treaty" to reform the legal foundation of the Soviet Union itself. He was the last person to speak to Gorbachev before the coup was launched. While the coup was ultimately unsuccessful, falling apart in three days, it was an inflection point.

No longer would the reform of the existing system suffice. Boris Yeltsin, the president of the Russian Republic, had led the opposition in the streets to the coup and mobilized supportive elements in the military. As the leader of Russia, he refused to defer to Gorbachev after the latter returned to Moscow. New leaders in the non-Russian republics, sensing the weakness of the central government, pressed ahead in asserting sovereignty or even declaring independence. On December 8, 1991, Yeltsin and the presidents of the Ukrainian and Belorussian republics annulled the treaty that formed the legal basis of the Soviet Union—effectively dissolving the country—and created in its place the Commonwealth of Independent States. Seventeen days later, on Christmas Day, Gorbachev resigned as president of the Soviet Union, and the Soviet flag was lowered for the last time above the Kremlin.

## Note

1 The conference was the second, and the last, of U.S.-Soviet dialogues organized by the International Research and Exchange Board (IREX), Columbia University's Research Institute on International Change, and the Soviet Academy of Science's Institute for International Economic and Political Studies. Its cochairs were Professor Charles Gati on the American side and Dr. Oleg Bogomolov on the Soviet side. Brzezinski was the most senior member of the American delegation. Other Americans at the second dialogue in Moscow also included Michael Mandelbaum, Strobe Talbott, Mark Palmer, Vernon Aspaturian, William Griffith, Jim Brown, and Angela Stent. The author, who was a fellow in international studies in Brzezinski's office in a Washington think tank, was included in the American group as an observer and note taker. This chapter is based on the author's extensive contemporary notes taken both at the conference and during Dr. Brzezinski's personal meetings with Soviet officials.

# CHAPTER 12

# Brzezinski and Iraq:
# The Makings of a Dove

## JAMES MANN

For the first several decades of his career, Zbigniew Brzezinski was known as a foreign policy hawk—an identification that derived from his tough-minded views on the Soviet Union. It seemed surprising to many, therefore, that during the administration of George W. Bush Brzezinski emerged in the forefront of public debate once again, this time as a determined dove. Starting in 2002, he became a leading opponent of Bush's war in Iraq. Brzezinski proceeded to speak out against the Iraq War earlier and more vigorously than other Democrats, many of whom declined to take a clear stand until a couple of years after the invasion.

What accounts for Brzezinski's migration from the right wing to the left wing of the Democratic foreign policy elite? The first answer that comes to mind is that the end of the cold war and the collapse of the Soviet Union changed the landscape in a way that freed Brzezinski to move on to other concerns and preoccupations. Yet a closer look at the evolution of Brzezinski's stance on Iraq shows that it grew out of some of the same concerns he expressed during the cold war—among them the importance of multilateralism, the strategic importance of oil, and the need for a Middle East peace settlement between Israel and the Palestinians. Opposition to the war in Iraq did not reflect a new Brzezinski, but the old one, cast in a different role.

Brzezinski's stance against the Iraq War of 2003 was noteworthy for a number of reasons. He was among the few foreign policy professionals to dispute the need for both the Persian Gulf War of 1991 and the Iraq War twelve years later. His opposition to both wars set Brzezinski apart from the many Democrats who came out against George H. W. Bush's Gulf War but then turned around and supported (or, at least, refrained from contesting) the Iraq War. At the same time, it also set Brzezinski apart from Republican realists such as Brent Scowcroft, who favored the war in 1991 but opposed the 2003 war in Iraq. Brzezinski's views and reasoning on Iraq, then, were virtually unique. He represented no particular faction and no political party, only himself. Yet he managed to achieve a position of considerable influence in the Iraq debate—a former national security advisor fervently opposing wars against the same country by two different American presidents in two different decades.

He modified his thinking on Iraq in some respects and from time to time. Yet he was, overall, surprisingly consistent in his outlook. What follows is a reconstruction of the evolution of Brzezinski's emergence as a leading opponent of George W. Bush's war in Iraq.

⁘ When the Carter administration took office in 1977, American policy toward the Persian Gulf seemed relatively settled. The United States sought to maintain access to oil from the region and to limit Soviet influence there, but it did so with only a limited military presence in the region. Since the 1950s, America had relied on its strong relations with Turkey, Iran, and Pakistan to block any Soviet drive south toward the Gulf. During the Nixon administration, the United States concentrated in particular on building up Iran as the region power, providing the shah with advanced weaponry.

This policy collapsed with the tumultuous events of the late Carter years: the Iranian Revolution that toppled the shah in 1979 and the Soviet invasion of Afghanistan later that year. In *Power and Principle*, Brzezinski's 1983 memoir of his service as Carter's national security advisor, he wrote that the impact of these upheavals "was a strategic revolution in America's global position."[1] Previously, the United States had focused on the central importance of two regions of the world: Western Europe and East Asia. Now, argued Brzezinski, the Middle East was becoming a critical region for the United States. In his 1980 State of the Union speech, President Carter set forth language drafted by Brzezinski and described as the Carter Doctrine: Any attempt by an outside force to gain control of the Persian Gulf "will be regarded as an assault on the vital interests of the United States of America, and such an assault will be repelled by any means necessary, including military force."[2] The United States began to build up a military presence in the Persian Gulf, starting with a new Rapid Deployment force. Military and strategic competition with the Soviets remained the focus of Brzezinski's thinking about the Persian Gulf throughout the last years of the cold war. In one 1987 article, Brzezinski urged that the United States shift about one hundred thousand troops from Western Europe to the Persian Gulf—an astonishing proposal for the United States, whose roots and early interests were in Europe. Brzezinski wrote this article primarily as a rebuttal to members of Congress who had called for a withdrawal of American forces from the Persian Gulf. At the time, Iran and Iraq were in the midst of their long war, and it appeared Iran could win. Brzezinski's main concern was the Soviet Union, not Iran or Iraq:

> If the Soviet Union were ever to achieve predominance over southwest Asia, Moscow would be able to exert tremendous leverage over our allies in Western Europe and Japan. . . . A U.S. pullout from the Gulf would demonstrate that [Ayatollah] Khomeini and his fellow things are now in control of the Persian Gulf—a strategic defeat ten times worse than the loss of Iran. The major beneficiary of a U.S. retreat would be the Soviet Union. Iranian control of the Gulf would at best be a transitional phase, to be followed by the expansion of Soviet influence, especially as [the] American presence receded. One can only speculate on the political stampede that U.S. failure to act would generate in the weak and valuable Persian Gulf states.[3]

The emphasis of this 1987 article was on unilateral American military power. "The United States must do whatever is necessary to assert Western interests in the Persian Gulf—alone, if necessary." Brzezinski had for years been a strong proponent of multilateralism; in the early 1970s, he had helped to organize the Trilateral Commission to forge cooperation among the United States, Europe, and Japan. But he assumed that America's allies wouldn't help protect the oil on which their economies depended. "In an ideal world," Brzezinski wrote, "U.S. forces patrolling the Persian Gulf would be joined by French, British, Italian, Belgian and Dutch forces, all financed by Japan. That would be a perfect solution. But if that is not possible, it does not necessarily follow that the United States should do nothing. We must recognize that the United States holds the status of a world power, and our allies are simply regional powers."[4]

At the time, Brzezinski made clear that all of his thinking about the Persian Gulf was based on the assumption that the cold war was a permanent fact of life. "My argument is based on the judgment that the American-Soviet conflict is an historical rivalry that will endure for as long as we live," he wrote. He could not imagine that the Soviet Union would endure only another three and a half years, and that his own career would extend more than two decades in a post-Soviet world.

❖ By 1988, Brzezinski had become so unhappy with the drift of the Democratic Party and especially with its presidential nominee Michael Dukakis that he came out in support of the Republican nominee George H. W. Bush. This was an extraordinary step: Bush was, after all, the loyal vice president to Ronald Reagan, who had thrown the Carter administration and Brzezinski himself out of office. Moreover, Dukakis's principal foreign policy advisor in the 1988 campaign was Madeleine Albright, a former member of Brzezinski's National Security Council staff and, before that, his former student at Columbia University. Yet Brzezinski considered Dukakis a novice in international affairs: "Mr. Dukakis's comments during the course of the primary campaign reveal a combination of extensive ignorance and very strong antimilitarist impulses," Brzezinski told the magazine *Defense Week* that fall. He said that Dukakis erred in attributing the Soviet Union's willingness to enter into arms control with the United States to Mikhail Gorbachev's goodwill, rather than the fact that the Reagan administration was bargaining from a position of strength. (In that same 1988 *Defense Week* interview, Brzezinski was asked who might be good candidates for secretary of defense or national security advisor. "Brent Scowcroft, John Tower [and] Don Rumsfeld are exceptionally able people," he replied.)[5]

The endorsement of Bush was a reminder, if any was needed, that Brzezinski's interest in foreign policy took precedence over partisan concerns. It provides perspective on his subsequent decision to take a strong stand against George H. W. Bush's Persian Gulf War. Other Democrats who opposed that war—such as Senators George Mitchell, Edward M. Kennedy, and Sam Nunn—could be accused of political calculation, namely, a need to find an issue against the Republican president they had opposed. For Brzezinski, who had endorsed Bush, such criticism didn't work.

In the weeks immediately after Saddam Hussein sent his forces into Kuwait on August 2, 1990, Brzezinski set down the outlines of the position to which he held throughout the half-year buildup to the war: America should go to war if Saddam Hussein were to go further and invade Saudi Arabia, but he was opposed to the use of force to dislodge Saddam Hussein's forces from Kuwait. "I think American interests ... are vitally engaged in the protection of Saudi Arabia, therefore assuring us of a stable access to reasonably priced oil," Brzezinski said in an interview on the *MacNeil/Lehrer NewsHour* on August 21, 1990. "That's the vital interest, one in which we cannot compromise, which we must defend ourselves." Getting Iraqi forces out of Kuwait would be "desirable, but it is not vital,"[6] he said. He envisioned that it might be possible for the Arab states to negotiate some sort of compromise—a withdrawal of Iraqi forces from Kuwait, "but also some arrangements giving the Iraqis some access to some aspects of Kuwaiti assets." Writing in the *New York Times* that fall, Brzezinski suggested an adjudication of Iraq's financial and territorial claims against Kuwait leading up to the invasion, "not all of which were unfounded."[7]

Brzezinski's opposition was based largely on broad strategic considerations, not on the details of the dispute between Iraq and Kuwait. He repeatedly called for the United States to act in partnership with other countries and not to be the "spearhead" of a campaign against Iraq. His broadest argument concerned the United States' role in the world after the cold war: "America is really riding high," he said in the August interview, "and the last thing I would like to see happen is the United States now become embroiled largely in an American war against the Arabs in the Middle East, which could happen if we go too far out front."[8] In another *NewsHour* appearance in January 1991, just after the start of the war, Brzezinski warned acidly, "We have to look critically beyond the slogan 'New World Order' we have been talking about and ask ourselves, is there really a new world order, or is there an order based on the supremacy of one superpower, namely the United States?"[9]

He warned about the harmful consequences of the use of force in the Persian Gulf. In doing so, he voiced concerns that seem farsighted, particularly in light of the second Iraq War a decade later. (He pointed to the costs of a prolonged war: up to $1 billion a day for American taxpayers—a figure that proved roughly accurate during George W. Bush's war but not in 1991.) He worried about destabilization of the Middle East and of Iraq itself. If Iraq was defeated and Saddam Hussein fell from power, Brzezinski asked, "how far do we go to establish a new authority [in Iraq]? I'm not sure we have really thought about that." Moreover, he added, if Iraq was devastated by war, "there is the risk that Iran will then be the No. 1 geopolitical power in the Persian Gulf. How do we accept that?"[10]

He was not prescient in all respects. In particular, Brzezinski's sense of strategy looks much better in hindsight than his military analysis. He helped give credence to the arguments of Democratic political leaders who were saying that a war would result in heavy American casualties. In an op-ed for the *New York Times*, he described the Iraqi Army as "battle-tested and experienced in defensive fighting. Since it is almost certain that the brunt of the military effort would have to be undertaken by American forces, one must expect therefore also thousands of deaths among American servicemen."[11] There was a certain irony in his underestimation of American military power: the new precision-guided weapons that were unveiled in the Gulf War and proved so important to its outcome were put into development by the Carter administration, in the Pentagon of Defense Secretary Harold Brown and a future defense secretary, William Perry.

In the months leading up to the Gulf War, Brzezinski condemned the use of strong rhetoric, such as in Bush's comparisons of Saddam Hussein to Adolf Hitler. He repeatedly urged a strategy of relying on economic sanction, rather than war. Even if Saddam Hussein were to develop nuclear weapons, Brzezinski said, the problem could be handled through deterrence, not the use of force. "America has lived for 40 years under the shadow of Soviet nuclear weapons, and Stalin or Khrushchev had no compunctions about killing those weaker than themselves," he said. "But deterrence worked, and America surely has the power to deter Iraq as well."[12]

As it happened, the Bush administration managed to pull together considerably greater cooperation between the United States and its allies than Brzezinski had envisioned, leading to a quick victory for the American-led coalition. Yet Saddam Hussein did not fall from power after the defeat, as the Bush administration believed he might. After the end of the war, and throughout the 1990s, Brzezinski continued to question American policy toward Iraq and the Gulf.

When the Bush administration in its final days in office launched another missile attack against Iraq, Brzezinski said the military strikes were "tactical in nature" and "do not deal with the heart of the problem, which is the feeling of frustration, embitterment of the Arab masses." He warned that the Gulf War coalition might erode, leaving the United States aligned only with the former colonial powers, Britain and France. "It's important to us to have the Egyptians, the Saudis, the Syrians and, further back, the Moroccans with us. And we can only sustain their support if we develop a wider policy toward the problems in the Middle East."[13] That was a reference to the need for a peace settlement between Israel and Palestine, an idea that became a frequent theme for Brzezinski.

Later in 1993, when the Clinton administration struck Iraq for the first time in retaliation for Saddam Hussein's plotting to assassinate former President Bush, Brzezinski put forward what became another frequent theme: the need to keep Iraq in perspective and to consider it not in isolation, but in relationship to Iran. "We have to be very careful to maintain some sort of a balance in the Persian Gulf, balance in our attitude regarding the threats posed by Iraq and by Iran," he said on CNN. "In fact, Iran poses the bigger threat, even though Iraq may be the bigger problem, and we should keep that distinction in mind."[14]

The Clinton White House seemed to heed this advice. During Clinton's first term, his administration adopted a policy of dual containment of both Iran and Iraq, along the lines Brzezinski had been proposing. After several years, however, Brzezinski began to have qualms about this policy and the way it was being applied.

In 1996, the Council on Foreign Relations (CFR) appointed Brzezinski as cochair of a task force to examine American policy in the Persian Gulf, along with another former national security advisor, Brent Scowcroft. The two men had taken strikingly different positions on the Gulf War; for Scowcroft, the overriding issue was that Saddam Hussein had invaded Kuwait, whereas Brzezinski viewed that fact as merely one of a number of strategic considerations in the larger Middle East. But by the mid-1990s, the two men were thinking along the same lines, each applying in similar fashion the ideas of foreign policy realism that they shared. Their partnership would reemerge in the George W. Bush administration, when the two became leading opponents of the American invasion of Iraq.

The triggering event that prompted the Council study appears to have been the Iran and Libya Sanctions Act of 1996 (ILSA), passed by the Republican-led Congress. The law imposed unilateral American economic sanctions on companies doing business with Iran; America's allies, particularly in Europe, were extremely unhappy with this new provision. The report of Brzezinski's and Scowcroft's CFR task force, issued in 1997, was given the title "Differentiated Containment." The study concluded that it was time to show more flexibility in policies toward both Iran and Iraq. "The international consensus on continuing the containment of Iraq is fraying," wrote Brzezinski and Scowcroft, along with Richard Murphy, the staff director of the task force. The "strident" American campaign to isolate Iran wasn't working, either, their report said. The United States needed "a more nuanced" approach, they wrote: "This new policy would keep Saddam boxed in, but would supplement such resolve with policy modifications to keep the Gulf War coalition united." The report also argued that Iran was of greater geopolitical importance than Iraq; the United States should recognize that "the United States' current attempt at unilateral isolation of Iran is costly and ineffective." One of their recommendations was that the United States explore "creative tradeoffs" with Iran, "such as the relaxation of opposition to the Iranian nuclear program in exchange for rigid and comprehensive inspection and control procedures." More generally, Brzezinski and Scowcroft said, "It is imperative that all parties understand an important strategic reality: the United States is in the Persian Gulf to stay. The security and independence of the region is a vital U.S. interest. Any accommodation with a post-Saddam region in Iraq or with a less hostile government in Iran must be based on that fact." Brzezinski was explicitly returning to the fundamentals of the Carter Doctrine.[15]

By the late 1990s, Brzezinski's own individual critiques of Clinton's Iraq policy were becoming ever more caustic. "We have lost our sense of balance and proportion regarding Iraq," he declared in late 1998, shortly after the Clinton administration launched a new round of intense bombardment of Iraq. "We talk of Iraq as if it was Nazi Germany. It's a poor, 22-million people country, devastated by the embargo and the strikes. It is a problem and a nuisance; it's not a major world threat."[16]

In fact, Brzezinski argued in the same television interview, Saddam Hussein's menacing rule in Iraq could ironically be said to serve America's larger purposes in the Middle East. "He's even useful to us, because it enhances the dependence of the Gulf States and of Saudi Arabia and others without protection—so it reinforces our position in the region, whereas otherwise the Arabs might be turning against us, in part because of the Israeli conflict and so forth."[17]

Thus, by the time George W. Bush arrived in the White House, Brzezinski had already demonstrated (1) more than two decades of advocacy for a strong American presence in the Persian Gulf, as a strategic requirement for secure access to oil; (2) a generally strong view that the United States should act in concert with its allies; (3) a determined belief in the need for an Israeli-Palestinian peace settlement; and (4) a frequent willingness to challenge U.S. policy toward the Persian Gulf in public, sometimes in biting language.

❖ Because Brzezinski eventually came to be known as one of the leading critics of the invasion of Iraq, it may seem as though he must have been opposed to military action from the moment the idea was broached. But that assumption does not bear scrutiny. A close examination of his public statements shows that in the three months after the September 11 attacks, as the Bush administration first began to mention the possibility of attacking Iraq, Brzezinski was open to the idea, at least under some conditions. It was only the following year, as U.S. officials began to move in more determined fashion toward an invasion and as the connection between Iraq and the September 11 attacks became increasingly attenuated, that Brzezinski became a staunch opponent of going to war.

Two weeks after the attacks on the World Trade Center and Pentagon, Brzezinski wrote an op-ed for the *Wall Street Journal* on how the United States should respond. In the short term, there should be immediate military action against al-Qaeda "to underline America's commitment to the campaign against terrorism and, to put it bluntly, to exact painful retribution." The more difficult question, he argued, was what should come after that initial stage of the war in Afghanistan. The Bush administration should "focus on governments that have tolerated tacitly or secretly supported terrorist organizations, or perhaps even colluded in terrorist acts," Brzezinski said. "*If collusion is reasonably determined—for example, if Saddam Hussein provided organizational or planning assistance to the recent outrage—direct U.S. military action to destroy such a regime would be not only justified, but required"* (emphasis added).[18]

Six weeks later, Brzezinski added a corollary: the case against Iraq for supposed involvement in the September 11 attacks wouldn't have to be proved beyond a reasonable doubt, either. "The explosive character of the Middle Eastern tinderbox, and the fact that Iraq has the motive, the means, and the psychopathology to provide truly dangerous aid to the terrorist underground, cannot be ignored on the legalistic grounds that conclusive 'evidence' is lacking of Iraq's involvement in September 11."[19]

At this point, Brzezinski seemed to be accepting some of the arguments of the administration's hawks concerning Iraq. In the wake of September 11, some commentators had predicted that the Bush administration would of necessity have to rely on allies and friends more than it did during its early months in office, when it had displayed a strong streak of unilateralism. In this op-ed, Brzezinski said he disagreed. "The bottom line is that in facing the challenge posed by terrorism, the heavy lifting will have to be done by the United States largely on its own," he asserted.[20]

Even during this initial phase, however, Brzezinski offered some views that diverged from those of the administration. He argued that the campaign against terrorists would have to deal with "some, if not all, of the political resentments that galvanize support for terrorism." He contended that in fashioning a long-term response to September 11, the administration should "focus on shaping a world-wide coalition of states."[21] Most significantly, Brzezinski warned that strong action against Saddam Hussein "could hardly be mounted in the context of continued Israeli-Palestinian violence."[22]

In the first half of 2002, several developments turned Brzezinski decisively against the administration. At the beginning of the year, Bush delivered the State of the Union address in which he lumped together Iran, Iraq, and North Korea as an "axis of evil." That was precisely the sort of moralistic language that tended to offend Brzezinski—much as he had objected a decade earlier to George H. W. Bush's efforts to compare Saddam Hussein to Adolf Hitler. Moreover, the "axis of evil" speech galvanized European opposition to the Bush administration and thus made it more difficult to form an international coalition, another of Brzezinski's concerns. Later that spring, there was escalating violence in and around Israel, the West Bank, and the Gaza Strip. Israel seized weaponry and rockets it said were being shipped from Iran to the Palestinians. There was a wave of suicide bombings by Arabs inside Israel, including one that killed twenty-nine Israelis as they were sitting down for a Passover Seder. The Israeli government of

Ariel Sharon countered by sending troops, tanks, and helicopters on a military offensive in the West Bank.

In Washington, members of the Bush administration were intensely divided over these events involving Israel—and over what they meant for the idea of possible military action against Saddam Hussein. The hawks, led by Vice President Dick Cheney, believed that the way to make progress toward a Middle East peace settlement was to make the Palestinian leaders more accommodating. Many of the hawks had been closely involved in the Persian Gulf War. The intimidating use of force there had for a time left Palestinian leader Yasser Arafat alienated from most other Arab states; the hawks of 2002 hoped to isolate Arafat again in similar fashion. Thus, they believed a war against Iraq should precede a drive for an Arab-Israeli peace settlement.[23]

The other faction within the Bush administration, led by Secretary of State Colin Powell, believed the opposite: that the United States should press hard for Middle East peace *before* it took on Saddam Hussein. Powell and others at the State Department contended that in order to succeed against Iraq, the Bush administration needed to win the support of other Arab governments. The Israeli military campaign and ensuing crackdown in the Palestinian territories made it impossible for the United States to put together a broad coalition against Iraq.

Cheney and Powell made separate trips to the Middle East in the spring of 2002. Powell recommended that Bush call for an international peace conference on the Middle East, but in the end, Cheney's view won out. In midyear the president delivered a major speech calling not for a peace conference, but for a new Palestinian leadership, chosen through democratic elections, to replace Arafat. Brzezinski had been on Powell's side of this argument. He was little more than a bystander to the back-and-forth inside the administration, but he was more than casually interested in the outcome. He had been closely involved in the Carter administration's Camp David Accords. In the aftermath of September 11, he had emphasized how important a Middle East peace settlement would be for American interests in the region.

In the summer of 2002, the administration started to make its case to the public and to Congress for military action in Iraq. The cutting-edge issue within the administration, in fact, was not whether to go to war but whether there was a need to go to the United Nations for authorization to do so. It was at that point that Brzezinski came out strongly in public opposition to the administration. He was working in parallel with Scowcroft, who had been only a few years earlier his cochair on the CFR's task force on the Persian Gulf. In mid-August, Scowcroft, who had been a mentor to Bush's national security advisor Condoleezza Rice, wrote an op-ed for the *Wall Street Journal* that carried the punchy headline "Don't Attack Saddam."[24] Three days later, in the Sunday *Washington Post*, Brzezinski launched his own broadside against the Bush team. It was his most important single article, encompassing virtually all the arguments he had been developing concerning Iraq, a few new ones, and some acerbic language as well. "War is too serious a business and too unpredictable in its dynamic consequences . . . to be undertaken because of a personal peeve, demagogically articulated fears or vague factual assertions," Brzezinski wrote. The president needed to offer the nation "a carefully reasoned case, without sloganeering, on the specifics of the threat."[25]

Moreover, Brzezinski went on, "as the United States positions itself for war, it must become more active in pacifying the Israeli-Palestinian conflict by pressuring both sides." If it failed to do so, he said, "there is a high risk that a U.S. assault on Iraq will be perceived in the region (and probably also in Europe) as part of an American-Israeli effort to impose a new order on the Middle East without regard for either Iraqi or Palestinian civilian casualties."

The new idea Brzezinski put forward was the importance of a plan for postwar Iraq. The Bush administration should start to talk with its allies, he said, "regarding possible postwar arrangements for Iraq, including a prolonged collective security presence and plans for international financing of the social rehabilitation of the country." Doing this would make the American position more credible with its allies. Finally, Brzezinski moved beyond Iraq to the broader strategic implications of unilateral action and to what it would mean for America's role in the world. "If it is to be war, it should be conducted in a manner that legitimizes U.S. global hegemony and, at the same time, contributes to a more responsible system of international security," he argued. "Ultimately, what is at stake is something far greater than Iraq. It is the character of the international system and the role in it of what is, by far, the most powerful state."[26]

His *Washington Post* op-ed set the tone for what followed. Appearing on a Sunday talk show two weeks later, Brzezinski was asked about Vice President Cheney's assertion that sending international inspectors to Iraq would merely result in false assurances that Saddam Hussein had no weapons of mass destruction (WMDs). Brzezinski's answer: "What the Vice President is saying is, we don't know if he has weapons, of what kind, we don't know where they are, we'll never find them—but we are going to go in there and destroy them. It just isn't very logical."[27] Over and over again through the fall of 2002 and early months of 2003, in a series of newspaper commentaries and television interviews, he questioned the rationale for war, insisted on the necessity of forming a broad coalition of nations to participate in it, and stressed the importance of moving toward peace between Israelis and Palestinians as crucial to obtaining international support. A decision by the Bush administration to act alone, without the support of the United Nations, "is more likely to leave America holding the bag during the possibly painful and expensive aftermath of the war," wrote Brzezinski. "The financial costs to America are likely to be enormous."[28] Still, and despite his continuing objections, Brzezinski always left open the possibility that there were some circumstances in which he could support military action: if the United States were to act in concert with other nations, in response to Saddam Hussein's clear and flagrant violations of United Nations resolutions.

That fall, the Bush administration obtained authorization from Congress for the use of force against Iraq. Their votes for this legislation would later come back to haunt Democratic senators John Kerry, Hillary Clinton, John Edwards, and Joe Biden. Yet, surprising as it may seem today, Brzezinski, the most prominent Democratic critic of the war, said he would have voted with them. In an interview on CNN, there occurred the following exchange:

> WOLF BLITZER. Dr. Brzezinski, had you been a member of the Congress and asked to vote on that resolution authorizing the use of force for President Bush if necessary against Iraq, would you have voted yea or nay?

> BRZEZINSKI. I probably would have voted yea, particularly because the vote came after [Bush's] September 12 speech, when the president made it clear that going to war unilaterally on a solitary basis was the last resort, and only (if) the threat was imminent, and the president went out of his way at the UN not to define the threat as imminent but as a grave and gathering one.[29]

On February 5, 2003, when Secretary of State Colin Powell made his now-famous presentation to the United Nations describing the American intelligence on Iraq's supposed possession of WMDs, Brzezinski voiced strong support for Powell. "I thought he made a very impressive presentation. I thought it was quite compelling," he declared on television that night. "I also felt this was the first genuinely effective case the administration has made that Iraq presents a long-term grave and gathering threat—and hopefully it lays the basis for more united international cooperation on Iraq to comply or for coercion if it does not."[30]

However, over the following weeks, as it became clear that the Bush administration was moving toward war without the international support he had recommended, Brzezinski came out finally and conclusively against military action, on grounds that there should be more time for diplomacy. "The United States should be willing to give the U.N. inspections and verification process in Iraq the several months needed to establish more clearly whether Iraq is grudgingly complying or deliberately evading," he wrote in the *Washington Post*.[31] He concluded one television interview with these words: "We are the number-one power. We have to lead. But our leadership depends also on being viewed as legitimate. We have to mobilize people on behalf of shared principles. And this is where we have really fallen down."[32] The Bush administration ignored such advice. Having failed to obtain a United Nations resolution in support of the immediate use of force, the United States launched the war on March 19, 2003, with modest support from British, Australian, and Polish forces.

✥ Virtually all of Brzezinski's writing about Iraq before the invasion occurred was aimed at answering a conditional question: *If* Iraq had WMDs, what should the United States do about it? Brzezinski had argued that the principal aim of American policy should be to deal with WMDs in Iraq, not to bring about regime change. He had raised the possibility that the problem of WMDs could be dealt with through a policy of deterrence rather than military invasion. And he had argued that any military action should be carried out by a broad international coalition.

Six weeks after American forces entered Iraq, Bush announced an end to major combat operations and in effect declared victory, standing in front of the famous banner that read "Mission Accomplished." But within a few weeks, it was becoming clear that the premise on which the entire prewar debate had been framed—the assumption that Iraq possessed nuclear, chemical, and/or biological weapons—was false. American forces occupying Iraq found no WMDs of any kind.

It was at this point that Brzezinski turned into the determined, vehement opponent of the Iraq War that Americans came to see on their television screens over the following five years. If others in the Washington foreign policy community found cause to hedge their criticisms, Brzezinski did not. The contrast with Henry Kissinger, another former national security advisor and Brzezinski's old Harvard classmate, was particularly striking. The two men appeared together on CNN in the summer of 2003. The question at hand was whether the Bush administration had misled the American public and the rest of the world in its claims about Iraq. CNN's Wolf Blitzer asked both of the former national security advisors whether anyone in the administration or in the intelligence community should resign. "I don't think anyone should resign," replied Kissinger. "We should analyze where the problem arose but I don't think this was a central element in the president's decision."

Brzezinski's response was biting:

The United States stated, at the highest level, repeatedly, without any qualification whatsoever, that Iraq was armed with weapons of mass destruction. Not just nuclear, but bacteriological and chemical. . . . And that is why we went to war. This is what we said to the world. This is what we said to the American people. It's clear that they weren't armed with these weapons. They didn't use them. We defeated their army in the field. We have control over their arsenals. We haven't found them. We're now maintaining that they may be hidden somewhere, which is kind of comical, actually. If they had them, and they were armed to the teeth with them, why didn't they use them? If they didn't use them and hid them, that means they were deterred. . . . Was the administration misled by very poor intelligence? In which case, some heads should roll in the intelligence community, absolutely, because an intelligence failure at this scale totally destroys American global credibility. Or was anyone in the administration hyping it while the intelligence was qualifying it? And that has to be established.[33]

Kissinger persisted, raising the question of whether the U.S. intelligence had been correct at the time it was gathered, but that the Iraqis subsequently destroyed or hid the weaponry. "I believe that, in essence, he [Bush] was right, even if it now turns out that some of these weapons may have been destroyed," Kissinger said. Brzezinski debunked that idea, too. He acknowledged that he, like many others, had believed the American intelligence briefings asserting that the Iraqis possessed WMDs. "The fact nonetheless—and we cannot evade it—is that they did not. . . . I mean, if they did, show them to me. They didn't use them. They weren't in their arsenals. We have been there for months, and we haven't found them."[34]

Over the following two years, Brzezinski further hardened his position. Writing in the *New Republic* in mid-2004, he asserted that the "increasingly messy Iraqi adventure" had its roots in "the extremist foreign policy pursued by this administration." In this piece, Brzezinski put forth what would become a new refrain: the United States should set a timetable for pulling out of Iraq. "Without a fixed and early date for U.S. troop withdrawal, the occupation will become an object of intensified Iraqi hostility," he asserted.[35]

Because the call for withdrawal later became commonplace for Democrats and liberals, it is hard to remember now how unusual it was for Brzezinski to have done so in mid-2004. At the time, there were vague and expectable calls for America to pull out from those who had opposed the war in the first place. But there were hardly any from members of the foreign policy elite, whose members generally accepted the old bromides about "staying the course." Having intervened, it was argued, the United States could not pull out without disastrous consequences.

Senator Edward M. Kennedy, perhaps the strongest opponent of the war in the Senate, called for an immediate withdrawal in early 2005. Later that year, Senator Russell Feingold attracted headlines by urging withdrawal in eighteen months—but news stories about Feingold's proposal pointed out that other prominent senators, including Hillary Clinton, Joe Biden, and Minority Leader Harry Reid, refused to join him. In the House, Minority Leader Nancy Pelosi took the lead in opposing the Iraq War, but she did not formally propose a withdrawal until the fall of 2006.[36] Brzezinski was at least a year or two in advance of most Democrats in calling for a withdrawal.

By the end of Bush's term, Brzezinski was regularly condemning the Iraq War in sweeping terms. "We were viewed by most people in the Middle East, particularly after World War II, as a liberating force," he observed in 2008. "That gradually changed, to the point that we've become the new colonialists, particularly through our military intervention in Iraq, our one-sided support for [Israeli Prime Minister Ariel] Sharon under George W. Bush, and a kind of generalized indifference to what is happening to the Palestinians."[37]

In sum, Brzezinski's views played a prominent role in the public debates over Iraq, lending high-level credibility to the opponents of the war. He became a frequent critic of American foreign policy, a hero to those on the political left who had (or would have) derided his strong positions against the Soviet Union during the cold war.

Not surprisingly, these views made him increasingly the target of right-wing attack. After he and Scowcroft came out against the war, columnist Charles Krauthammer accused the two men of "exhibiting nostalgia for containment and nuclear deterrence." They seemed to long for the cold war, Krauthammer said, when the Soviet Union could be inhibited by the threat of retaliation, in a way that wouldn't work with Saddam Hussein.[38] On the eve of the invasion, the *Weekly Standard* called Brzezinski "demented" and accused him of having been afflicted with *"algoreitis simplex,* the mysterious brain infection so named for its most obvious manifestation: the eagerness of its victims to indulge in ludicrously exaggerated condemnations of George W. Bush's war on terrorism."[39]

His detractors sometimes dwelled on Brzezinski's role in the Carter administration, blaming Brzezinski for its sins and straining to explain its relevance to contemporary circumstances. "As for Mr. Brzezinski's indictment [of Iraq policy]—most of us would still prefer the United States of 2005 to the chaotic America of 1977–80 under an administration that did little to confront the rise of Islamic fundamentalism," wrote Victor David Hanson.[40] The *Wall Street Journal*, referring to Brzezinski's birth in Warsaw, at one point accused Brzezinski of applying different standards to Iraq than he would have to his homeland. "We get even Zbigniew Brzezinski, who spent his career fighting for the freedom of his native Poland, dismissing its prospects in Baghdad," said the newspaper in its European edition. "What a disappointing spectacle."[41]

American liberals began to treat him as their guiding light. In 2004, the Center for American Progress, which had just been formed as a new Washington think tank expressly devoted to promoting liberal views, chose Brzezinski as its keynote speaker for a conference on developing a new national security policy for the United States. (In his address, Brzezinski denounced the George W. Bush administration for "extremist demagogy" and for promoting a "paranoiac view of the world" through its with-us-or-against-us philosophy.)[42] Liberal magazines such as the *American Prospect* and the *Nation* regularly praised Brzezinski for his wisdom.[43]

Perhaps the most fitting tribute to Brzezinski's influence over the Democrats on Iraq came from one of his neoconservative critics. In the spring of 2007, just as the next presidential campaign was beginning, the Middle East specialist Reuel Marc Gerecht lamented the unwillingness of the Democrats to support Bush's decision for a surge in new American troops to Iraq. "This is not the time for talk of timetables for withdrawal—much less talk of a war that is lost," wrote Gerecht in a signed editorial for the magazine. "Do thoughtful Democrats really believe that the Middle East, America's long fight against Sunni jihadism, and our standing in the world against potential aggressors and bullies will be improved by a precipitous and mandated departure from Mesopotamia? The Democratic Party is beginning to sound like an echo chamber for Zbigniew Brzezinski."[44]

## NOTES

1  Zbigniew Brzezinski, *Power and Principle: Memoirs of the National Security Adviser 1977–1981* (New York: Farrar, Straus, Giroux, 1983), 454.

2  Jimmy Carter, State of the Union Address, January 23, 1980.

3  Zbigniew Brzezinski, "We Need More Muscle in the Gulf, Less in NATO," *Washington Post*, Outlook section, June 7, 1987, B-1.

4  Ibid.

5 David J. Lynch, "Jimmy Carter Confidant Brzezinski Tells Why He Jumped Ship For Bush," *Defense Week*, October 3, 1988, 8.

6 Zbigniew Brzezinski, interview, *MacNeil/Lehrer NewsHour*, PBS, August 21, 1990.

7 Zbigniew Brzezinski, "Patience in the Persian Gulf, Not War," *New York Times*, October 7, 1990, A-19.

8 Brzezinski interview, *NewsHour*, August 21, 1990.

9 Zbigniew Brzezinski, interview, *MacNeil/Lehrer NewsHour*, PBS, January 17, 1991.

10 Ibid.

11 Brzezinski, "Patience in the Persian Gulf."

12 Ibid.

13 Zbigniew Brzezinski, interview with David French, CNN, January 17, 1993.

14 Zbigniew Brzezinski, interview with Frank Sesno, CNN, January 28, 1993.

15 Zbigniew Brzezinski, Brent Scowcroft, and Richard Murphy, "Differentiated Containment," *Foreign Affairs* 76, no. 3 (May/June 1997): 20–30.

16 Zbigniew Brzezinski, interview, *NewsHour with Jim Lehrer*, PBS, December 21, 1998.

17 Ibid.

18 Zbigniew Brzezinski, "A Plan for Political Warfare," *Wall Street Journal*, September 25, 2001, A-18.

19 Zbigniew Brzezinski, "A New Age of Solidarity? Don't Count on It," *Washington Post*, November 2, 2001, A-29.

20 Ibid.

21 Brzezinski, "Plan for Political Warfare."

22 Brzezinski, "New Age of Solidarity?"

23 See James Mann, *Rise of the Vulcans: The History of Bush's War Cabinet* (New York: Viking Press, 2004), 322–27.

24 Brent Scowcroft, "Don't Attack Saddam," *Wall Street Journal*, August 15, 2002, A-12.

25 Zbigniew Brzezinski, "If We Must Fight . . . ," *Washington Post*, August 18, 2002, B-7.

26 Ibid.

27 Zbigniew Brzezinski interview, *This Week with Sam Donaldson and Cokie Roberts*, ABC News, September 1, 2002.

28 Zbigniew Brzezinski, "The End Game," *Wall Street Journal*, December 23, 2002, A-23.

29 Zbigniew Brzezinski, interview, *CNN Late Edition with Wolf Blitzer*, CNN, October 20, 2002.

30 Zbigniew Brzezinski, interview, *NewsHour with Jim Lehrer*, PBS, February 5, 2003.

31 Zbigniew Brzezinski, "Why Unity Is Essential," *Washington Post*, February 19, 2003, A-29.

32 Zbigniew Brzezinski, interview, *Early Show*, CBS News, March 10, 2003.

33 Henry Kissinger and Zbigniew Brzezinski, interviews, *CNN Late Edition with Wolf Blitzer*, CNN, July 13, 2003.

34 Ibid.

35 Zbigniew Brzezinski, "Lowered Vision," *New Republic*, June 7, 2004, 16.

36 Peter Baker and Shailagh Murray, "Democrats Split over Position on Iraq War," *Washington Post*, August 22, 2005, A-1; Adam Nagourney, "Democrats Turned War into an Ally," *New York Times*, November 9, 2006, A-1.

37  Zbigniew Brzezinski and Brent Scowcroft, *America and the World: Conversations on the Future of American Foreign Policy*, mod. David Ignatius (New York: Basic Books, 2008), 93.

38  Charles Krauthammer, "The Obsolescence of Deterrence," *Weekly Standard*, December 9, 2002.

39  "Profiles in Chutzpah," *Weekly Standard*, March 18, 2003.

40  Victor Davis Hanson, "An American 'Debacle'?," *National Review Online*, October 14, 2005, www.nationalreview.com/articles/215681/american-debacle/victor-davis-hanson.

41  Unsigned editorial, *Wall Street Journal* (Brussels), January 31, 2005, A-8.

42  James Traub, "The Things They Carry," *New York Times Magazine*, January 4, 2004, 28.

43  See, for example, Ari Berman, "The Democrats: Still Ducking," *Nation*, March 27, 2006, www.thenation.com/article/democrats-still-ducking; "A Conversation with Zbigniew Brzezinski," *American Prospect*, June 2007, 12.

44  Reuel Marc Gerecht, "On Democracy in Iraq," *Weekly Standard*, April 30, 2007.

# CHAPTER 13

# Solving
# the Arab-Israeli Conflict

DAVID IGNATIUS

It's telling that Zbigniew Brzezinski became a committed supporter of Jimmy Carter in 1975 after the two men talked about the need for Arab-Israeli peace. As Brzezinski recounts the story in his memoirs, he and Carter attended a meeting of the Trilateral Commission in Kyoto, Japan. "Carter spoke forcefully and clearly on behalf of a fair Middle East settlement as very much in the U.S. national interest" and, later, propounded his candidacy at a press conference to which he invited Brzezinski.[1] This was a "turning point," says Brzezinski, and when he returned home he told his wife about the Middle East comments and "how impressed I was by Carter generally."[2] That set the ball rolling, in ways that altered history.

Brzezinski's commitments to Arab-Israeli peace, and his willingness to make political enemies in trying to achieve it, are among the defining themes of his career. Though he began as a specialist in the Soviet Union, with little early interest or experience in the Middle East, the region came to be a primary concern. This is a terrain where many American foreign policy intellectuals trim their views for fear of offending powerful interest groups, but Brzezinski has been outspoken, occasionally to a fault. And he has been consistent, ever since he began to think seriously about the issue in the mid-1970s, in advocating a comprehensive settlement that includes an eventual Palestinian state, rather than a more limited "step-by-step" approach.

Brzezinski has a contrarian streak—a feisty side of his personality that seems to relish a principled fight, all the more if it's an unpopular cause. This quality has been evident in his involvement with the Arab-Israeli issue. One story, from his pre–White House days, illustrates this contrarianism: Like scores of prominent politicians and analysts over many decades, Brzezinski in 1976 was given a tour of Israel and meetings with top officials. The message the Israelis wanted to impart, which has been embraced by most of the Americans who have taken the tour, is that this tiny country, with barely defensible borders, should not be pressed to make territorial concessions to the Arabs who surround the Jewish state on three sides. Brzezinski took away a quite different lesson, as he explains in his memoirs: "Probably contrary to the expectations of my Israeli hosts, my trip to the Golan and my travels within the country convinced me of the futility of seeking security through the acquisition of territory. It became clear to me that Israel could never acquire enough territory to compensate for Arab hostility—and that therefore the question of Israeli security would have to be decoupled from the question of territorial sovereignty. The extension of Israeli sovereignty would not in and of itself create security, especially if that extension generated greater Arab hostility."[3]

Brzezinski's views about the Arab-Israeli issue began to form after the 1967 war. As he watched U.S. officials struggle with the consequences of Israel's lightning victory and its conquest of the Sinai Peninsula, the Golan Heights, and the West Bank, Brzezinski recalls, "I was struck by the challenge to U.S. interests from the Soviet Union and the challenge for U.S. policymaking because of differences among President Johnson's advisors—some viscerally pro-Israel, some viscerally anti-Israel."[4] Johnson's national security advisor, Walt Rostow, represented the pro-Israel view; the pro-Arab side was embodied by Under Secretary of State George W. Ball. Brzezinski remembers worrying that "emotions were shaping policy," and he decided, "Here's a problem one had better get involved in."[5]

Brzezinski viewed the Arab-Israeli problem as a subset of the cold war through the Nixon years. In 1973, a month after the Yom Kippur War, he wrote an op-ed piece in the *Washington Post* arguing that "the victors in the Yom Kippur were the Arabs and the Soviets." He argued that the Arabs had won politically by avoiding another outright defeat, and that the Russians had gained by helping broker a cease-fire. Interestingly, in an early expression of his skeptical view of Israel, he also observed that "the leverage that the United States has gained over Israel is about the only thing that it has obtained from the crisis."[6]

Brzezinski was early among U.S. policy intellectuals to endorse the idea that the best way out of the Arab-Israeli impasse was through the creation of a Palestinian state. He made this argument in a January 1974 peace proposal published in the *New Leader*. He advocated an autonomous Palestinian state in the West

Bank, federated with Jordan, and a hybrid status for Jerusalem that would allow it to be both the Palestinian and Israeli capital.[7] This was well beyond the step-by-step diplomatic approach that Henry Kissinger would pursue.

The 1974 article is worth noting for its expression of basic themes that Brzezinski has maintained ever since. "What is needed in the present situation is to decouple security from the possession of land," he wrote, arguing for removal of Israeli settlements in the West Bank and Gaza and demilitarization of the occupied territories after they were returned to the Arabs. He also argued for a formal U.S. guarantee of Israel's security, "making the consequences of any aggression against Israel much more serious." By offering his detailed peace plan, Brzezinski was doubtless hoping to be seen as a Democratic advisor who could play at Kissinger's level of diplomatic maneuver. But it's a remarkably farsighted document, staking out positions that are still sound nearly forty years later.

Brzezinski reiterated his argument for a comprehensive settlement—and his critique of Kissinger's more cautious iterative approach—in a 1975 article in *Foreign Policy*.[8] Seeing the Middle East through the prism of his abiding interest in the Soviet Union, Brzezinski argued for a diplomacy that included the Soviets as co-guarantors of peacemaking. This would be a continuing Brzezinski theme in the White House, where he spent his first year as national security advisor trying to organize a U.S.-Soviet-backed peace conference in Geneva.

He refined his critique of Kissinger's approach in a subsequent exchange in *Foreign Policy*, warning that incremental bargaining "expends on marginal settlements Israel's major bargaining assets, and it also uses up American leverage without resolving the central issues (a Palestinian state, Golan, and Jerusalem). As a consequence, the 'step-by step approach' is likely to produce either a stalemate or bitter Arab disunity. . . . That is why we urged that the United States outline explicitly the broad principles of an eventual settlement."[9]

It is noteworthy (if also depressing) that three decades later Brzezinski would make this same argument—for launching negotiations with a broad statement of principles for a settlement—to President Barack Obama. Once more, his proposal was rejected in favor of yet another step-by-step round, this time led by Sen. George Mitchell, Obama's special envoy. Brzezinski made the argument to Obama again, in March 2010, when it was clear that Mitchell's effort was failing. This time he was joined by Brent Scowcroft, another former national security advisor. Once again, this effort failed, and for the same reason: a reluctance to appear to be dictating conditions to Israel. But we are getting ahead of our story.

Brzezinski's growing interest in the Middle East led to his appointment in 1975 to a high-level group organized by the Brookings Institution to study the problem. This panel included some prominent doves in the American Jewish community, including Rita Hauser and Phillip Klutznik, as well as Mideast scholar William Quandt, who would later join Brzezinski's National Security Council staff. Their report called for a "comprehensive settlement," including "Palestinian self-determination" through either an independent state or an entity federated with Jordan.[10] The report and its authors were sharply criticized by pro-Israel supporters, who felt it went too far. Brzezinski saw the Brookings study group as an important formative experience in shaping policy.[11]

Asked in 1976 how his view of the Middle East differed from Kissinger's, Brzezinski gave an interesting answer: "I am perhaps more inclined to stress the need to focus on the questions of what might constitute the basic principles of an eventual settlement, including the necessary trade-offs."[12] He has invoked that rubric often since then, but never entirely successfully. The "basic principles" for resolving the Arab-Israeli dispute have turned out to be harder to implement than anyone could have imagined.

❖ Brzezinski joined the Carter campaign as a foreign policy advisor in 1975, to the consternation of some pro-Israel Democrats who feared a pro-Arab tilt if Carter were nominated and elected. Such was the anxiety in the American Jewish community that Carter was quizzed at a fund-raiser in Philadelphia about having an Arab advisor. When Carter asked who the questioner meant, he was told "Rafshoon"—a reference to Atlanta advertising executive Gerald Rafshoon, who, in fact, was Jewish.[13]

Carter was attracted by Brzezinski's strong views on the Middle East and other issues. He explains in his memoirs: "A few of the people who knew him well cautioned me that Zbig was aggressive and ambitious, and that on controversial subjects, he might be inclined to speak out too forcefully.... Knowing Zbig, I knew that some of these assessments were accurate, but they were in accord with what I wanted."[14]

Carter's initial peacemaking approach was straight from Brzezinski's playbook—an effort to draw the Israelis and Arabs together under the umbrella of a U.S.-Soviet-sponsored peace conference in Geneva. Brzezinski outlined his strategy at the first Policy Review Committee (PRC) meeting on the subject, on February 4, 1977: "My argument was essentially as follows: the time was ripe for a new U.S. initiative and we should seek to develop a comprehensive framework of principles that would serve to guide the ensuing negotiations."[15] But a White House visit by Israeli prime minister Yitzhak Rabin in March went badly, with

Rabin brushing off Carter's attempt at the personal touch by refusing an offer to look in on daughter Amy asleep in her bedroom. Rabin's stiff response no doubt reflected how hard Carter was pushing. Brzezinski quotes from notes he took immediately after the March 7 meeting: "He made it very clear that the U.S. was in favor of rapid negotiations, favored minimum border changes, and that the Palestinians (including the PLO [Palestine Liberation Organization]) would have to be somehow included in the discussions."[16]

The Israelis were unhappy with Carter's peace approach, as well as with his refusal to sell cluster bombs and some other weapons to Israel. Pro-Israel groups in the United States were also upset and launched an initial volley of protests. In contrast, Egyptian president Anwar Sadat's visit to the White House in April went "extremely well,"[17] framing the parameters that would prevail through the next two years of peacemaking.

⋯ From the beginning, Brzezinski was worried about political pressure. He recalls in his memoir "the intensifying attacks by the Jewish community on Carter and, to a lesser extent, on me" during 1977,[18] which led to what he describes as "a large-scale pressure campaign launched by the American-Israeli Political Action Committee." Brzezinski didn't enjoy being a lightning rod: "Hints of this started appearing in *Time* and *Newsweek* magazines and also in the [daily] press. I was presented as anti-Israeli, perhaps even worse than that, and references to my Polish and Catholic background became increasingly pointed in some of the commentaries on the subject of the Middle East."[19] When he protested to Carter, Brzezinski recalls, "he kind of laughed and . . . in effect said that 'this is exactly what we want you to be, the fall guy' or something to that effect."

This suspicion that Brzezinski's Polish Catholic background had made him reflexively anti-Israel has dogged him ever since. In public comments, Brzezinski sometimes confronts it directly, noting as he did in a 2011 appearance at the Metropolitan Club in Washington that because he has argued so emphatically for a comprehensive settlement and a Palestinian state, he has been accused of anti-Semitism, a criticism he strongly denies. Rafshoon, a Jew who worked with Brzezinski in the White House, agrees that Brzezinski is "not a bigot," however strong his views on the Mideast.[20]

A crucial new player emerged when Menachem Begin, a hard-line conservative, was elected prime minister of Israel in May 1977. Carter began to trim his sails. He promised Begin he would stop talking about an Israeli return to the 1967 borders with minor modifications and stop calling for a "Palestinian homeland."

Carter asked Begin, in return, for restraint in building settlements, but in August Begin's government announced approval of three more—the opening round of a battle that has continued for thirty-five years.

Carter kept pushing the Arabs and Israelis toward a Geneva peace conference and comprehensive negotiations, including an October 1, 1977, U.S.-Soviet "joint statement" calling for such talks—which was blasted by Israelis and their U.S. supporters. To ease Israeli pressure, Brzezinski stressed that the PLO would not be able to participate in the Geneva conference unless it agreed in advance to accept UN Security Council Resolution 242, with its implicit recognition of Israel's right to exist.[21]

But the game changer would prove to be not Brzezinski's framework for superpower-brokered peacemaking, but the dream in the mind of Anwar Sadat for breaking free of Soviet tutelage and regaining the Sinai through his own bold diplomacy. As Brzezinski aptly titled this section of his memoirs, the destination turned out to be "Not Geneva, but Jerusalem" and a separate peace between Israel and Egypt. The first signpost came in early November, when Sadat informed the White House that "he was prepared to go to Jerusalem to talk to the Israelis about peace."[22]

⁕ Sadat took his brave journey to Jerusalem on November 20, 1977, and immediately upended all the planning Brzezinski had done for broad negotiations. Though discussions about the Palestinian issue and other elements of a general peace continued, the action was now on the Egyptian-Israeli bilateral front. Sadat was the man of the hour, as he had dreamed he would be, and Jimmy Carter was his counselor and guide. Though it would not become obvious until more than a year later, Sadat's brave journey had the effect of shelving Brzezinski's goal of brokering a settlement of the Palestinian problem.

At the end of Carter's first year in office, Brzezinski offered him a written assessment of his Middle East policy. Because of its frank self-criticism, it is worth quoting briefly: "The most controversial of the points in your approach proved to be the idea of the Palestinian homeland.... By fall [1977], there was a very intense domestic reaction.... It seems fair to conclude that the Palestinian issue was introduced too early and without adequate care to keep it in perspective. This resulted in a loss of domestic support for our policy which came at a particularly unfortunate time in terms of the peacemaking efforts."[23]

The momentum of Sadat's trip to Jerusalem carried him and Begin toward the Camp David negotiations in September 1978 and the eventual signing of the Egyptian-Israeli peace treaty in March 1979. This story has been widely told, and it is outside the scope of this chapter. On the American side, it was largely a one-man show, starring Jimmy Carter. The national security advisor played a peripheral role. The peacemaking embodied a peculiar dynamic: Sadat was alone among his entourage in really wanting to make peace with Israel; Begin was the converse—the only member of the Israeli entourage who seemed genuinely hesitant about signing a peace treaty with an Arab state. Carter was in the center, playing a role that had elements of marriage counselor, campground preacher, and diplomatic intermediary.

Brzezinski was a visible figure at Camp David, if not a decisive one. The diplomatic gamesmanship of the moment was captured in a famous picture of him and Begin playing chess outside the Israeli prime minister's cabin. As Brzezinski tells the story, when the wily Begin began the game, he announced that it was the first time he had played since 1940, when his match was interrupted by his arrest by the Russian secret police. A little while later, Mrs. Begin wandered by and said, "Menachem loves to play chess."[24]

The real game at Camp David was the pretense that it could be the prelude to a broader settlement. As the negotiations were about to start, Carter told Brzezinski that he planned to "go for it all the way."[25] But it was not to be, as Brzezinski admitted in his memoirs: "The issue of linkage between an Egyptian-Israeli settlement and the West Bank–Gaza negotiations, which had been flagged at the outset of Camp David as the single most important issue, was not resolved, largely because Carter in the end acquiesced to Begin's vaguer formulas."[26]

Though Carter would continue to struggle in the run-up to the formal Egypt-Israel peace treaty the next year for some commitment on the Palestinian issue, Brzezinski admits now that "it turned out to be a fig leaf."[27] As he conceded in his memoirs, "Camp David had created the impression that a separate peace between Egypt and Israel was acceptable to both the United States and Egypt."[28]

❖ The basic driver in these negotiations was the self-interest of the two parties. In a recollection in 2012, Brzezinski summarized the dynamic this way: "Sadat wanted the Sinai back without any compromises. The Israelis wanted to bust up the Arab military coalition so it would never form again." Both sides got what they wanted in a treaty. But the effect of this separate peace arguably was to delay a Palestinian agreement so long that all sides eventually lost faith in the peace process.

Brzezinski argued in later years that rather than just blasting Sadat, the Arabs should have seized the opening provided by Camp David to insist that the Palestinian issue be addressed. This was the theme of his argument in a 1984 interview with the Palestinian journalist Ghassan Bishara which appeared in the *Journal of Palestine Studies*: "The wiser strategy for the Arabs would have been to try to get the peace process moving forward beyond the Israeli-Egyptian accommodation. . . . If the Arabs, in one fashion or another, had been willing to join the process of negotiations which were initiated by Sadat, it would have been very difficult for Mr. Begin to sustain the stalemate regarding the Palestinian issue."[29]

My own assessment of Brzezinski's role in the Arab-Israeli diplomacy of the Carter years focuses on several points:

- First, in his pursuit of a comprehensive approach, Brzezinski emphasized too much the idea of the Geneva conference backed by Moscow and Washington and too little the desires motivating the parties themselves. With relatively little background in the region, he didn't have the feel for Sadat, King Hussein, or Hafez Assad that a more experienced Middle East player might have had. Had he known the region better, he might have mobilized Arab support for a comprehensive peace strategy to accompany Sadat's opening to Israel—and headed off the "rejectionism" of Egypt's separate peace that came to dominate the Arab debate for a generation.

- Second, Brzezinski was right that without a real Palestinian component, an Egyptian-Israeli settlement might freeze the larger peace process rather than foster it; he saw this problem clearly but couldn't alter the bilateral logic of peacemaking at Camp David or deter Carter from negotiating a glamorous, celebrated treaty—but one Brzezinski knew was also limited and in some ways counterproductive.

- Third, Brzezinski was not a smart political player. He let himself and Carter become the object of pro-Israeli political pressure, without having a sound counterstrategy. Brzezinski recognized this problem early. In June 10, 1977, in one of his private weekly reports to the president titled "Domestic Aspects of the Middle East Issue," Brzezinski wrote, "We should give those Jewish Americans who believe that Israel must take risks for peace more encouragement. We should carry our case to the American people, but be careful not to overreact or to be overly optimistic and thereby contribute to a crisis atmosphere."[30] But he never found a way to help Carter follow through.

Begin well understood the political weakness of the Carter-Brzezinski position and tellingly brought it up at Camp David in a private meeting with Brzezinski: "He started by telling me that he knows that I have been attacked in the Israeli press and by American Jews as being anti-Israeli, that he always defends me."[31] What better way to signal a counterpart's vulnerability than by saying that you always defend him! Brzezinski was always playing from this position of political weakness, in part because of statements that, while always principled, were not always wise.

A fitting last word on Brzezinski's White House diplomacy comes from Hamilton Jordan, perhaps Carter's closest advisor, who wrote in his memoirs of telling Brzezinski that he played tennis the same way he conducted foreign policy. When Brzezinski responded genially that this must mean he hit every shot cleanly and well, Jordan replied that it meant that the national security advisor hit the hell out of every ball, and that some of them stayed within the lines.[32]

⁘ In the years after his service as national security advisor, Brzezinski became an increasingly outspoken advocate of the approach he had championed since the mid-1970s but failed to implement, namely, a comprehensive solution based on a clear U.S. statement of principles for resolving the Palestinian conflict. As a result, he continued to be a target of attacks from pro-Israel groups in the United States. But Brzezinski seemed to take this criticism with relative equanimity, as the price of advocating policy positions he knew were correct.

Brzezinski criticized the Reagan administration in 1983, for example, for allowing the Israeli war in Lebanon and its aftermath to overwhelm the Middle East peace process. "Lebanon cannot be restored without serious and tangible progress in the Arab-Israeli dispute. It was that dispute that destabilized Lebanon in the first place and produced the destructive chain of events of the last year," he wrote in October 1983 in the *New York Times*.[33] He warned that America was increasingly perceived by Arabs as a "protagonist" in the region and a "military proxy of Israel" and was losing its ability to act as a mediator.

After the withdrawal of U.S. Marines from Lebanon in early 1984, following the disastrous terrorist bombings of the previous year, Brzezinski argued in the *Washington Post* for a frank reassessment of U.S. policy in the region. He contended that the United States should recognize that Israel's 1982 invasion of Lebanon had been a mistake, as had much of America's effort to fashion a Lebanese settlement; in his eyes, the United States had become a combatant rather than a mediator.[34]

Brzezinski, not surprisingly, liked the aggressive peacemaking of President George H. W. Bush at the 1991 Madrid peace conference. This effort, in its way, was vintage Brzezinski: an international peace conference aimed at pressuring Israel and the Arabs toward a settlement whose basic principles the United States had outlined. Brzezinski enthused in the *New York Times*, "This is the first time in the modern age that only one power is dominant in the Middle East, the United States. The Arabs have nowhere to go. Israel has to take American views extremely seriously, especially since the president has demonstrated over the housing loan guarantees that he will not be jerked around. . . . Above all, the United States has to keep the pressure on, and make it clear that there are definite penalties for any party that disrupts the process."[35] The Madrid process helped launch the eventual Jordanian-Israeli peace treaty. But on the Palestinian issue, it was once again, as at Camp David, the bilateral "Oslo process" that stole the show from the comprehensive, American-organized effort.

Brzezinski continued to make his case forcefully for a comprehensive Palestinian settlement in books, articles, and television appearances. His ruminations on U.S. mistakes in the region could fill a library shelf, especially in the books published after September 11, 2001, as he moved from being a foreign policy "hard-liner" to an increasingly sharp critic of the Bush administration's policies in the Middle East, especially its failure to address the Palestinian problem.

Notable among these books are *The Choice* (2005), which urges a U.S. diplomatic surge to counter Islamic populism and the rise of what he calls "the global Balkans," and *Second Chance* (2007), which bemoans "America's failure to move decisively on the Israeli-Palestinian problem during the fifteen years of its supremacy" and assigns grades for Middle East peacemaking to the Bush I, Clinton, and Bush II presidencies of "B–," "D," and "F," respectively.

❖ I had a special chance to witness Brzezinski thinking aloud about Arab-Israeli issues in my role as moderator of a 2008 book called *America and the World: Conversations on the Future of American Foreign Policy*, which was a series of discussions with Brzezinski and Brent Scowcroft, the national security advisor in the Gerald Ford and Bush I administrations. Brzezinski was emphatic on the need for the approach that he had been championing for more than thirty years: "If we want progress today, we have to be willing to state publicly at least the general parameters of a settlement, and then say, 'The rest is up to you as you negotiate the details.' "[36] He went on to list the four parameters for a settlement: no right of return for Palestinians, real sharing of Jerusalem, 1967 borders with mutual adjustments, and a demilitarized Palestinian state.[37]

Over the months and years that followed publication of the book, I would hear Brzezinski repeat this list of conditions for peace literally dozens of times. And when he and Scowcroft visited the Oval Office in March 2010 to make the same case privately to President Obama, I wrote a column in the *Washington Post* revealing their private pitch. Looking back, I fear that my public revelation of their private advice to the president probably derailed any chance that Obama would actually follow it; my column made it too easy for the Israelis and their supporters to attack what they claimed were repetitions of well-known arguments by the two "pro-Palestinian" former national security advisors.

Perhaps inevitably, Brzezinski got caught up in the controversy surrounding the 2006 publication of *The Israel Lobby and U.S. Foreign Policy*, by John Mearsheimer and Stephen M. Walt. In a comment on the book that appeared as part of a roundtable in *Foreign Policy* magazine, Brzezinski argued that the authors "have rendered a public service by initiating a much-needed public debate on the role of the 'Israel lobby' in the shaping of U.S. foreign policy." He cited the shift since his days in the White House "from relative impartiality (which produced the Camp David agreement) to increasing partiality in favor of Israel, to essentially the adoption of the Israeli perspective on the Israeli-Arab conflict."[38]

Given Brzezinski's experience in and out of government, it would have been surprising if he had said otherwise. But he closed his brief article in *Foreign Policy* with a gratuitous attack on critics in the American Jewish community: "Of course, stifling such debate is in the interest of those who have done well in the absence of it. Hence the outraged reaction from some to Mearsheimer and Walt."[39] This provocation had a predictable effect. Alan Dershowitz, a strongly pro-Israel professor at Harvard Law School, called on President Obama to publicly dissociate himself from Brzezinski's endorsement for the book.

❖ What's striking, reviewing Brzezinski's record on the Arab-Israeli issue, is the continuity of his views. Against the ebb and flow of events, and the waxing and waning of America's standing in the region, he has stood by the argument that America's national security interests are served by a comprehensive settlement in the Middle East, including creation of an independent Palestinian state. When others pulled back from expressing such views, often for reasons of political expediency, Brzezinski stood his ground—and often paid a personal price in terms of public criticism.

My own judgment is that historians will view Brzezinski's positions to have been correct, and America's failure to achieve a comprehensive settlement as a significant mistake, however understandable in terms of domestic factors. Brzezinski's political moves may not always have been the best—and he sometimes may have displayed the pugnacity that, in other circumstances, leads people to get into bar fights—but his policy analysis and strength of character on the Arab-Israeli issue have been steadfast and admirable.

## NOTES

1  Zbigniew Brzezinski, *Power and Principle: Memoirs of the National Security Adviser 1977–1981* (New York: Farrar, Straus, Giroux, 1983), 5–6.

2  Ibid., 6.

3  Ibid., 84.

4  Zbigniew Brzezinski, interview with author, March 2012.

5  Ibid.

6  Zbigniew Brzezinski, "The Mideast: Who Won?," *Washington Post*, November 21, 1973.

7  Zbigniew Brzezinski, "Plan for Peace in the Middle East," *New Leader*, January 7, 1974.

8  Zbigniew Brzezinski, Francois Duchene, and Kiichi Saeki, "Peace in an International Framework," *Foreign Policy*, no. 19 (Summer 1975): 3–17.

9  Zbigniew Brzezinski et al., "An Exchange on Mideast Guarantees," *Foreign Policy*, no. 21 (Winter 1975–76): 218.

10  Brzezinski, *Power and Principle*, 85–86.

11  Ibid., 84; Brzezinski interview.

12  *Bulletin of the American Professors for Peace in the Middle East*, June 1976, 75.

13  Gerald Rafshoon, interview with author, May 2012.

14  Jimmy Carter, *Keeping Faith: Memoirs of a President* (Little Rock: University of Arkansas Press, 1995), 52.

15  Brzezinski, *Power and Principle*, 86–87.

16  Ibid., 91.

17  Ibid., 93.

18  Ibid., 96.

19  Ibid., 98.

20  Rafshoon interview.

21  Zbigniew Brzezinski, interview on *Face the Nation*, reprinted in *Department of State Bulletin*, vol. 77, no. 2006, 800–805.

22  Brzezinski, *Power and Principle*, 111.

23  Ibid., 234.

24  Ibid., 255.

25  Ibid., 254.

26  Ibid., 273.

27  Brzezinski interview.

28  Brzezinski, *Power and Principle*, 277.

29  Zbigniew Brzezinski, "Peace at an Impasse," *Journal of Palestine Studies* 14, no. 1 (Autumn 1984): 4–6.

30  Brzezinski, *Power and Principle*, 558.

31  Ibid., 263.

32  Hamilton Jordan, *Crisis: The Last Year of the Carter Presidency* (New York: Putnam, 1982), 84.

33  Zbigniew Brzezinski, "America's Mideast Policy Is a Shambles," *New York Times*, October 9, 1983, E19.

34  Zbigniew Brzezinski, "Lebanon: The Aftermath in America," *Washington Post*, February 12, 1984, B8.

35  Zbigniew Brzezinski, "An Ocean Away, Pundits and Former Players Offer Views of Madrid Talks," *New York Times*, November 3, 1991, 23.

36  Zbigniew Brzezinski and Brent Scowcroft, *America and the World: Conversations on the Future of American Foreign Policy*, mod. David Ignatius (New York: Bantam Books, 2008), 81.

37  Ibid.

38  Zbigniew Brzezinski et al., "The War over Israel's Influence," *Foreign Policy*, no. 155 (July–August 2006): 63–64.

39  Ibid., 64.

# CHAPTER 14

# The Strategic Thinker

ADAM GARFINKLE

Zbigniew Brzezinski finds himself among fewer than half a dozen widely acknowledged American strategic thinkers. Along with Henry Kissinger, George Shultz, and Brent Scowcroft, Brzezinski is clearly a top-tier intellectual celebrity, his views on U.S. foreign policy and global affairs sought avidly by media in the United States and abroad. Since the appellation *strategic thinker* rests to some degree in the eyes of beholders, we can extend and perhaps bend Descartes just a bit: if people think you are a strategic thinker, therefore you are. Zbigniew Brzezinski therefore is.

In an odd way, Brzezinski's current status is both one of the most overdetermined phenomena imaginable but also one of the most accidental. It is overdetermined because Brzezinski was born to a family of aristocrats and diplomats in his native Poland, experienced both Nazi Germany and Stalinist Russia as an impressionable youngster, and then endured a peculiar forced exile in Canada only to land in perhaps the most bizarre environment of all—Harvard University. His native intelligence and keen analytic facility ensured his eventual rise into the elite in the United States, and his disciplined mind and work ethic guaranteed he would stay there. But Brzezinski's status is accidental, too: had he not been denied a scholarship to Britain based on a technicality, he might have ended up working for the Canadian Foreign Ministry, or in time perhaps the British one as the citizen of a Commonwealth country. In those countries, where the power structure was less open to the foreign-born than in the United States, he might have labored long in relative obscurity, his many talents notwithstanding.

As matters have turned out, Brzezinski's status is secure; he already resides in the history books, and there he will stay. He is one of the few twentieth-century Americans to have gone from not one but two prominent universities (Harvard and Columbia) into government (John Kennedy's National Security Council [NSC] and Lyndon Johnson's State Department Policy Planning Staff), back to academia and the world of think tanks, once again into senior government service (as Jimmy Carter's national security advisor), and then living many years thereafter to tell the tales and occasionally pull a policy string or two acquired from experience. Brzezinski is in his mid-eighties. There is plenty to be said in this regard for simply staying healthfully alive and alert for a long time. At Robert Strausz-Hupé's 95th birthday party at the Union League in Philadelphia, a young woman eagerly asked the aged ambassador and professor, "To what qualities, sir, do you owe your long and active life?" Without missing a beat, Strausz-Hupé answered, "My dear, I owe my long, and perhaps active life to the fact that I have not yet died."

Humor here hides a serious observation, which is that genuine wisdom comes only with experience and the opportunity to reflect upon it. Youth is unkind to its attainment; as Michael Oakeshott observed, "Politics is an activity unsuited to the young. . . . Everybody's young days are a dream, a delightful insanity, a sweet solipsism. . . . There are no obligations to be observed; there are no accounts to be kept."[1] Brzezinski, who would undoubtedly affirm Oakeshott's observation today, would not claim that he understood as much at age 30 or 40 as he did at 60 or 70, or that he does now. He wrote some things fifty years ago, as a junior member of President Kennedy's NSC, that do not stand up particularly well against the historical record, such as a long-since-declassified memo, written in the immediate wake of the Cuban Missile Crisis, in which a 34-year-old Brzezinski exuberantly prophesied imminent Western victory in the cold war.

Every strategic thinker has at least a few sartorial failures in his conceptual closet from earlier times; it goes with the territory. If one does not extend oneself, one cannot be meaningfully correct—one cannot in the sense we mean it here really be said to think at all. Humans still grow intellectually and emotionally even in the third third of their lives, and the keen perspective that age often brings forth may still be recognized even in a society in which respect for elders is much lacking. Zbigniew Brzezinski's status as strategic master is testimony to the fact.

❖ Aside from being acknowledged a strategic thinker, there are obviously certain less subjective criteria that are necessary if not entirely sufficient to acquire the status. What are they?

One of Brzezinski's friends (and one of my mentors), Owen Harries, once quipped that if you want to be a sage observer of international politics, it is a good idea to start by not being an American, and by not being young.[2] Having already covered the second condition, let us look now to the first.

Harries was not referring to American citizenship, of course, but rather to the natural intellectual misanthropies of being born into a political culture that, for various historical reasons, he considered monolingually insular to the point of self-absorbed, arrogant due to its self-avowed exceptionalism, Manichaean by way of secularized religious disposition, too prone to trust "grand" but ironically narrow theories as opposed to studied experience, and therefore, not coincidentally, impatient and historically ignorant to boot. Above all, however, the problem with being an American, as Harries expressed it, is that Americans lack the instinctive sense of danger and the possibility of tragedy that, say, Polish, or Belgian, or Jewish, or Korean children acquire virtually at birth. Americans have long had unthreatening and undefended frontiers, no history of having their mainland invaded or attacked over nearly two centuries, and power both continuously rising and ultimately unmatched. They have acquired so much confidence and optimism, according to Harries, that it is difficult to get them to see the world as an intrinsically dangerous and differentiated place that ought to be approached with caution and restraint. If we flip this list of temperamental shortcomings, we get a reasonably serviceable checklist of virtues for any aspiring strategic thinker.

The opposite of insular, in this respect anyway, is to be capable of understanding multiple viewpoints. It is to understand what it means to be foreign and to be a foreigner. It means making oneself aware of the underlying predicates of one's own society so that those of other societies can be appreciated in context. It means, too, not making the mistake of unwittingly projecting one's own frames of reference onto others. Monolinguality conduces to insularity; knowing more than one language fluently conduces to a facility for intellectual pluralism. This is why many of the greatest thinkers about society and politics who have lived in the United States were not born here. Zbigniew Brzezinski is no less an obvious example than are Henry Kissinger and Hans Morgenthau, Arnold Wolfers and Bronisław Malinowski, and many others going all the way back to Carl Schurz. All learned English as a second, and sometimes as a third, language. This did not make any of these people less patriotic as Americans; it merely made them less innocently so.

The opposite of arrogance is humility. Humility is a critical characteristic of a genuine strategic thinker. A genuine strategic thinker understands the satyr of contingency in human affairs, the inability to vanquish structural uncertainty, and the limits of planning. Brzezinski has been categorical on this point: "global politics do not lend themselves to pat formulations and clear-cut predictions," and he has long been a critic of abstract formal models that pretend otherwise.[3]

There are two kinds of American exceptionalism. One is revelational exceptionalism, which, when folded into American Protestant evangelicism, posits the superiority of the United States to be a decree of God on high. The other form is fortuitous exceptionalism: history, geography, and biography all came together to produce a great experiment in modernity and democracy. By both revealing and promoting the highest aspirations of human dignity, America truly qualifies, as Abraham Lincoln put it in 1862, as mankind's last best hope. As such, it is a moral imperative as well as a strategic one to keep America safe, prosperous, and powerful. But there are no guarantees here; as Machiavelli knew, fortuity (*fortuna*) is a fickle dame. What happenstance gave, happenstance can take away.

No one who believes in revelational exceptionalism can be a sound strategic thinker. When doing God's work, concern for detail tends to go out the window. When the God-talk starts in American foreign policy, whether from the likes of Woodrow Wilson with his Thirteen Points or from the likes of George W. Bush with his "forward strategy for freedom," big trouble and much carnage cannot be far behind—e.g., in Wilson's case, allowing a fit of idealism to destroy centuries-old pillars of the European balance of power, paving the way for an even more destructive war; in Bush's case, playing into the hands of Iran, the Middle East's most dangerous and aggressive actor. As the old saw suggests, God may protect drunks, fools, and the United States of America, but banking on divine protection is no substitute for policy.

Brzezinski is no adherent of revelational exceptionalism. We have never discussed the matter, but being Catholic rather than Protestant—and taking a somewhat skeptical view of all ecclesiastical associations with politics—the whole idea seems to appall him. He does, I think, affirm fortuitous exceptionalism. He has said many times that he prefers realist means to achieve idealist ends, and those ends in his view obviously require a strong American role in the world, to the extent that America as a society continues to deserve it. I am not certain that being a strategic thinker requires an emotional as well as an intellectual commitment to a side in a consequential struggle, but in Brzezinski's case it is foundational in his thinking.

The opposite of Manichean and excessively theoretical thought—the characteristic quality of political theology or of any attenuated religious mode of thinking, whatever it calls itself—is a mode of analysis that appreciates the complexity, subtlety, and protracted open-endedness of most real-world circumstances. It is the ability to see early on, for example, that the Communist world was not monolithic, so that U.S. policy toward Warsaw Pact satellite governments should be carefully and deliberately distinguished in tone from policy toward the Soviet Union. This was perhaps Brzezinski's earliest burden of advocacy, and it was an enormously heavy one when the likes of John Foster Dulles bestrode the halls of Foggy Bottom.[4]

It is the ability to see that there were more than two sides—pro-democratic or proto-democratic and anti-democratic—in a country like pre–March 2003 Iraq, and that none of the sides there could be usefully defined by such terms. It is the ability to see that, in places like Afghanistan and Pakistan, there are more than just two sides and that none of them fit the made-in-the-American-imagination description of a "good guy." But perhaps the most vivid exemplar of Brzezinski's assessment on this score comes from a conversation the two of us had around 2007. I began by recalling his answer to a question put some weeks before by another magazine editor about the presumed mistake of the U.S. government ever having aided the Afghan *mujahidin* against the Soviet Union because this created al-Qaeda and caused 9/11. Brzezinski replied that this was "a crazy question," as indeed it was, not least because of the host of unpredictable events that transpired between the winter of 1979–80 and the emergence of an al-Qaeda presence in Afghanistan after 1996. At one point, Brzezinski said in agreement that the "blowback" accusation

> is a totally ahistorical argument which seems to be premised on the notion, maybe implicitly, that it would be better if the Soviet Union still existed. That way we would not be waging "World War IV," as some of the crazies among the neocons call it, against Islamofascism.

I then replied,

> It seems to me that the real animus behind the "blowback" argument is not that its proponents want the Soviet Union to continue to exist, but that everything that goes wrong in the world is somehow the fault of the U.S. government, as manifested in some antecedent decision.

Upon hearing this, Brzezinski said,

> Right, and that everything should again be black and white. It's complicated to think that some Muslims, like the majority of Afghans, work with America against other Muslims. It would be so much simpler if we were waging war against some sort of

united Islamic, Muslim fascist enemy, but it's a mistake to think that, whether that thought comes from the Left or the Right.

I then pressed the point:

> The forces that issued forth from the *mujahidin* experience included not just Muslims who don't like us, but also the several constituents of the Northern Alliance, who were also *mujahidin* but were on our side during the war. This is a complicated part of the world. It isn't easily divisible into good guys and bad guys. There aren't just two sides but often three or four sides.

Brzezinski's rejoinder was both expansive and telling as he remarked on the American inability to acknowledge complexity or to care about the historical record that illustrates it. He said in part,

> I think you're putting your finger on a major weakness of contemporary America. The weakness is that we're more democratic than we've ever been before in the sense that popular pressures translate into policy pressures very quickly. And we're probably as ignorant as ever about the rest of the world, because everybody now lives in a kind of simplistic, trivialized virtual reality in which fact and fiction, impressions and impulses, are mixed up in an incoherent fashion.[5]

Similarly, his resolutely anti-Manichean attitude accounts for Brzezinski's ability to have seen that the end of the cold war was no time for complacency or excessive defense budget cuts, because the competitive nature of world politics was never wholly subsumed by the ideological dimension of the cold war and would not therefore become extinct upon its termination. Geopolitics, he has always insisted, does not become obsolete. This dovetails nicely with Brzezinski's most "un-American" trait: his capacity to imagine tragedy.

It is a hallmark of a temperamental realist to fear anyone who says with any sense of conviction that we should try doing this or that because "things can't get any worse." Things can always get worse, and they often do. There is no Pole born in the twentieth century—whether in Poland or displaced to another land—who does not know this in his or her bones. These are people who have watched a progression of events that nearly beggars imagination: from national rebirth in 1919–20 to a slide into petty authoritarianism in the 1930s, then to murderous Nazi occupation and decades of brutal Soviet Russian domination, the latter shift punctuated by one of the most ruthlessly premeditated acts of political cynicism in historical memory—the summer 1944 Warsaw uprising, which Stalin's armies watched contentedly from the far side of the Vistula.

Even Zbigniew Brzezinski's biggest boosters do not deny the power of his Polish identity in the way he sees the world. All throughout the cold war this identity paralleled in practice the U.S. orientation to that struggle. When Brzezinski acted—in the words of one of his former NSC colleagues—"like the desk officer for Poland" on President Carter's trip to Warsaw in 1977, the "charge" was not very far from the truth. But Brzezinski's European focus, and his special focus on the Soviet Union, was such a perfect fit during cold war times with the genuine locus of maximum feasible tragedy in world politics that such parochial indulgences could be overlooked. More than that, in an administration in which the likes of Cyrus Vance, Andrew Young, and Patricia Derian had significant influence, even those who disagreed with Brzezinski on many discrete issues were thankful that he (and Defense Secretary Harold Brown) was there to limit the damage that such idealists, ministering to a president with little foreign policy experience, could do.

Brzezinski's antipathy to allowing one's thinking to be dominated by rigid and abstract ideological categories at the expense of a close, hard look at social reality highlights another aspect of his prowess as a strategic thinker. Brzezinski is really a master not just of strategy but of statecraft. Americans usually throw these two words around as though they were synonyms, but there is a profound—and unappreciated—distinction between the two terms. Strategy is about foreign policy, how a state manages its relations in a dangerous world over time. It is about matching resources to goals in the context of a state's relation with other states. Statecraft concerns itself with the critical coordination of internal (domestic) with external (foreign) aspects of the nexus between challenge and opportunity. In current circumstances, for example, the United States needs a strategy for dealing with China and East Asia, but we also need statecraft in order to relate our economic challenges, which are partly domestic and partly a function of the international environment, to that strategy. A true strategic thinker is really a statesman, then, someone who is mindful of what is proverbially called the big picture that breaks through the ultimately artificial barrier between "foreign" and "domestic."

A genuine strategic thinker needs to know what is going on at the Federal Reserve and the Treasury Department as much as he needs to know what is going on at the State and Defense Departments. More than that, a strategic thinker needs to appreciate changing social and cultural variables below the line of everyday political sight. It is not enough to know chronicle; one must know history in the true sense of the term: we are interested not only in what happened when but in what events tell us about human nature, and especially about human nature as it applies to politics and social conflict within and among peoples. Brzezinski's first book to show a keen appreciation for such concerns was *Between Two Ages: America's Role in the Technetronic Age* (1970); it may be his best book overall, for in it he tries his hand at what amounts to a practical application of social science to American statecraft on a fully global scale.[6] While others were captive of their supposedly "grand" ideological narratives, which were in truth highly truncated pictures of social reality, Brzezinski starts in philosophy and expands into the history and sociology of science and technology. Technology, and especially cybernetic technology, was severing stabilizing connections between the way people lived and the values they espoused. The technetronic age, he insisted, would be as different from the industrial age as the industrial age was from the agricultural age. The growing misalignment between social realities and belief systems, and how state leaderships understood and tried to cope with them in both the West and the Communist world, would drive social organization in directions common in some ways but dangerously dissonant in others. There were not many people at that time, nor are there many today, who think in such broad, syncretic ways about global affairs and yet are able to drive their insights down to practical conclusions in discrete realms of policy formulation.

Brzezinski has maintained his determination to see the big picture within the solid context of global social data. Trained as a social scientist rather than as a historian or an economist, mindful of data but not mesmerized by it, Brzezinski has always believed that what goes on out of political sight, deep within societies, is ultimately the key to seeing around the elusive corner we call the future. As an example, in his signature essay in the inaugural issue of the *American Interest*, he reemphasized an old theme of his—the phenomenon of a global political awakening—which would complicate but also hold out great opportunity for American foreign policy in this century.[7] Brzezinski's approach was, and is, therefore somewhat akin to social forensics, only for the purpose of looking forward, not back. Another way to describe it is as not a "whole-of-government" approach, but a whole-of-social-world approach to the causal ingredients of international reality.

Whether in his earlier incarnation as a Soviet expert or in his latter persona as a global strategic thinker, Brzezinski has always entertained a wider band of causal agents than most analysts. All genuine strategic thinkers have this in common: they seek a Kantian unity in the manifold, and they acknowledge the manifold to be expansive. The trick here, of course, which few ever master, is to hone one's intuition for how the various causal threads come together to form the whole cloth of reality. There is no formula to follow here, no foolproof equations or shortcuts that can be known. Mastery comes from an open orientation to the subject matter, in particular the ability to learn from one's mistakes (or excessive enthusiasms) and to avoid the laziness inherent in too-quick-to-close analogical thinking. To watch Brzezinski field a question or think through a problem is to see his intuitive facility in action. One can almost hear the gears turning and witness the critical distinction between quickness and haste. There is a certain look in his eyes when he is thinking that communicates his respect for the difficulty of the subject matter, a respect that is incumbent on anyone who would be a strategic thinker.

Finally, genuine strategic thinkers tend to be prophylactic optimists, or, put a bit differently, betting types who are not afraid of the game. This is a matter of temperament, not intellect. It is a trait that cannot be taught. But it is a trait that government service strongly develops for a reason few outsiders appreciate: it's your job to make the policy work, and you can't do your job well working on behalf of a course of action you don't believe can, or in some cases should, succeed. The benefit of this attitude is that it is indispensible to success; the bane of it is that insiders are often the last to recognize an ill-fated course of action for what it is. So it goes; the dynamics of cognitive dissonance are agnostic on matters of efficacy.

In Brzezinski's case, his prophylactic optimism has been earned. The major struggle of his lifetime, the cold war, ended in success, not just for the United States and the West in general, but also for the country of his birth, Poland. That experience shows that not only is incremental success possible, but thoroughgoing triumph is too. This experience has also bequeathed a major achievement within that larger success—the fact that Brzezinski helped keep his party from falling headlong into the clutches of Democrats who had lost their strategic balance and verve. He supported George H. W. Bush for president in 1988 against the candidate of his own party, a strategic judgment of a sort that could not have been very easy to make. Indeed, overcoming the McGovernite wing of the Democratic Party may have been a more difficult strategic objective in Brzezinski's private view than delivering the USSR to Trotsky's proverbial dustbin of history.

Either way, Brzezinski's guarded optimism has clearly not flagged. In his newest work, he calls on the United States to drive hard ahead to build a wider West that includes a more unified European Union and also encompasses a genuinely reformed Russia and a still-democratic Turkey, to create a universalist democratic culture from Vancouver eastward all the way around the globe to Vladivostok. This goal echoes his 1965 argument in *Alternative to Partition* in favor of a reunited European political and cultural space. At the same time, he adjures the

United States to play the role of offshore balancer in Asia, triangulating wisely between China and Japan, as well as China and India. He acknowledges that playing this dual role requires first getting our domestic house properly restored, but he spends little time with this prolegomenon before painting the larger canvass of an America as—at the same time—builder of the West, balancer of the East, and master of the twain.[8]

There are those who might characterize this vision as excessively optimistic, and so it may be. Brzezinski posits "after 2025" as the date for the *annus mirabilis* to come, 360 years after Dryden's original: not so far into the future as to be fanciful, but not too soon to be thought unserious. Imagining a more unified and effective Europe is hard these days. Imagining a democratic Russia is hard, too. Imagining Turkey remaining pro-Western and still genuinely democratic a decade hence is very hard, and one wonders if Brzezinski has taken the full measure of the changes in Turkish society these past two decades. Imagining the United States being able to broker a lasting Sino-Japanese conciliation, or to run interference between Chinese and Indians, even as the U.S. military presence recedes from the region under the pressures of fiscal austerity and its economic clout becomes occluded, is, well, also hard. Imagining we can do all of this, and do it in simultaneous, harmonious balance, is—what is that handy speechwriter's euphemism?—a challenge.

That said, *someone* has to postulate a winning scenario; *someone* has to think through what it will take to manage American fortunes effectively in the new New World of the twenty-first century. *Someone* has to define the stretch goals. That a man in his mid-eighties is leading the pack is cause for some embarrassment, or it should be. We at least ought to thank the man for trying before we pick and peck at his envisioned edifice.

Of this, then, is a strategic thinker composed: he is comfortable with plural perspectives; facile with multisided circumstances so as to privilege distinctions over conflations; not averse to moral and emotional commitment, but wary of excessive moral or theoretical abstraction; mindful of danger and tragedy, but not given over to pessimism or cynicism; patient and undemanding of a generically recalcitrant reality, rarely willing to tolerate the best becoming the enemy of the adequate, but quick to seize opportunity when it knocks; respectful of difficulty, but hopeful of success, even major success; and perhaps, above all, not too young. Zbigniew Brzezinski is all of these. And it stands to reason that he admires those who come closest to this ideal and saves his sharpest barbs for those who wander farthest from it.[9]

Being qualified as a strategic thinker does not necessarily make a person right, of course, all or even most of the time. If it did, then all those who qualify as strategic thinkers would take the same view on all consequential issues, and of course they do not. Brzezinski supported U.S. military intervention in the Balkan Wars of Yugoslav Succession, which I believe is the best name for them, but he opposed the 1991 Gulf War to liberate Kuwait. Others equally entitled to the sobriquet of strategic thinker took the opposite positions, and my own views align with them, not with Brzezinski. However, whatever the differences in case-by-case prudential judgment, strategic thinkers do tend to agree on how to pose the question, for experience has taught them how to home in on core stakes and not be distracted by the peripheral, the emotional, or the telegenic in an age of media immersion. Sometimes, too, all or nearly all strategic thinkers within a given political community take a broad consensus view on a particularly impor-tant issue—the U.S. intervention into Vietnam, for example—only to regret it to one degree or another later on. Thus, having the qualities of a strategic thinker constitutes a necessary but not a sufficient condition for getting the big judg-ments right.

Alas, it comes down to temperament, experience, and the just biases that se-rious thinkers earn (as opposed to the flippant ones that the insecure use as de-fense mechanisms). There is always a danger, too, that with age one can think a bit off-key past one's sell-by date. As Henry Kissinger has, I think, been flattered too successfully by the Chinese, and as Brent Scowcroft was so temperamen-tally conservative a thinker in that other *annus mirabilis*, 1989, that he could not imagine the world without the Soviet Union, so Zbigniew Brzezinski may remain Euro- and Russocentric in a world that has outgrown that orientation as a proper grounding strategic assumption. Though Brzezinski would probably contest the point, it is this orientation, I think, that at least partly explains his support for U.S. military intervention in the Balkans, but not in the Middle East. What hap-pens in the Balkans reverberates directly into Europe's post-Communist space, including space occupied by Poland and Russia. What happens in Kuwait or Iraq does not.[10]

This favored cockpit for viewing the world has saved Brzezinski from several common errors—such as exaggerating the global strategic importance of the Middle East, as so many have done, and, more recently, dismissing the continu-ing strategic significance of Europe. (It is true, as some have pointed out, that he feels no special warmth for Israel, but it is often forgotten that he also feels no special warmth for Israel's regional enemies and critics either.) Nor has his preferred orientation stunted his hopes that Russians will one day freely join the

West; he harbors nary a scintilla of crude ethnopolitical determinism—or if he does, he hides it well.

Sitting in that cockpit, however, one must strain to comprehend a world rapidly moving into a post-Western normative environment, a world in which the stabilities of the state system itself are now more vulnerable to challenge than since before Westphalia. In Brzezinski's recent writing his analogies invariably base themselves in European experience and then move outward toward Asia. He does this, one suspects, not because he is indulgent of Western readers' weaknesses with Asian history, but because this is honestly and naturally the way he thinks. Alas, many of these analogies do not travel well from West to East.

There is no accounting for temperament. That leads some to conspiracy theories, and from his days associated with the Trilateral Commission no one has been the archvillain of more loopy conspiracy theories than Zbigniew Brzezinski. Among the more serious of mind, Brzezinski's reputation is mixed. McGovernite Democrats and their present-day scions have thought him too hawkish; many Republicans have thought him too reticent about the use of force. Some think him obsessed with Russians and accuse him of not being able to find South America on a map; others wish he were more obsessed with China. You can't please everyone (and you definitely shouldn't try). Time will tell whose vision falls truest to the historical mark. As Chou En-lai famously said when asked his view of the French Revolution, so it is with any definitive assessment of Zbigniew Brzezinski as a strategic thinker: "It's too soon to say."

## NOTES

1 From Michael Oakeshott, *Rationalism in Politics* (London: Methuen, 1962).

2 Owen Harries, conversation with author, 1997.

3 See Zbigniew Brzezinski, *Between Two Ages: America's Role in the Technetronic Era* (New York: Penguin Books, 1970), xiv, and note on xvi.

4 Note Zbigniew Brzezinski, *Alternative to Partition: For a Broader Conception of America's Role in Europe* (New York: McGraw-Hill, 1965).

5 This exchange comes from "'I'd Do It Again': Talking Afghanistan with Zbigniew Brzezinski," *American Interest*, May/June 2008.

6 It was certainly a formative book, for Brzezinski picks up on many of the same themes in *Out of Control: Global Turmoil on the Eve of the Twenty-First Century* (New York: Macmillan, 1993).

7 Zbigniew Brzezinski, "The Dilemma of the Last Sovereign," *American Interest*, Autumn 2005.

8 Zbigniew Brzezinski, *Strategic Vision: America and the Crisis of Global Power* (New York:

Basic Books, 2012). A précis of the book's argument appeared as "Balancing the East, Upgrading the West," *Foreign Affairs*, January/February 2012.

9   This explains, I think, the tone as much as the substance of Brzezinski's *Second Chance: Three Presidents and the Crisis of the American Superpower* (New York: Perseus, 2007).

10   One sees this same general bias, and in my view also its analytical limitations, in Brzezinski's *The Grand Chessboard: American Primacy and Its Geostrategic Imperatives* (New York: Basic Books, 1998).

# PART IV

# Portraits

# CHAPTER 15

# The Professor

## STEPHEN F. SZABO

Zbigniew Brzezinski was a brilliant teacher who cared about his students and used Harvard, Columbia, the Council on Foreign Relations, and the Trilateral Commission to prepare himself for the policy world. Nonacademics may find it surprising to learn that he only spent six years in government service, with the remainder in academia or in think tanks. The latter included direction of the Trilateral Commission and decades of association with the Washington-based Center for Strategic and International Studies. After leaving government, think tanks offered him an opportunity—in his words—to shift "from policy making to policy analysis and advocacy."[1]

In important ways, however, Brzezinski remained an academic. He was always studious and precise. In lectures and in interviews, he spoke in perfect paragraphs. Much as he found "political science" empty of serious content, his policy analyses and advocacy grew out of serious and systematic scholarly study, something he had learned at his academic homes: at Montreal's McGill, Harvard, Columbia, and Johns Hopkins University's Nitze School of Advanced International Studies (SAIS). Of these four major universities, Brzezinski's formative years were spent at Harvard. It was there that he learned what it meant to be an academic and a policy analyst, as well as the tension between these two worlds. In this respect his experience was similar to that of his famous colleagues at Harvard, Samuel Huntington and Henry Kissinger, both of whom were viewed by some of their faculty colleagues as insufficiently serious due to their outside policy interests and networks.

Brzezinski was always fascinated by ideas, but unlike most academics, he wanted to translate ideas into policy, theory into practice. This orientation, and especially his pervasive interest in the Soviet Union, was the result of his biography. The son of Polish émigrés, he grew up when his family's country was under the domination of the Soviet Union. As he describes it, "My writing was always connected with some fundamental political and philosophical premise. I started out focusing on the Soviet Union. I thought of the Soviet Union as a menace in the same category as Hitlerism. I then broadened to think about what were the implications for American foreign policy."[2]

When he was at Harvard in the 1950s, there was considerable interest in Washington in this kind of work. In response to the competition with the Soviet Union, the U.S. government provided major support for area studies through legislation such as the National Defense Educational Act. In this initial phase of the cold war, in particular, universities provided an ideal match between Brzezinski's personal interests and ambitions and those of the U.S. government. He was not alone, as other students at Harvard were also interested in relating ideas and theory to policy. What made them different in the academic world was their disdain for abstract quantitative methods and conceptual approaches far removed from any relation to the real world—methods and approaches favored by most university departments then and now. (The exceptions, where area studies are still accepted as legitimate and important, are academic havens such as Columbia, the Fletcher School at Tufts, Georgetown, SAIS, and the Elliot School at George Washington University.) As Brzezinski notes, "If you look at the [American] Political Science Review, it is very hard to discern how you apply any of that to real life. Some theorists postulate that America and China have to go to war. My view is that they don't have to go to war. If they are wrong a new theory has to be developed and theory is always retroactive. If conditions change and the right choices are made the theory has to be amended."[3] One result of this emphasis on abstractions in academic political science has been to move policy discussions out of the university and into think tanks, mostly in Washington.

❖ Brzezinski entered Harvard in 1950 after completing both his BA and MA at McGill University. He had written his master's thesis on Soviet nationalities policies and came to Harvard with the conviction that the nationalities question was Moscow's Achilles heel.[4] At Harvard, he wrote his dissertation on the role of the political purge in the Soviet Union under the supervision of Merle Fainsod, a giant in the field of Soviet studies. Brzezinski was a PhD student at Harvard during the 1950s and taught there until he was denied tenure in 1960. He admits, "I of course wanted to be given tenure, but I did not campaign for it, which in retrospect I realize was naiveté. But when I learned I did not get tenure, I decided not to let it get to me and my wife, and I threw a big costume party called shipwreck, and it was one of the best parties that year at Harvard."[5]

The denial of tenure at Harvard was a crucible moment in Brzezinski's life. He had spent the most formative decade of his life in Cambridge, developing both ideas and friendships there. Up until that point, everything had come easily for him at Harvard, and this rejection came as a surprise and a shock. Harvard, as always, was overflowing with talent, and its Department of Government included such stars as Brzezinski, Kissinger, Huntington, and Stanley Hoffman. Harvard was then, and still is, notorious for denying tenure to gifted scholars, sending them off to brilliant careers elsewhere; it is only a slight exaggeration to say that the best thing that could happen to a promising academic was to be cast out by Harvard. This was clearly the case with Brzezinski (and with Huntington, too).

He moved to Columbia in 1960, where he directed the Research Institute on Communist Affairs (RICA). He remained at Columbia until entering government as national security advisor to President Jimmy Carter in 1977 (and returned to Columbia after his service in Washington came to an end in 1981). In New York, he quickly discovered the city's attractions, which included the prestigious Council on Foreign Relations and *Foreign Affairs* magazine, as well as television. In March 1962 he appeared as the first lecturer in a television series organized by Columbia on world problems. The *New York Times* review of the series stated, "The meaning of the international stresses besetting communism . . . were discussed by Professor Brzezinski with a lucidity that consistently held the attention."[6] When Harvard tried twice in the 1960s to lure him back to Cambridge, including an offer of a full professorship with half time off for research, Brzezinski was torn:

> I said to myself, look Harvard is a better university than Columbia, just as Oxford is a better university than the Sorbonne, but the Sorbonne is in Paris and Oxford is in Oxford. Harvard is in Cambridge and Columbia is in New York City. I would have been more of a scholar if I had stayed at Harvard, but I said to myself do I want twenty years from now to be walking across Harvard Yard wearing a tweed sports jacket carrying a folder with the latest adapted version of a lecture I had given over the years with the text of the opening joke with class reactions in brackets underneath and asking would that satisfy me?[7]

By 1989 Brzezinski had grown tired of the commute to New York. Although he remained loyal to Columbia, he began to look for an academic home in Washington. He was courted both by the School of Foreign Service of Georgetown and by

SAIS. Although he and Paul Nitze had disagreements over Nitze's strong opposition to the START treaty, Brzezinski and the SAIS dean, George Packard, were friends and regular tennis partners. After one of their matches, Brzezinski mentioned that he had tired of the demands of the weekly commute to New York, and Packard offered him the Osgood Chair at SAIS. While it did not carry tenure, Brzezinski was delighted, as it meant that he would not have to attend committee meetings and become involved in endless faculty politics, something he had tried to avoid throughout his career. He told Packard he wanted bright students and to be part of a first-rate academic institution; ultimately, he chose SAIS over Georgetown because he thought the latter was too academic while SAIS was more policy oriented. Brzezinski taught at SAIS from 1989 through 1997, teaching one seminar a year and a large lecture course every now and then. He proved to be an extremely popular teacher, whose classes had to be limited to twenty carefully selected students.

He also led a biweekly luncheon series that combined SAIS faculty with Washington-based foreign policy specialists, including such luminaries as Helmut Sonnenfeld, Kissinger's top European aide at the National Security Council (NSC); Fritz Ermarth, a former high-level CIA analyst; Ambassador Phyllis Oakley and Toby Gati, both former heads of the Bureau of Intelligence and Research at the State Department; and SAIS faculty Francis Fukuyama and Charles Gati (the latter a member of Brzezinski's similar seminar, then focusing on communist affairs, at Columbia in the 1970s). Brzezinski chaired these sessions, inviting top-level policy makers and analysts of different political persuasion to speak for thirty minutes. He would also ask the first question, which was always unfailingly comprehensive in its sweep of understanding the heart of the matter under discussion. Those invited by Brzezinski to take part in these seminars were expected to attend regularly—or they were not invited back the following year. The waiting list was long. George Packard noted many years later that "hiring Zbig was one of the best decisions I made as Dean. He brought policy experience to a faculty that needed it and was an immensely popular teacher."

❖ Brzezinski has always been an inspired and gifted teacher. He remembers being introduced to a class as a Soviet military attaché at West Point, where he compared the war-making styles of the Soviets and the Americans, claiming that the former was superior. The audience became increasingly angry until the end, when it was revealed that he was an assistant professor at Harvard. The audience erupted with a roar of approval. Later, while at Columbia in 1968, he met with students protesting the Vietnam War. He was a major target for the students because of his support for the war—through both advising the Johnson administration and then serving on Hubert H. Humphrey's campaign. He confronted the students on the steps of the building where RICA was located, with an apple in hand, from which he would take an occasional bite in a gesture of insouciance. At the end of this heated session, he told them that he hoped they didn't have any further questions because he had "other genocides to go ahead and plan."[8] In a forthcoming study, Justin Vaïsse notes that Brzezinski did not hold these students in high regard as they had not been sufficiently critical of the Soviet invasion of Hungary in 1956 and the Soviet crackdown in Czechoslovakia in 1968. However, Brzezinski himself says that he always liked his students but was not intimidated by them.

Protesters notwithstanding, Brzezinski established himself as both a powerful lecturer and a well-organized and insightful professor at Columbia. F. Stephen Larrabee, a former student and later a junior colleague at the NSC, describes Brzezinski as a "terrific professor, well organized, knowledgeable and disciplined."[9] He was also a conscientious taskmaster:

> During my time at Columbia four graduate students, myself being one, were interested in the cold war and wanted to set up a special class. We asked Brzezinski if he would teach the class, a daunting task which involved creating a whole new reading list, syllabus etc. Brzezinski graciously accepted. After week two or three of the class, Brzezinski came up to me and said, "Are you doing any work for this class?" I was a conscientious student and replied "Yes, why?" He then brought me in to his office where about twenty books from Columbia's library for the class were lying on a table and said, "How could you, if I have all the books?"[10]

The late Lt. Gen. William Odom, initially a student and subsequently an NSC colleague and close friend of Brzezinski's, was also impressed: "Brzezinski's lectures were an event,"[11] he said. His long-time colleague Charles Gati recalled, "When I met my [future] wife at Columbia she was in one of Brzezinski's courses, and she was his research assistant too, and I remember how hard she studied. She didn't have time for me. To get an 'A' from Brzezinski was truly a mark of excellence."[12]

Future secretary of state Madeleine Albright was also one of Brzezinski's students at Columbia. This is how she remembers him as a professor:

> I first met Brzezinski when, as a young Harvard professor, he had come to give a lecture at Wellesley. In the interim he had published *The Soviet Bloc*, a perceptive analysis of how Stalin had put together his empire.

He was still only in his mid-thirties but was already being quoted everywhere and was increasingly visible in policy circles. I thought it essential to get into a seminar he was offering on comparative Communism, itself a novel idea. With all respect to my other former professors, I judged it the best course I took in graduate school. The professor was challenging, the material totally new, and the students all thought they were the best.

Brzezinski assigned lengthy readings in Russian without questioning our ability to understand them. Because he was a good friend of my friends the Gardners [Professor and Mrs. Richard Gardner] and I was older than most students, I was able to see his human side. To most of his students, however, he seemed unapproachable. He was brilliant, did not put up with blather, and while he spoke with a Polish accent, he did so in perfect, clear paragraphs. Even at this time there was little doubt he was going to play an important role in U.S. foreign policy.[13]

While at SAIS, Brzezinski's classes were always in high demand. After teaching a class with fifty-six students, he limited his seminars to twenty students, each of whom had to go through a rigorous screening process to get into the course. He took his teaching obligations seriously and, despite all the demands on his time and numerous requests to speak, never missed a class. His SAIS students have exceptionally warm memories of him as a teacher. Here are a few recollections:

In the 1992 policy seminar, Dr. Brzezinski pushed us hard for clarity of thought and expression on a series of strategic policy issues. We were on pins and needles to a degree beyond any other class—no one wanted to let him down, and he brought out the best in us. One teaching detail I recall and often cite was his insistence that our papers be no more than 2 pages long—horrifying for grad students being asked to shape policy approaches to big, mega issues (mine was policy toward the former Soviet Union). His valuable insight into the minds of policymakers in this regard went along the following lines: "I hope many of you join government service, in this country or your home country (he had handpicked a good international mix), and provide advice to key policymakers. If you cannot express the essence of your approach in two pages, no policy maker is going to read it, so do more thinking." I certainly found that to be the case in the course of my State Dept career, whether it was Richard Holbrooke as an Assistant Secretary in the 1990s limiting cables from the field to no more than 1000 words, or various secretaries of state requiring all info and action memos to be no more than two pages (and for one secretary, it was a single page).[14]

In my educational experience, I've found that any educational organization, regardless of prestige, can have certain teachers who are gifted. They are able to create an environment in which students both learn a lot and are excited to do so. Zbigniew Brzezinski was such a teacher. It surprised me because my impression of him from the Carter Administration had been as a rather harsh, uncompromising cold warrior. His seminar was exceptional. He made clear at the outset that he would start classes on time and would not accept extensions—because that's how things are in real life. What impressed me most is that he actively encouraged and respected a diversity of views among his students, ranging from conservative realism to advocacy for more influence by the United Nations versus national governments. He really didn't appear to favor one over the other based on his own views, but instead focused on the quality of the argument. In my experience, that is rare in academia.[15]

"Zbig," a reference of endearment and dread among some of his students, was an upright man, who was neither upbeat nor uptight in person. He was methodical in his way of teaching, a man of discipline, purpose and preparedness. Small talk is not easy with him. He was a policymaker who taught, not a teacher who used to make policy. In my encounters, Zbig was not set out to be a mentor but he nevertheless taught. What I took away from his courses are perpetual tools for life and livelihood. All problems of the world can be solved if we do not insist on ideal solutions. Zbig's method of teaching and analysis was adapted from his National Security Advisor years under President Carter. His approach was reductionist, pragmatic and reliable. Above all, he approached all problem areas as a patriotic American. It was through America's lenses of national interest that we broached perennial problems of international affairs.[16]

Brzezinski was not very self-conscious about his teaching technique ("I just taught instinctively in the way I related to the students"). He never studied teaching; his style came out of his interaction with a class: "Out of my instinctive way of engaging students, somewhat intimidating them but also pushing them to do better. Making them appreciate the fact that they did well. I confined A's to something they would appreciate. I made a point by sending a letter saying you were one of a few from a large class getting an A."[17]

Brzezinski stopped full-time teaching at SAIS in 1998, but this did not mean he stopped teaching. He maintains an office at SAIS, and he meets colleagues and students there. In a sense, he has broadened his classroom through occasional (and extremely well attended) lectures at SAIS, as well as through his books, articles, and television commentary. Well into the ninth decade of an extraordinary life, he remains one of the wisest and most effective observers of world affairs—and a professor who is remembered by his students with awe and admiration.

## NOTES

1  Zbigniew Brzezinski, interview with author, February 24, 2012.

2  Ibid.

3  Ibid.

4  Patrick G. Vaughan, "Zbigniew Brzezinski: The Political and Academic Life of a Cold War Visionary" (PhD diss., University of West Virginia, 2003), 26–27.

5  Brzezinski interview.

6  Jack Gould, "TV: Preview of International Affairs," New York Times, March 26, 1962.

7  Brzezinski interview.

8  Justin Vaïsse, De Harvard à la Maison Blanche, Zbigniew Brzezinski et l'ascension des universitaires dans l'establishment de politique tangère américaine pendant la guerre froide. Habilitation à diriger recherché histoire (Paris: Sciences Po, 2011). (To be published in English in 2013 as Justin Vaïsse, Zbigniew Brzezinski: A Complete Biography.)

9  F. Stephen Larrabee, interview with Jeff Raider, March 31, 2003.

10  Brzezinski interview.

11  William E. Odom, interview cited in Jeff Raider, "Leadership Case: Zbigniew Brzezinski," unpublished paper prepared for the seminar "Leadership in Europe," School of Advanced International Studies, Johns Hopkins University, April 2003.

12  Charles Gati, interview with Jeff Raider.

13  Madeleine Albright with Bill Woodward, Madam Secretary: A Memoir, Madeleine Albright (New York: Miramax Books, 2003), 57.

14  George Kent, interview with Jeff Raider.

15  Daniel Hildreth, interview with Jeff Raider.

16  Thitinan Pongsudhirak, interview with Jeff Raider.

17  Brzezinski interview.

# CHAPTER 16

# An Appreciation

FRANCIS FUKUYAMA

My own appreciation of the life and intellect of Zbigniew Brzezinski has been shaped not only by his books and articles, but even more by the personal interactions I have had with him over more than two decades, primarily as a regular participant in the biweekly Current Issues seminar that he ran at the Johns Hopkins School of Advanced International Studies (SAIS) in Washington. Through the collapse of communism and the denouement of the cold war, the conflict in the Balkans, the Oslo Peace Process and first Gulf War, and then on through September 11 and all of the tumultuous events of the past decade, this seminar gave its participants a forum for exchanging views, hearing from outside speakers, and always benefiting from Zbig's incisiveness as the inevitable poser of the first question. His ability to keep the discussion focused on national interest and the big picture was a constant throughout these interactions, as was the extra dimension of wisdom born of personal experience with Washington and policy making. I regret that these luncheon seminars are no longer part of my life.

I believe that there are two broad accomplishments that will constitute Brzezinski's longer-term legacy. The first was his moral opposition to the former Soviet Union and its domination of Eastern Europe, as well as his consistent recognition of the threat that it posed to the democratic values and institutions of the West. The jaundiced view of Russian power came of course naturally to a Pole and an émigré from that part of the world. But his identity as a Pole served him rather as an anchor and not a bias in thinking about how to deal with the USSR.

His contribution began with the classic book he wrote with Carl Friedrich while still a young academic, *Totalitarian Dictatorship and Autocracy*, which became the lens through which Westerners saw totalitarian regimes in subsequent years. It established firmly the view, taken for granted in later years, of the essential difference between totalitarian and authoritarian regimes, based on the former's control of the "circular flow of power." The marriage of ideology to tyrannical political power redefined the struggles of the twentieth century in terms very different from anything that had come before.

The totalitarian model started fraying from the moment of Khrushchev's secret speech in 1956, but Brzezinski in his later analysis of the Soviet system was never trapped by that concept. He understood full well the extent to which the Soviet Bloc (to take the name of another of his foundational books) comprised heterogeneous interests, interests that might one day be used to undermine the system as a whole. This was, in many respects, the theme that tied together much of his early career.

The 1970s saw a rush toward détente on the part of Germany and other NATO countries; Zbig played an important role in the Carter administration moderating that impulse and making sure that considerations of power factored into our dealing with it. The final denouement of this course of events was, of course, the collapse of the Warsaw Pact, the end of the Soviet Union, and the liberation of Zbig's native Poland from communism and its integration into NATO and the European Union. It is hard to imagine an individual more vindicated by the actual course of historical events.

The second major area in which Brzezinski contributed importantly to the national debate was the Middle East. He has taken a consistently realist view of the region: that the interests of the United States were hurt by the prolongation of the Israeli-Arab conflict and by Israel's post-1967 occupation of the West Bank and Gaza, and that the parties themselves were incapable of coming to a solution on their own. He himself was a participant in the negotiation of the Camp David Accords that led to the Israeli-Egyptian peace treaty, which transformed the conflict from one between states to one between peoples.

In the face of the American commitment to Israel as a democratic ally and the seeming intractability of the conflict, there has been a long-standing temptation by the United States to downplay the importance of this issue relative to other threats and regions. Like Brent Scowcroft, Zbig understood that whatever else the United States did in the region, whether opposing the projection of Soviet power, or containment of Iran after the 1979 revolution, or dealing with radical Islamist terrorism, was made more difficult by this unresolved conflict. The kind of settlement he would have liked to see the United States impose might have worked had it been undertaken early on. Unfortunately, through missed oppor-

tunities and distraction with other issues, this never happened, and in the meantime the positions of the parties continued to polarize. Arafat and the secular
Palestine Liberation Organization were replaced with an Islamist Hamas, while
the Israeli public has shifted far to the right, and the prospects of a U.S.-brokered
peace have drifted farther away than ever.

In a way, Zbig's finest moment may have been his early and consistent opposition to the 2003 Iraq War. He was no stranger to the hardheaded use of American power—his Carter administration had, after all, initiated the Rapid Defense
Force that later evolved into Central Command, which was the basis for U.S.
power projection into the Persian Gulf. But he never bought into any of the apocalyptic scenarios of the global conflict with "Islamofascism" propagated by many
on the right in the aftermath of the September 11 attacks, and he remained deeply
skeptical of the willingness and ability of the United States to reshape the politics of the region through its deployment of hard power. Indeed, in his writings in
this period he warned of a broad-based global mobilization of social forces that
were transforming the politics of the region and that the United States would
have great difficulty controlling. These premonitions of an impending disaster
for U.S. influence in the Middle East were borne out by subsequent events as the
United States got sucked deeper into the Iraqi morass and the original apparent
success in Afghanistan turned into a grinding insurgency.

Like his contemporary and sometimes rival Henry Kissinger, Zbig was capable
of thinking strategically. Where he differed was in his straightforwardness and
courage in staking out positions. While Kissinger's views on any given subject,
from the Iraq War to George Schultz's initiative to eliminate nuclear weapons,
seem often driven by complex calculations on how he was to position himself
with regard to the political winds blowing at the given moment, Zbig always said
forthrightly what he thought, even when those views earned him considerable
opprobrium. He had blinders of his own: he was always far more interested in
what was going on in tiny Georgia than in giant Mexico next door, and one looks
in vain in his books for any sustained interest or insight into Latin America as a
whole. But there are in the end very few individuals who could match his breadth
of vision and engagement in the ongoing policy debate, sustained over an extraordinarily long and productive lifetime.

# CHAPTER 17

# A Self-Assessment

*In conversation with Charles Gati* *

CHARLES GATI: One way to start this conversation is to cite Max Ascoli, who was the founder and then editor of a now-defunct weekly called the *Reporter*. Like you (and I), he was an immigrant. He came to this country from Italy on the eve of World War II. Many years later, Ascoli said that some people may have been born abroad but their personality made them "born American." Do you feel that way?

ZBIGNIEW BRZEZINSKI: I don't feel I was "born American," but my homeland was denied to me after the end of World War II and I craved something I could identify with. When I became a student at Harvard in the 1950s, America very quickly filled the vacuum. I felt I was American, but I think it's more revealing of America how quickly others here accepted me.

CG: Who made an impression on you? I know you were close to the late Bill Odom. Would you talk about your relationship, and perhaps also relate that phone call he made to you at 3:00 a.m. on November 19, 1979?

ZB: Bill Odom was a military guy. After he had come back from a stint in Vietnam, we first met at Columbia University. I asked him to make a presentation at a lun-

---

* This is a condensed and edited version of two conversations. One was held in front of a small group of SAIS students and faculty on February 22, 2012. The second conversation took place at Professor Brzezinski's office on May 4, 2012. With the assistance of Bree Bang-Jensen, the text was edited for publication by Charles Gati and approved by Zbigniew Brzezinski.

cheon I was running, and I was quite struck how analytical and intelligent he was. In the early 1970s, he spent several years at Columbia. We stayed in touch. By the time I went to the White House, he had become a colonel. I decided to have him as my military aide, and we worked very closely together.

Our friendship ran the gamut from our professional relationship to playing tennis regularly, to sharing a common interest in the Soviet Bloc, to traveling to the former bloc shortly after it collapsed and celebrating the independence of the new countries. It was almost a victory lap as we traveled from capital to capital.

And I also remember him for waking me up one night. It was, as you say, on November 19, 1979. He was my military assistant, but he was also my crisis officer. My job was to coordinate the president's decision in response to a nuclear attack on the United States. Odom woke me up at 3:00 a.m. When I picked up the phone, I could hear him say: "Sorry, sir. We are under nuclear attack." That kind of wakes you up. I said, "Yes? Tell me," and he says, "30 seconds ago, 200 Soviet missiles have been fired at the United States." According to the rules, I had two more minutes to verify this information and then an additional four minutes to wake up the president, go over the options in the so-called football, get the president's decision, and then initiate the response. So, I said to him, "Call me back when you have the information verified," and I remember sitting there. It was a strange feeling because I'm not some gung-ho hero, physically. When I would fly into turbulence, for example, I'd be very nervous. This time I was totally calm. Somehow or another, I knew everybody would be dead in 28 minutes—my wife, my kids, everybody else. If that was the case, I was going to make sure we had lots of company. So, I said to him, "Make sure the Strategic Air Command proceeds to take off." Then I waited for confirmations. With one minute left, we waited for one more confirmation. Bill called back and said, "Canceled. Wrong tapes. It never took place." I remember saying to him, "Make sure the Strategic Air Command is called back."

Bill Odom was an intellectual and a fighter at the same time, a combination I liked.

CG: Would you talk about your father? I'd be particularly interested in the role he played in helping Central and Eastern European Jews escape persecution in the years before World War II.

ZB: Not long ago, I got a letter from a woman who lives near Washington, in Bethesda, Maryland. She started off by saying, "I'm 93 and I meant to write to you much earlier, but I am doing it now, before I pass away. I want you to know that your father [a Polish consul in Germany, 1931–35] saved me and my late husband by issuing my father passports for our family. He certified that we were Polish citizens." In fact, they were German citizens. My father's actions were contrary to his diplomatic status.

CG: Did he ever talk to you about his views?

ZB: He was a profoundly liberal person who was offended by the semi-fascist manifestations of Polish anti-Semitism. The first time I remember it coming up was when in the mid-1930s we were walking together down the streets of a city called Lodz. I was about 6. We saw a bunch of right-wing fanatics. They had a huge sign in Polish that said, "All Jews and swine live only in Palestine. Warsaw and Krakow are only for the Poles." My father was using a cane, not because he needed it but because it was a stylish European habit at that time, and he charged at them with it. As for the passports he'd issued, while I was a child I didn't really know that he was issuing them. I know that he did it because the Israeli government recognized him and several years ago he was honored for what he did.

CG: During the war, your father was transferred and the family moved to Montreal. As a teenager you met the famous Jan Karski there, who was on his way to Washington from Poland to relate what he knew about the holocaust. He and I became friends when he was a professor, for some forty years, at Georgetown University. Posthumously, he received the Presidential Medal of Freedom from Obama in 2012.

ZB: During the war, our house in Montreal became a kind of a getaway for people my father knew from Poland. I recall that Jan Karski was in our house, about to meet President Roosevelt. Karski was the emissary for the Polish underground, on his way to report to the world what had been happening to the Jews. I remember noticing he had scars on his wrists.

He had put on the uniform of an SS officer in order to observe the conditions in the concentration camps firsthand. He was caught at the border between Poland and Slovakia. He was supposed to travel through Poland to Hungary, to occupied Yugoslavia and then to the west, but the Gestapo caught him and tortured him. He couldn't take it anymore, so he slashed his wrists, trying to commit suicide. He was quickly placed by the Nazis in a hospital because they knew he was valuable. He passed word to some nuns in the hospital that he was an emissary from the underground, asking to meet a priest to talk about his mission and to pass a message back to the underground. They brought a priest to speak with him. Karski explained who he was, and the priest said, "I deal with spiritual matters, not human matters." But several hours later, some armed men showed up to smuggle him out. So the priest wasn't so bad, he was just fearful of exposing himself to a stranger.

I remember my father asking Karski, "Well, what's happening in Poland to the Jews?" Karski said, "They are being murdered." My father came from the eastern part of Poland where there was a large and vibrant Jewish community. He said, "What do you mean by that?" Karski said, "Just what I'm telling you. They're all being killed." And I remember my father asking, "Well, what do you mean by 'all'? Men? Women? Children?" Karski said, "Yes, that's exactly what I just told you." And my father was shocked. Even though he knew Hitler hated the Jews, initially he still couldn't conceive what Karski had to say.

I've since read that when Karski went to Washington and talked to Felix Frankfurter [Roosevelt's friend and advisor], the conversation was similar. Frankfurter even turned to the Polish ambassador and said, "I cannot believe this." And the Polish ambassador exploded, "Felix! How can you say that to this man? Look at his wrists!" And Frankfurter replied, "I didn't say I don't believe him; I'm unable to believe what I hear." When I read this account, it was so reminiscent of my father's reaction in Montreal.

CG: Another key figure in your life was Pope John Paul II.

ZB: At the beginning of his career, during World War II, he was a worker priest. He subscribed to a notion of social justice. He wasn't against the free market system, but he wasn't devoted to capitalism. He emphasized social responsibility and some sort of balance in the distribution of wealth. I happen to share that point of view. The pope was a fascinating combination of spirituality and political sensitivity. He was infectious in his religious convictions, which were spontaneous and deeply felt. They were expressed in very simple words, which he demonstrated when he assumed the papacy.

I went to his coronation as the U.S. representative, in part for symbolic reasons due to the Polish connection. We sat outside St. Peters. Some sixty thousand people were there. When he walked out, he had a theatrical manner, he was charismatic. He raised his hands, and he reached out and said to this huge crowd, "Do not be afraid," and then he gave his talk. In a way, with that one sentence, he touched on the ultimate mystery and sense of anxiety inherent in the human condition. This is so because we really don't know who we are. We don't know how long we exist. We don't know what exists, if anything, beyond our physical existence. That's the mystery of life, and it introduces elements of fear. And his message was *do not be afraid*; that there is something transcendental that gives more meaning and significance to your existence.

At the same time, he was a very political person, and he certainly disapproved of communism. He understood, in that context, America's role as a counterweight to the Soviet Union, but he didn't necessarily glorify, say, the Strategic Air Command. Spiritually we were all on the same side. And in that context, it was very easy for me to talk to him, both about politics and to some extent about questions of theology and faith. I said to him once that I'm a Catholic because I was born a Catholic, but if I was born in China I would have been a Buddhist. And to me, there are many ways to reach a sense of what is beyond us, and not just one. And I thought he would disagree, but he said, "No, you're absolutely right."

I used to see him whenever I was in Rome, and during one visit I went to his apartment for lunch. I walked to the room where we were supposed to sit down, and there was a little chapel on the side. It was the middle of the day; he was lying on the floor, all by himself. It wasn't a show for anybody. He was lying on the floor with his arms stretched out in a cross position in front of the altar, praying.

CG: The Soviet leadership believed that you engineered his election.

ZB: Sure. The Soviet politburo was briefed on the proposition that I allegedly got Cardinal Krol of Philadelphia to organize American cardinals. Then the American cardinals organized the German cardinals in an American-German Coalition of Cardinals, then some others, and therefore I was responsible for his election. The pope had heard of this "grand conspiracy." I remember saying good-bye to him once and he said, "Come and see me soon." I said, "Oh, I can't do that so often. This is too much. You know, it's a privilege." And he replied, laughing, "You elected me. You have to come and see me."

CG: Before I ask you about presidents you met or knew, talk a bit about the last Soviet leader, Mikhail Gorbachev. What did you think of him in 1985 when he rose to prominence, and what do you make of him now?

ZB: In 1985, I thought of him as a breath of fresh air, especially compared to his predecessors. At that point, it was clear to all that the previous Soviet leadership had profoundly deteriorated. And he was different, he was younger, he was intelligent, he was congenial, and he didn't even talk like a convinced or practiced Communist. But I also thought he was a bungler in terms of his inability to give his idea of perestroika some sort of political and social coherence. I think that judgment actually remains justified, but what I had failed to recognize in 1985 was that he was introducing a different style of decision making and a willingness to experiment. Subsequently, as I got to know him a little bit better, I also began to see him as a person who was really thoughtful and intelligent, quite daring, had a sense of humor and even a little bit of flexibility.

Let me tell you a little anecdote here, too. After he lost his positions in Russia, we used to meet at different conferences around the world. I was registering in a hotel the evening before one such conference when all of a sudden I heard someone shouting my name, "Zbeeeg! Zbeeeg!" I turn around. It's Gorbachev. So he gave me a hug. I gave him a hug. This was the first time when I met him when he was no longer Russian president, and I said to myself, "Well, if he calls me 'Zbig,' I'm going to call him 'Mikhail.'" I said, "Mikhail! Mikhail!" I could tell he stiffened. It wasn't such a big deal though. Next day, however, in his speech he said, "Talk to Brzezinski here. Of course, he's longing for the good old days of the cold war which he so enjoyed." So, after the event was over, I went over to him, put my arm around him, and said to him, "Mikhail, why did you say that about me? It had nothing to do with my speech." He replied, "Zbeeeg, Zbeeeg, they paid us. They expected us to argue."

CG: Were you paid that well?

ZB: Not really, but he seemed to think we were.

CG: Let me ask you about five of the presidents you met, some you knew well. What did you think of them when you encountered them, and what do you think of them now, looking back? The first one is JFK, I think.

ZB: I met him in the 1950s when I was at Harvard, and I thought the world of him. I was greatly inspired by him when he became president, I found his Inaugural Address moving, I liked that special sense of vigor and enthusiasm that he injected into an America that seemed to be a little bit uncertain of itself, especially after the launch of the Sputnik. And I was profoundly shocked when he was shot. I remember that moment vividly, but I have to add that the more I learned about him later on, the more I became inclined to temper my enthusiasm for him. I began to see that he was much more manipulative, much more opportunistic, much more self-serving, much less guided by any profound sort of code of conduct or standard than I had believed. So it was, in a way, a disillusioning reassessment.

CG: President Carter is next. When it comes to foreign policy, there are some critics who think he's just about the weakest modern president. This is strange because during his tenure—and yours, of course—the United States normalized its relations with China, the Camp David Accords were signed, there was agreement about SALT II, Panama, no major wars occurred. True, you failed to bring home the hostages from Iran. But is Carter getting a raw deal now? Is his current critical view of Israel a source of these criticisms? Is this, at least partly, a retroactive judgment?

ZB: First of all, I don't think that the prevailing national opinion is that hostile, but it's certainly true that segments of our society feel negatively about him, especially those who believe in the unilateral use of force, and also what you mentioned with respect to his views on Israel. I would argue that on balance he might be seen as a president who anticipated the serious problems we have now with energy and who dealt very effectively with a number of critical foreign policy issues. If George W. Bush or Barack Obama had accomplished half as much during their time in office, it would be viewed as a great success. I also think a lot of the interpretation of Carter's legacy has to do with emotions. Let's face it: the Jewish community is the most active political community in American society. And people within that community were very upset by Carter asserting that Israel was becoming an apartheid state.

CG: That upset me, too.

ZB: Well, it may bother you, it bothers me in the sense that I wish it wasn't happening. But you know who else has said that? [Former Israeli prime minister] Ehud Barak, among others. Word for word. When it comes to Jewish sensitivity, I don't find the proposition compelling that non-Jews have no right to comment. We all have the right to comment about each other. And I object when people say that these comments are motivated by anti-Semitism. It's a much more complicated issue, and it actually trivializes anti-Semitism.

CG: Saving Soviet Jews by letting them emigrate to the United States was an idea that preceded the Carter administration, but whose idea was Carter's human rights policy? Did you embrace it in order to play up and advertise Soviet oppression?

ZB: He bought my commitment to human rights and I shared his, except that mine had a special twist when it came to the Soviet Union. Carter was initially hesitant but eventually approved my recommendation that we undermine Soviet cohesion by supporting the national aspirations of the non-Russian peoples in the Soviet Union—even though the State Department came in with a counter-recommendation not to do it, which they justified on grounds that were unbelievable. State maintained that just as there is an American nation made up of people of different ethnic origins, there is a Soviet nation made up of people of different ethnic origins. I remember asking someone at State, "Do you happen to know what language the 'Soviet nation' speaks? Is it the Soviet language?" There is no common language. The Ukrainians speak Ukrainian. The Turkmanis speak Turkman. The Kazakh speak Kazakh, and the Balts didn't consider themselves to be part of the Soviet Union. This is not America where we individually adopt the American version of English as a common language. We have become part of America as individuals, not as territorially inhabited nations subjected to rule from Washington.

CG: My reading is that President Reagan was receptive to your perspective on Moscow. I imagine you briefed him during the transition.

ZB: Yes, I briefed him on occasion because some people in the White House thought I was a good briefer. According to [Reagan advisor and future CIA head William] Casey's memoirs, he even considered keeping me on as his national security advisor, but that never would have worked. However, I have an anecdote that seems to confirm what Casey was saying. I got a phone call once from [another Reagan associate and future attorney general Edwin] Meese saying that a three-day war exercise was being planned involving a collision between the United States and the Soviet Union. The president would preside. But the president didn't want to preside for three days, he wanted to preside for two hours and then walk out and announce that I was taking over on his behalf. I was totally surprised, and I said, "Why does the president want me to do this?" and Meese replied, "Well, he said that you have a presidential perspective."

My head was swimming at this point, and then something stupid occurred to me—stupid from the point of view of my personal self-interest. I said that I would do it, of course, but I wanted to know if he had asked [Reagan aide and future secretary of state Alexander] Haig and [Secretary of Defense Caspar] Weinberger. I don't know how they would react if I were to substitute for the president. After a moment of silence, Meese replied, "That's a very good point. Let me check with them." He called back in the afternoon and said, "There has been a change of plans. We are going to ask [former secretary of state] Bill Rogers to preside. It will be less difficult." But this tells you something about my relationship with Reagan. And he did adopt some of my ideas, particularly on Afghanistan.

CG: For the younger generation, you are best known as a strong, insistent critic of President George W. Bush. What did you think of him in 2001? What do you think of him now?

ZB: What I thought of him in 2001 is not fundamentally different from what I think of him now. The only difference is that there is a lot more evidence to sustain my original point of view. I think he contributed very directly to the fact that the status of America as the world's only superpower lasted for twenty years at most.

CG: The last of the five presidents on my list here is Barack Obama. You endorsed him early on. What did you think of him in 2008, and what do you think of him now?

ZB: We met a couple times about a year before the elections, and I traveled with him and we had a chance to talk. I was impressed that he had a very perceptive grasp of how the existing international reality has fundamentally changed and how much more complex the global scene has become. He understood that America ought to pursue its national interests in that broad context and with great sensitivity. The speech in Cairo, the speech in Istanbul, the Brandenburg Gate speech before the elections, the Prague speech, all confirmed my original judgment about him. He understood that for a variety of reasons global hegemony by a single power and particularly a Western power is no longer possible. There has been a shift within the global system, from west to east. The global political awakening we've witnessed in recent years has created a situation that is so volatile that America has to be both intelligent and appealing in order to be effective.

I tend to be more critical now because while he has proven that he preaches very well, he has not demonstrated that he strategizes very well. The current mess we have in the Middle East, for example, could turn into an explosion that will be region-wide and terribly damaging to the global economy and to our national interest. Here I see a failure of strategic determination, maybe strategic vision, on his part. This may be the consequence of the economic and financial problems at home that he has had to confront; in other words, maybe he got diverted. But it's probably worse than that. At a critical juncture he failed to show he had steel in his back, he failed to follow through. He spoke on the record and very sensibly about the settlements, but when a confrontation developed between him and [Israeli prime minister Benjamin] Netanyahu, Obama caved in. That has contributed significantly to the general mess we now have in the Middle East.

I'm sympathetic to his dilemma; he didn't want to jeopardize his reelection. Yet I also think that when really great issues are at stake, sometimes you have to take a chance and do what you think is right. We could be sliding to a really bad explosion, the consequences of which would be detrimental to our interests.

CG: The next controversial issue I'd like to probe has to do with human rights and China and the infighting within the Carter administration. Your critics claimed that you were more than willing to put détente and arms control with the Soviets on the backburner because you felt you would get better results if you had better relations with China. But this was not the view of Vance, it was not the view of Marshall Shulman, our colleague at Columbia. They disagreed with you, and they really didn't like you at the time. Leslie Gelb called you a street fighter...

ZB: I consider that to be a compliment.

CG: From today's perspective, how do you assess the Carter administration's China policy?

ZB: First of all, I question the word you used to describe the American-Soviet relationship at the time. You referred to it as détente. It really wasn't détente. It was a time of increased tensions as the Soviet Union began to engage in military operations in Africa and so forth, claiming as well that they had superior military and economic capabilities. It is almost humorous to recall that today. But those were the circumstances. We lived every day with the possibility of nuclear war. In that context, the relationship with China obviously had enormous strategic significance, and that is what was guiding me. Of course, the critics raised the issue of "abandoning" Taiwan, but they conveniently forgot that this issue was resolved years earlier during the Nixon-Kissinger visit to China when the United States acknowledged the fact that we respect China's view that there is only one China.

CG: So your negotiations reinforced what Kissinger had approved?

ZB: We didn't reinforce it, we translated it into a normal relationship that not only gave us diplomatic leverage but initiated an intelligence-sharing policy and some de facto geopolitical cooperation against the Soviets. And subsequent to all of that, the new relationship permitted a flowering of Chinese economic reforms after we were out of office, something that Deng Xiaoping couldn't have otherwise undertaken. In other words, we began with what was a promising but increasingly tense partnership between the United States and China. We managed to have a major breakthrough. I could not understand why some people at the State Department wanted to drag their feet on it.

CG: You were willing to take human rights off the table in your relationship with China.

ZB: We didn't have much of a relationship with China until the very last year [1980]. There was some discussion of human rights between President Carter and Deng Xiaoping. Since then, it has become an issue within China. Obviously, there has to be some balance between our ability to promote what we might call an abstract good, on the one hand, and the necessity of promoting the national interest, on the other. It's a long-standing dilemma that no one can resolve with any degree of mathematical precision.

CG: Whether the United States should approach human rights concerns quietly or through public confrontation is a subject of perpetual controversy. Where do you stand on this?

ZB: I'd add one more dimension to it, domestic perception. Is it politically advantageous or fashionable to be doing this and so on? There is no simple formula, in every case you have to make a judgment: what is at stake? How useful is it to the national interest to promote human rights? How counterproductive may it become? And in every case the answer varies.

CG: How about expressing it publicly, even if you know that in the short run it will not produce results, but by expressing such concerns we—Americans—might feel better? "Standing up" for human rights may sustain a favorable self-image of American idealism or altruism.

ZB: I don't think that's a very good argument. Foreign policy should not be justified through making oneself feel good, but through results that have tangible consequences. There may be circumstances in which damaging our relationship with countries over human rights is counterproductive and the benefits to human rights may be very small because of our limited capacity to enforce our stance. That was the dilemma the United States faced after Tiananmen Square. The cost was very brutal, but the benefit was our improving relationship with China. Could we really have changed the fate of the students or changed the Chinese political system through pressure? The answer is probably not. Was the positive relationship with China worth it? Probably so. It's a case-by-case decision.

CG: Do you think China is still as useful as when the Soviet Union existed, especially now that we're effectively mortgaged in this relationship?

ZB: Useful is not necessarily the right word. I think it's a fact of life that we'll have a relationship with China; without such a relationship each of us would be worse off. Our interests wouldn't be served by a policy that was designed to prevent China from becoming economically and socially more successful. It's a country of almost a billion and a half people, extremely intelligent and energetic; what conceivable benefit would there be in trying to make China weak, disorganized, and hostile?

We have a close relationship with China, and it is our most important relationship in Asia and probably in the world. I have no apologies to make for pushing for a relationship with China that helped us end the cold war with Russia. To some degree, the relationship has also helped bring China into the world as a whole, with an attitude that is significantly different from the attitude that used to motivate the Soviet Union. What we see, in short, is an unprecedented historical experiment. Can the United States and China—can two preeminent powers—coexist? I reject the proposition that they cannot, and I reject the normative proposition that they shouldn't. I think we should try to make it work, and I think that if we're both intelligent we can succeed. I hasten to add, however, that there are clouds on the horizon. There's an unfortunate tendency to engage in mutual demonization.

CG: To pursue your more controversial views, let's turn to Israel. While the neocons and others too criticize you, and the Netanyahu government is certainly very upset with you, a growing number of Americans have come to embrace the two-state solution. Do you foresee a settlement in the next five years?

ZB: I do. Whether it's possible in five years, I can't say. I had expected a settlement in the first four years of the Obama presidency and it didn't happen, but I still think that the good sense of the Israeli people will prevail. I think that the majority of Israelis have good common sense and strong principles that would make a settlement possible.

CG: Do you think the criticism directed against you is because the critics disagree with you on the feasibility of a two-state solution that you've suggested or on your four points as the basis for negotiations, or is it founded on prejudice against a Polish Catholic?

ZB: I think that plays a role. Martin Peretz [for many years owner and editor of the *New Republic*] never fails to identify me as "the Catholic Polish-American national security advisor" and describes me explicitly as anti-Semitic. I never exploited my father's role in helping Jews avoid the concentration camps, for example. It was you who prompted me to talk about it earlier in this conversation.

CG: When you were at Columbia, you told me that most of your friends were Jewish. Is that still true?

ZB: It is, but it sounds like that awful joke, "Some of my best friends are Jewish...." But the fact is yes, because I grew up in an intellectual environment and Jews are intellectually in the premier class. Maybe half of those who attended my wedding in a Catholic church were Jewish. My friend at Harvard, Dean Henry Rosovsky, was once approached by a Jewish publication that asked for some evidence of my anti-Semitism. His reply: "Oh, yes, I can tell you a story about that. You know, he made me kneel on this horrible floor during his wedding. Why don't you get the hell out of my office?" I have no patience for those in the American Jewish community who just go around slandering people as anti-Semites without realizing that what they're doing is really trivializing anti-Semitism. I hope—actually, I think—that it's beginning to change now.

Just one more thought: You know, the only country, apart from Poland, where I feel really at home when I'm abroad is Israel. That's where I remember—even relive—my childhood. In Israel, there are so many people there from Poland, and we speak Polish together.

CG: Another charge against you, quite widespread in the 1960s and 1970s among Democrats, was that you were a Russophobe, that everything you did and said reflected deep-rooted hostility toward not only Communists or totalitarians but Russia. How do you address the Russophobe charge?

ZB: To some extent, I question the first part of your question suggesting that some Democrats were suspicious of me. Consider the following: I served as co-chairman of Young Americans for Lyndon Johnson, so that particular Democrat didn't seem to share the view you cite. Another Democrat, Hubert Humphrey, asked me to be his principal foreign policy advisor, so he didn't have that view of me either. And then, in the early 1970s, and I say this even though it sounds very immodest, I had my pick of whoever I wanted to advise on foreign policy. So, obviously, they had a different view than the "Democrats" you're referring to. That said, I know there was a segment in the American foreign policy establishment that viewed me with suspicion. That group wasn't solely Democratic; it was both Democrats and Republicans, including many from the traditional WASP elite that believed that you had to be a third- or fourth-generation American to understand and speak on behalf of the national interest.

[Former New York governor W. Averell] Harriman was one of the old-timers who expressed this view [for details, see chap. 1 in this volume—CG]. I took him head-on. "You are questioning my credentials as a foreign-born Pole. What about you, a multimillionaire who owns this and that in Russia, mines in Georgia?" He wrote me an apology.

CG: I'm glad you took him on. He was a good governor, as I recall, but he was both naive and condescending about the Soviet Union—a terrible combination. What about post-Soviet Russia? You sound more optimistic about its future these days.

ZB: I think we have the emergence of a new reality in Russia, and it's the dominant reality. It's mushrooming, and its chances of intensifying are very high, mainly through the beginnings of a civil society. We see not just heroic individuals as in the past, isolated and often persecuted dissidents we could admire as individuals, but increasingly we're witnessing a broader phenomenon. The younger members of a growing new middle class are evidence of a genuine urban-based civic society with its own aspirations and expectations. There are also some other symptoms of this new reality. I don't think we understand it here in America, because we often follow events in such a shallow fashion, just how diversified the mass media has become in Russia, how different facts and perceptions can be found in different newspapers and on the Internet. Even political satire is part of the new reality there.

My impression is that in the West our perception of change in Russia is overly dominated by the shadow of Putin, his nostalgia for the past. It obscures the pattern of deeper change, which I think makes his tenure problematic. It's hard to tell which way he'll react; he may try to resist it or go with the flow.

Here's a somewhat complicated story that tells you a great deal about today's Russia. Bear with me. You may remember the time when the Chechens supposedly blew up residential houses in Moscow and Putin used that as an excuse to attack them. According to one interpretation of what happened, the bombings were actually instigated by the Federal Security Service of the Russian Federation (abbreviated from the Russian as FSB, today's KGB), and Putin exploited that. Of course, to most Westerners this seems far-fetched. How could a leader of a country blow up or arrange to have blown up apartment houses in which his fellow citizens lived?

But then consider this. There was a Russian who fled to London with some additional information on the bombings. It was Alexander Litvinenko, a former FSB agent, and he was murdered. Was he murdered because of what he knew? We don't know exactly what he knew. But we know that his sponsor in London was a Russian oligarch, Boris Berezovsky. And Berezovsky made a documentary film that suggests that the FSB and presumably Putin were responsible for the blowing up of these apartment houses. Now comes my punch line: Do you know that this film is being shown in three movie houses in Moscow? For me who experienced the rise of the Soviet Union, its outreach for global power, and then its disintegration, this is of monumental symbolic significance. At the least, this story shows two things: first, that Russian minds are now opened (and they cannot be shut again), and second, that fear has disappeared. To bring fear back would require monumental effort that may be beyond Putin's capacity to deliver. To paraphrase Pope John Paul II: If you have no fear, you have the makings of change.

CG: As we're coming to the end of these conversations, I'd like to ask if you have any regrets about what you wrote, said, or did. Vietnam?

ZB: Yes. I supported the war in Vietnam until I went to Vietnam myself in 1968, and I changed my mind after being there. So, yes, in a sense, I regret it. I don't really regret it very much because at the time I didn't have much influence at all. Still, I certainly underestimated—in fact, not only underestimated but totally missed—the critical disconnect between Vietnamese nationalist aspirations and the Communist movement.

CG: Any regrets about supporting the mujahedeen in Afghanistan?

ZB: No. No, no. It would be far worse if we had not. First, after 9/11 we would have encountered much more hostility from them. Second, if the Soviet Union had prevailed then—at a time when Iran was collapsing and the Pakistan government was as unstable as it was—you can use your imagination to figure out what the situation would be. So, you know, the choice was either to be engaged or not to be engaged, and the engagement at least contributed to the eventual defeat of the Soviets in Afghanistan.

CG: Speaking of Afghanistan but actually throughout the cold war, you were widely seen as a hawk. But now, in this book, chapter 12 refers to you—in its subtitle at that—as a dove. I also recall that in 1989 you gave an interview to *Time*; its subtitle was "The Vindication of a Hard-Liner."

ZB: Let me first address the dichotomy between hawk and dove. I don't see myself as ever having been a hawk. I don't see myself as being a dove right now, either. I was always for a policy which allowed us to prevail in the cold war, and to do it by a strategy of what I called peaceful engagement. We engage them. We deal with the regimes. We penetrate the societies. We begin to exploit the fissures between the Central Europeans and the Russians. We eventually break up the Soviet Union from within.

President Reagan continued the programs I instituted as national security advisor. Among other measures, we let Radio Free Europe grow and aided the non-Russian nationalisms to weaken Soviet power. Broadly speaking, I think history has confirmed the validity of my concept.

When it comes to the more recent years, and specifically the war in Iraq, I just thought it was "justified" by falsehoods. It's as simple as that, and I don't think a democracy should make a commitment of its youth and its resources to fight a war based on falsehoods. What was Saddam Hussein going to do to us after he was effectively disarmed by Bush Senior? He was in a state of impotence after that. So I was against that war. When it comes to Afghanistan, I was for immediate intervention after 9/11. But I also remember writing a note to [Secretary of Defense Ronald] Rumsfeld—and some of it I actually incorporated into an op-ed—that we should go in, we should knock off the Taliban from power, we should destroy al-Qaeda if we can do it, but we should not get involved in a prolonged effort to create a democratic modern society in Afghanistan because if we try to do that we'll be repeating the mistake the Soviets made when they invaded Afghanistan in order to create a socialist or Communist society. So there, I differed.

CG: After our first conversation you told me—as kindly as you could—that I'd make a good interrogator. So let me throw you a softball at long last: Of all your accomplishments, what are you most proud of?

ZB: I guess I feel best about the way the cold war ended, without bloodshed and with success, and I think that was something to which I made a contribution. I'm not claiming it was thanks to me, but I think I contributed to the eventual outcome. And ending the cold war without something like World War III was a blessing, and that's historically as important, perhaps even more important, as prevailing. So I feel very good about that.

I feel good about the relationships I've had with my students. It was never very loving and tender, because I'm not that kind of a person, but I tried to give them my best. In some cases, it worked out okay.

I probably can't add very much to this. I'm not the kind of person who spends too much time reflecting about myself. I don't assess things in my own past.

CG: My very last question is about your name. When you became a U.S. citizen in Boston in 1958, the judge gave you a chance to change your name. Did you consider the offer?

ZB: I considered it, but I decided to keep my original name for two reasons. It was a good time for me, personally and professionally, I was feeling confident about my future, and I said to myself, why change my name? I was also confident about America and the idea that in America people can become American without masking their ethnic identity.

This was confirmed for me soon when I began to appear on the public scene. Sometime early in the 1960s, out of the blue, *Newsweek* ran a very complimentary article about me. I was just over 30, but the article talked about my influence on American foreign policy, ending with the comment that America is the only country where someone called "Zbigniew Brzezinski" can make a name for himself without changing his name.

# ACKNOWLEDGMENTS

I am grateful for the generous support of Johns Hopkins University's Nitze School of Advanced International Studies and the Smith Richardson Foundation. Christine Kunkel of the School's Foreign Policy Institute handled administrative details with skill and care. Bree Bang-Jensen served as my and several contributors' research assistant. Her help was indispensable. Her willingness to respond to my queries any time of the day or night, and to do so with both understanding and deep interest, made it possible to complete this book on time. My wife's extensive notes of the conversation recorded in chapter 17 proved to be very helpful, and I thank her for that. Last but not least, readers and reviewers should blame me for the book's shortcomings and praise the authors for their expert contributions.

# CHRONOLOGY

| | |
|---|---|
| 1928 | Born in Warsaw, Poland |
| 1931 | Brzezinski's father, Tadeusz, a member of the Polish Foreign Ministry, is posted to Berlin |
| 1936 | Tadeusz is posted to the Soviet Union |
| 1938 | Tadeusz is posted to Montreal as consul-general, the family moves to Canada |
| 1945 | Graduates from Loyola High School, enters McGill University in Montreal |
| 1949 | Receives BA from McGill |
| 1950 | Receives MA from McGill, writing thesis on "Russo-Soviet Nationalism," begins doctoral program at Harvard University, Cambridge |
| 1953 | Receives PhD from Harvard, begins work as an instructor at Harvard |
| 1955 | Marries sculptor Emilie Anna Benes |
| 1956 | *The Permanent Purge* and *Totalitarian Dictatorship and Autocracy* (with Carl Friedrich) are published |
| 1957 | Visits Poland for the first time since childhood |
| 1958 | Becomes a U.S. citizen in Boston |
| 1960 | Leaves Harvard for Columbia University in New York, advises John F. Kennedy's presidential campaign, receives Guggenheim Fellowship |
| 1961 | Becomes a member of the Council on Foreign Relations |
| 1962 | *Ideology and Power in Soviet Politics* is published |
| 1963 | Ian Brzezinski is born |
| 1964 | Chosen as one of the U.S. Junior Chamber of Commerce's "Ten Outstanding Young Men of 1963," serves as cochair of Young Americans for Lyndon Johnson |

| | |
|---|---|
| 1965 | Mark Brzezinski is born; *Alternative to Partition* is published |
| 1966 | Joins the Policy Planning Council (S/P) for the Department of State |
| 1967 | Mika Brzezinski is born |
| 1968 | Serves as principal foreign policy advisor for Hubert H. Humphrey's presidential campaign |
| 1970 | *Between Two Ages* is published |
| 1971 | Spends six months in Japan on a Ford Foundation fellowship |
| 1973 | Starts the Trilateral Commission with David Rockefeller |
| 1973 | Invites Governor Jimmy Carter of Georgia to join the Trilateral Commission |
| 1974 | Joins Middle East study group at Brookings; group releases a report with a plan for peace in the Middle East |
| 1975 | Begins advising Carter on foreign policy |
| 1977 | Serves as President Carter's national security advisor |
| 1978 | Travels to Beijing to lay the groundwork for normalization; Polish Cardinal Karol Wojtyla elected Pope John Paul II; Camp David Accords |
| 1979 | Iran hostage crisis; Soviet invasion of Afghanistan |
| 1980 | Solidarity labor union is formed in Poland |
| 1981 | Resumes academic career at Columbia University, joins Center for Strategic and International Studies (CSIS), receives Presidential Medal of Freedom; martial law imposed in Poland |
| 1983 | *Power and Principle* is published |
| 1985 | Serves as a member of the Chemical Warfare Commission |
| 1987 | Joins the National Security Council–Defense Department Commission on Integrated Long Term Strategy, serves on President's Foreign Intelligence Advisory Board |
| 1988 | Endorses George W. H. Bush over Michael Dukakis, serves as cochair of the Bush National Security Task Force |
| 1989 | Leaves Columbia University to teach at SAIS Johns Hopkins in Washington, D.C. |
| 1989 | *The Grand Failure* is published; travels to Moscow in October |
| 1990 | Opposes the Gulf War |
| 1992 | *Out of Control* is published |
| 1997 | *The Grand Chessboard* is published |
| 2002 | Becomes a leading opponent to the Iraq War |
| 2004 | *The Choice: Global Domination or Global Leadership* is published |

| | |
|---|---|
| 2007 | Endorses Barack Obama for president; *Second Chance: Three American Presidents and the Crisis of American Superpower* is published |
| 2012 | *Strategic Vision* is published |

# SELECTED BIBLIOGRAPHY

## BOOKS BY ZBIGNIEW BRZEZINSKI

*The Permanent Purge: Politics in Soviet Totalitarianism.* Cambridge, MA: Harvard University Press, Russian Research Center Studies, 1956.

*Totalitarian Dictatorship and Autocracy.* Cambridge, MA: Harvard University Press, 1956. With Carl Friedrich.

*The Soviet Bloc: Unity and Conflict.* Cambridge, MA: Harvard University Press, 1960.

*Ideology and Power in Soviet Politics.* New York: Praeger Books, 1962.

*Political Power: U.S.A./U.S.S.R.* New York: Viking Press, 1964. With Samuel Huntington.

*Alternative to Partition: For a Broader Conception of America's Role in Europe.* New York: Published for the Council on Foreign Relations by McGraw-Hill, Atlantic Policy Studies Series, 1965.

*Between Two Ages: America's Role in the Technetronic Era.* New York: Viking Press, 1970.

*The Fragile Blossom: Crisis and Change in Japan.* New York: Harper and Row, 1972.

*Power and Principle: Memoirs of the National Security Adviser, 1977–1981.* New York: Farrar, Straus, Giroux, 1983.

*Game Plan: A Geostrategic Framework for the Conduct of the U.S.-Soviet Contest.* Boston: Atlantic Monthly Press, 1986.

*In Quest of National Security.* Boulder, CO: Westview Press, 1988. With Marin Strmecki.

*The Grand Failure: the Birth and Death of Communism in the Twentieth Century.* New York: Scribner, 1989.

*Out of Control: Global Turmoil on the Eve of the 21st Century.* New York: Scribner, 1993.

*Differentiated Containment: U.S. Policy towards Iran and Iraq, Report of an Independent Task Force Sponsored by the Council on Foreign Relations.* Washington, DC: Brookings Institution, 1997. With Brent Scowcroft and Richard Murphy.

*The Grand Chessboard: American Primacy and Its Geostrategic Imperatives.* New York: Basic Books, 1997.

*The Geostrategic Triad: Living with China, Russia, and Europe.* Washington, DC: Center for Strategic and International Studies, 2000.

*The Choice: Global Domination or Global Leadership.* New York: Basic Books, 2004.

*Second Chance: Three Presidents and the Crisis of American Superpower.* New York: Basic Books, 2007.

*America and the World: Conversations on the Future of American Foreign Policy.* New York: Basic Books, 2008. With Brent Scowcroft and David Ignatius.
*Strategic Vision: America and the Crisis of Global Power.* New York: Basic Books, 2012.

## BOOKS ABOUT ZBIGNIEW BRZEZINSKI

Lubowski, Andrzej, *Zbig. Człowiek, który podminował Kreml* (*Zbig: The Man Who Undermined the Kremlin*). Toronto, ON: Agora, 2011.
Vaïsse, Justin. "De Harvard à la Maison-Blanche. Zbigniew Brzezinski et l'ascension des universitaires dans l'Establishment de politique étrangère américaine pendant la guerre froide" ("From Harvard to the White House: Zbigniew Brzezinski and the Rise of Universities in the Foreign Policy Establishment during the Cold War"). Institut d'études politiques de Paris, 2011.
Vaughan, Patrick. *Brzezinski: A Life on the Grand Chessboard of Power.* Warsaw: Polish Scientific Publishers, 2010 (in Polish).
Ziollowska-Boehm, Aleksandra, *Korzenie Sa Polskie* (*The Roots Are Polish*). Warsaw, 1982.

# CONTRIBUTORS

*Jimmy Carter* was president of the United States from 1977 to 1980.

*Warren I. Cohen* is Professor Emeritus at the University of Maryland, Baltimore County, where he taught courses in American diplomatic history and American–East Asian relations. Some of his most recent books include *America's Response to China*; *Empire without Tears*; *America in the Age of Soviet Power*; *East Asia at the Center*; *America's Failing Empire: U.S. Foreign Relations since the Cold War*; and his latest book is *Profiles in Humanity*.

*David C. Engerman* is a professor of history at Brandeis University. He has written two books on American ideas about Russia/USSR, including most recently *Know Your Enemy: The Rise and Fall of America's Soviet Experts*. His long-standing interest in modernization and development programs in the Third World has led to two coedited collections (including *Staging Growth: Modernization, Development, and the Global Cold War*) and a current project on American and Soviet aid to India.

*Francis Fukuyama* is a Senior Fellow at the Center on Democracy, Development, and the Rule of Law at Stanford University. Before that, he served as a professor and Director of the International Development program at the Johns Hopkins School of Advanced International Studies. His books include *The End of History and the Last Man*; *Trust: The Social Virtues and the Creation of Prosperity*; and *The Origins of Political Order: From Prehuman Times to the French Revolution*.

*Adam Garfinkle* is founding editor of the *American Interest*. In 2003–5 he served as a principal speechwriter for the Secretary of State (S/P, Policy Planning). He has also been editor of the *National Interest* and has taught at the Johns Hopkins School of Advanced International Studies (SAIS), the University of Pennsylvania, Haverford College, and other institutions of higher learning. He served as a member of the National Security Study Group (as chief writer) of the U.S. Commission on National Security / 21st Century (the Hart-Rudman Commission) and as an assistant to Senator Henry M. Jackson.

*Charles Gati* is a professorial lecturer of Russian and Eurasian studies and a Foreign Policy Institute Senior Fellow at Johns Hopkins University's School of Advanced International Studies. He is Professor Emeritus at Union College, has taught at Columbia University for fifteen years, and served as a senior member of the Policy Planning Staff of the U.S. Department of State in the early 1990s. In addition to many articles and chapters on Russia, U.S. foreign policy, and the politics of Central Europe, Gati is the author of two prize-winning books (*Failed Illusions: Moscow, Washington, Budapest and the 1956 Hungarian Revolt* and *Hungary and the Soviet Bloc*), *The Bloc That Failed*, and numerous other books.

*Robert Hunter* is Director of the Center for Transatlantic Security Studies at the National Defense University. Prior to that, he was Senior Advisor at the RAND Corporation. He was National Security Council Director of West European Affairs and later Director of Middle East Affairs in the Carter administration and United States Ambassador to NATO during the Clinton administration. He was President of the Atlantic Treaty Association from 2003 to 2008 and is currently Chairman of the Council for a Community of Democracies and serves on the Secretary of State's International Security Advisory Board.

*David Ignatius* is an associate editor and columnist for the *Washington Post* and the author of eight novels. He cohosts Post Global, an online discussion of international issues at www.washingtonpost.com. He has received numerous honors, including the Legion of Honor from the French Republic, the Urbino World Press Award from the Italian Republic, and a lifetime achievement award from the International Committee for Foreign Journalism.

*Mark Kramer* is Director of Cold War Studies at Harvard University and a Senior Fellow of Harvard's Davis Center for Russian and Eurasian Studies. He has taught international relations and comparative politics at Harvard, Yale, and Brown Universities and as a visiting professor at Aarhus University in Denmark. He was formerly an Academy Scholar in Harvard's Academy of International and Area Studies and a Rhodes Scholar at Oxford University. His latest book, *Deterrence and Coercion in Soviet-Polish Relations: The USSR, the Warsaw Pact, and the Solidarity Crisis of 1980–1981*, will appear in late 2013.

*James Mann* is an award-winning author and former journalist. His books have focused on American foreign policy, including *The Obamians: The Struggle inside the White House to Redefine American Power*; *The Rebellion of Ronald Reagan: A History of the End of the Cold War*; and *Rise of the Vulcans*. He has also written three books about America's ties to China: *The China Fantasy*; *About Face*; and *Beijing Jeep*. He currently is an author-in-resident at SAIS Johns Hopkins and previously was the senior writer-in-residence at the Center for Strategic and International Studies and served as staff writer for the *Los Angeles Times*, including a stint as the Beijing bureau chief.

*Robert A. Pastor* is a professor of international relations at American University, where he established and directs the Center for Democracy and Election Management and the Center for North American Studies. He was Director of Latin American Affairs at the National Security Council in 1977–81, and he has been a consultant to the Departments of State and Defense. He has a PhD from Harvard University and is the author or editor of seventeen books, including *The North American Idea: A Vision of a Continental Future*; *Exiting the Whirlpool: U.S. Foreign Policy toward Latin America and the Caribbean*; and *A Century's Journey: How the Great Powers Shape the World*.

*William B. Quandt* is a professor in the Department of Politics at University of Virginia. He previously served on the National Security Council during the Nixon and Carter administrations and was a Senior Fellow in the Foreign Policy Studies program at the Brookings Institution. His writing is concentrated on America's role in the Middle East and includes *Peace Process: American Diplomacy and the Arab-Israeli Conflict since 1967*; *The United States and Egypt: An Essay on Policy for the 1990s*; and *Camp David: Peacemaking and Politics*.

*David J. Rothkopf* is CEO and Editor at Large of *Foreign Policy* magazine and is a visiting scholar at the Carnegie Endowment for International Peace, where he chairs the Carnegie Economic Strategy Roundtable. He is also CEO and President of Garten Rothkopf, an international advisory firm. He was formerly Chief Executive of Intellibridge Corporation, Managing Director of Kissinger Associates, and U.S. Deputy Under Secretary of Commerce for International Trade Policy. He is the author of *Power, Inc.: The Epic Rivalry between Big Business and Government and the Reckoning That Lies Ahead*; *Superclass: The Global Power Elite and the World They Are Making*; and *Running the World: The Inside Story of the National Security Council and the Architects of American Power*.

*Marin Strmecki* is Senior Vice President and Director of Programs at the Smith Richardson Foundation. Before joining the foundation in 1994, Dr. Strmecki served as a professional staff member of the Senate Select Committee on Intelligence and the Senate Foreign Relations Committee from 1990 to 1991, a member of the Policy Planning Staff at the Department of Defense in 1992, and a legislative assistant to Senator Orrin Hatch from 1993 to 1994. He also worked as a Research Associate and Fellow in International Studies at the

Center for Strategic and International Studies from 1985 to 1990, where he followed U.S.-Soviet issues and provided research and editorial assistance to Dr. Zbigniew Brzezinski.

*Stephen F. Szabo* is the Executive Director of the Transatlantic Academy with the German Marshall Fund. Before joining the German Marshall Fund, Szabo had been with the Paul H. Nitze School of Advanced International Studies, Johns Hopkins University, where he served as Academic and Interim Dean as well as a professor of European studies. Prior to that, he had served as a professor of national security affairs at the National Defense University and Chairman of West European Studies at the Foreign Service Institute, U.S. Department of State.

*James Thomson* served as the President and CEO of RAND from 1989 to 2011. Prior to this, Dr. Thomson was a member of the National Security Council during the Carter administration, where he focused on defense and arms control. He was on the staff of the Office of the Secretary of Defense during the Ford and Nixon administrations. Thomson earned a PhD in physics from Purdue University.

*Nancy Bernkopf Tucker* is a professor of history at Georgetown University and at the Edmund A. Walsh School of Foreign Service. In 2007 she received a National Intelligence Medal of Achievement for distinguished meritorious service as the first Assistant Deputy Director of National Intelligence for Analytic Integrity and Standards and Analytic Ombudsman in the Office of the Director of National Intelligence. She recently received Georgetown University's Career Researcher Award for 2012. Some of her books include *Strait Talk: U.S.-Taiwan Relations and the Crisis with China*; *Uncertain Friendships: Taiwan, Hong Kong and the United States, 1945–1992*; and *Patterns in the Dust: Chinese-American Relations and the Recognition Controversy, 1949–1950*.

*Justin Vaïsse* is a Senior Fellow in Foreign Policy at the Brookings Institution and an adjunct professor at Johns Hopkins's School of Advanced International Studies. A specialist of transatlantic relations, he is also a historian of American foreign policy and is the author of many articles and books, including *Neoconservatism: The Biography of a Movement*. He is currently working on a biography of Zbigniew Brzezinski, based on his private papers.

*Patrick Vaughan* is a professor of transatlantic studies at Jagiellonian University in Krakow, Poland, where he focuses on the cold war and the American exercise of "soft power." His published works include "Beyond Benign Neglect: Zbigniew Brzezinski and the Polish Crisis of 1980" and "Zbigniew Brzezinski and the Helsinki Final Act." He has published the first full biography of Brzezinski in Polish.

# INDEX